MW01167091

Other Works by Mollie Moncrieff

Miss Rosamund's Jewels
> A children's story.

IMPACT
> A Second World War memoir, being a true account of the transference of evacuees from bombed areas to reception areas.

The River Aire
> A travel book written for walkers. The course of the river is explored from source to mouth. Includes descriptions of scenery and landmarks of historic interest. Photographs.

The Devil and Dundee
> The true story of the life of John Graham of Claverhouse, Viscount Dundee, 1648-1689.

A Bribe for Judge Jeffries
> A play. Based on a true incident in England's West Country during the Monmouth Rebellion.

England's Notorious Highwaymen: Robbery Was Their Job
> True stories of the infamous highwaymen (and highway-women) who plundered merchants, clergy, and gentry alike, from medieval times through to the nineteenth century. Wit, elegance, guile, gaiety and courage marked their style.

Prisoners of Time: A Simplified Cosmo-Conception
> An exposition of Ancient Wisdom designed for the initial understanding of such. A primer. Topics include: the origin and purposes of the planets and of ourselves; the nature of time; the importance of karma; our relationship with animals.

Call Joshua

    The theme of this volume is Evolution—our collective resistance to Evolution, and the movements for Reform which have arisen periodically, throughout the ages.

True Tales of Reincarnation and Astral Rescue
More Astral Rescues
Where Do We Go From Here?

    A trilogy outlining the mechanics of reincarnation. All three volumes include word-for-word records of communications with discarnates—royals, Ancients and ordinary figures trapped in astral fixations.

Manifest Destiny: The Birth of a Nation

    The esoteric story of the American Red Indian. Their origin, romance on Earth and Fate. Includes many lesser-known legends about animals and the elements.

Oglethorpe and Wesley of Georgia

    Two short biographies of extraordinary Englishmen who left their marks on America. Oglethorpe carried a gun and respected the American Indian culture; Wesley carried sermons and attempted conversion of the Indians, while discouraging Slave Trade on both continents.

The British Monarchy and the Divine Right of Kings

    Traces the esoteric foundations and significance of the British monarchy from early times until now, and on into future likelihoods. Symbols, royal jewels, crowns and coronation rituals are explained in accordance with their original, spiritual origins. Many historical anecdotes.

Memoirs

of An Esotericist

Memoirs
of An Esotericist

Mollie Moncrieff

Saunders & Rakauskas
Publishing Company, Inc.
Atlanta, Georgia, USA

_____ 1996 _____

Published
by
Saunders & Rakauskas Publishing Company, Inc.
Atlanta, Georgia, U.S.A

Copyright © 1996 Saunders & Rakauskas Publishing Company, Inc.

Library of Congress Cataloguing-in-Publication Data
Moncrieff, Mollie
Memoirs of An Esotericist/by Mollie Moncrieff - 1st ed.
CIP 95-072385

British Library Cataloguing-in-Publication Data available on request.

ISBN 1 888477 008

Typesetting by *Susan L. Moiles,* Worcester, Massachusetts, U.S.A
Printing by *Ambrose Printing Co.,* Nashville, Tennessee, U.S.A

Manufactured in the United States of America

First Edition

To Julie Robertson,
whose inestimable help and care
has made this book a reality.

Memoirs of An Esotericist

Contents

You'd think it would be the easiest thing in the world to write an autobiography. Surely it should just flow. Do like Alice—begin at the beginning, go on till you come to the end, then stop.

But it is not as simple as that. Because we have no beginning and no end. We have always been here, and always will be. We are God, and in the end we are all one. Man the microcosm, God the macrocosm. And accordingly excerpts from other incarnations are bound to creep in, and digressions occur as we pause to describe other people, our karmic contacts, ships that pass in the night, those we meet and part from and meet again, and call our "relatives," or our friends, or even our enemies. But as the Bahai scripture reads, *"No man is your friend, no man is your enemy. All are alike your teachers."* They are with one accord travelling the same road, each at a different stage along that road, wearing each his or her appropriate label 'John' or 'Mary,' with its accompanying *personality-surround*, which are merely disguises to mask the true identity or reality, the definition being Latin *Persona*, meaning *mask*. We use them as long as we need them, to express ourselves and our astral counterparts, until we are ready to render up our quota of experience to the semi-monad, male or female as the case may be, prior to mergence with our opposite polarity.*

Accordingly these *Memoirs* will be recorded mainly from the viewpoint of the current *personality*, and will be mainly about *me*. Such a fleeting, transitory term!** Biographies of famous people are compiled by others, from a fund of information culled from a wide variety of sources, and much can be infiltrated from the sayings of the celebrity in question. Otherwise they are merely hearsay or the result of observation, and neither of these is invariably accurate.

People write their *Memoirs* for a variety of reasons. Either they are serving a prison-sentence, are in hospital, or are old, and have nothing to look forward to, perhaps cannot afford to speculate in property, and make themselves comfortable, or beguile the heavy time, or circumnavigate the world as they vowed they would do when they retired, or they do not enjoy meeting other old people to imbibe

---

*All this is explained in my tape-recordings. This is not the place for esoteric dissertations. I have left the tapes for Ian. He did not want them while I was "alive," but will want them sooner or later. Everyone wants them sooner or later. They outline the whole *process* from start to finish.
**We come into physical existence, we age, we disappear.

cups of tea and talk about their grandchildren, when, in fact, they have come to the end of the line, and grown aware, like Wordsworth, of shades of the prison-house beginning to close.

General de Gaulle averred that old age is like a shipwreck. Very apt. You lose everything, salvaging only memories, and they are of no use to you, but only to posterity and even then only if posterity wants them. If you wrote them earlier, they would not be *Memoirs.* You would still, like Elvis, have a lot of living to do, and the emotional content would not have gone out of them, so that you would not be able to discuss them dispassionately, and view them in perspective, or resist the temptation to dramatise them or dwell upon your matrimonial skirmishes, whose prototypes are adequately dealt with in the tabloid press, or your aches and pains, which no one wants to hear about, or the world chaos or the political situation, about which your opinion is as good, or as bad, as the next person's. So you indite them as an antidote to demise from boredom or to preserve your sanity. Then, and then only, can you affirm, like Seneca, *"When the State is past cure, the wise man must retire into solitude and work for Posterity."*

The State is assuredly past cure now. We stand right in the midst of the prophecised Armageddon situation, wherein every man and woman is constrained to learn to stand alone, and draw upon his or her own resources. We have no leaders. The last one for us in England was Churchill; no *"Government."* Today's so-called *"Governments"* consist solely of financiers. We have to *govern* ourselves, and lots of people are failing to do it . . . hence the access of criminality and lawlessness. Most of our life in this dimension is a lonely journey. Sometimes we may acquire a *"companion of a mile."* But it is only a mile, and he or she duly falls away, to resume his or her own appointed path.

Thus much of my life has been spent *"wandering lonely as a cloud,"* and I have to go far back in time to find its beginnings both astrally and linearly. For the latter, to mediaeval times, when according to legend a monk in Ireland put a curse on our family on the maternal side. Like the Lady of Shalott, I know not what the curse may be, and so I can only weave steadily at the tapestry of my life—that ridiculously minuscule portion of it that is *down here* (for want of a better term) in physical manifestation.

Mollie Moncrieff
Bristol, England

The Curse of the O'Connors

Our family is descended from the Kings of Munster, the High Kings of Erin. High they may have been, but low inasmuch as all too often they behaved like brigands, and no doubt the O'Connor in question richly deserved the curse he incurred, though that is small consolation to his descendants who bore the brunt of it. Some of us were doomed to tragic, untimely death, others to a rootless existence and "No Fixed Abode."

Details are scarce, records sparse, and all I know is that until the year 1836 my grandmother's forebears were still living in their castle in Kerry built in 1100 by King Tearlach O'Connor, i.e. "Of Conahar." O'Connors are now two-a-penny, but our branch of the dynasty proudly retained that distinction. The castle was doubtless what James I would have dubbed "a hurrock o' stanes" for there is no mention of the family's means to maintain it in the pristine grandeur of the original owners.

This notwithstanding, my grandmother, Alice O'Connor, the last of the "militant O'Connors," decamped to England and married a dull Victorian merchant, with explosive consequences. My recollections of this redoubtable scion of royalty are of the vaguest, since I was only seven years old when she died. They are of a talkative lady, with a fiery temper, penetrating dark eyes, but quite an endowment of charm, if it suited her. Later my mother told me that she had a caustic wit. She was the proverbial matriarchal martinet, ruling the family with a rod of iron, whose often unreasonable word was law, addicted to family feuds, in the good old Irish tradition, and wholly intractable and uncompromising. Before the onslaught of such a formidable character, others tend to take the line of least resistance. She had six children: Edith, Ethel, (*Queenie*), Grace, Doris, Ernest and Olive. The trammels of suburbia must have irked her intolerably, the wide open spaces of Kerry were in her blood; she needed space, lots of it, in which to throw her weight about. The Curse, cramped into a villa in Streatham, began to do its deadly work.

Of the six children listed, Edith, the eldest, was an alcoholic, who drank herself to death at the age of fifty-two. The next, my mother, swung the pendulum fanatically to the extremity of Temperance, even to the extent of declining a glass of sherry at a party. Her lifespan was fifty years.

Then Auntie Gay, actually *Grace*, (I was named after her). She was stone-deaf all her life, and of her three children, Phil, the eldest, survived the war, mine-sweeping, and marriage. Within a year, his wife died of a brain tumour. Eric, the middle one, was killed in the R.A.F. In the very first air raid of World War II, at the age of nineteen. The youngest, Joan, an athletic girl, training to be a ballet dancer, was crippled with polio from the age of twelve. Despite this, she had three children, the eldest of whom, Dierdre (meaning *sorrow* in Irish), died of a brain tumour at the age of twelve. Joan lost her Irish husband at the age of fifty, and today lives on at Gerards Cross, a hopeless cripple.

The next, Ernest, was involved, for the duration, in the First World War, with no let-up. Because he was not physically injured, he was sent back and back again, remorselessly, to the Front, his shattered nerves wholly, disregarded. He committed suicide, racked with nightmares of the trauma of the trenches, the mud, the cockroaches, the rats gnawing at his toes, the constant, unremitting shelling, the death and mutilation of his comrades, the limbs of men trampled into the sodden earth. He was forty-four when he hanged himself in a hotel room, not willing to do it at home to spare his mother and sisters.

The next of my mother's siblings, Doris, was like Grandma, but without the wit and charm. She had inherited the caustic tongue, and made everyone's life a misery with whom she came in contact, especially mine.* She possessed a vitriolic temper. She was a Sagittarian, and I, likewise a Sagittarian, have always impressed upon myself the necessity for never getting like that, as I easily might have. She lived to a horrendous age, but her husband, similarly a victim of World War I, had his lungs virtually destroyed by the poison gas.

The youngest, Olive, died of a heart attack at age forty-seven.

* The almost venomous animosity she directed at me could only be explained karmically, and I did not understand it until considerably later, when details of our past lives were communicated to me. It certainly did not stem from the present life, for I had never consciously done or said anything to upset her, and in fact exerted every endeavor to avoid doing so, a difficult feat. It took the form of a smouldering jealousy and envy of *Sarah Whittaker*, a cousin in the seventeenth century, when as *Jennifer Butler*, residing in the saje farmhouse at Luddendenfoot in West Yorkshire, I would roam about the countryside alone, which she would have liked to do but dared not; she was likewise suspicious and resentful of my interest in the "occult," and the acquaintances I made in the pursuit of it, and spitefully predicted that I would "come to a bad end."

Auntie Edith had two daughters. Viola, my eldest cousin, lost her husband in middle life, and had only one son, Graham, who married and decamped to Australia, leaving her alone in her remote bungalow in the country at Clandon in Surrey, where she died of a brain tumour, while her sister, whom we called "Bunny" died in a mental institution, having sustained a total breakdown. Thus in one family, three brain tumours and two cases of polio, one of whom was myself. Cousin Joyce's husband was killed in a car crash (Joyce was Auntie Doris's daughter), and my brother, Bernard, at forty-nine, in a similar car accident; his daughter Anne, standing at the gate of their house near Brighton, helplessly watched him die. The family dubbed itself "the Ten Little Nigger Boys," not knowing who was to be next.

Because of the family feud engendered by Grandma, I was debarred from meeting my great aunts Kate and Sophie. Uncle Edward had offended Grandma Alice and the edict went forth that no one, but *no one* was ever to speak to Uncle Edward again, *or* his two daughters.

Kate was a fine artist, Sophie a well-known novelist. Sophie Cole was extensively read in the early years of this century, and along with Marie Corelli, is still read. The deprivation affected me profoundly. Kate came to me years later in spirit, a tall, auburn-haired, Edwardian figure. She said, "What a pity we never met. Sophie would have helped you with your writing."

And, of course, she would have helped. Her publisher was Ward Lock. She left a great deal of money, and I was as poor as a church mouse. Not that that matters. It was just one section of my part of the Curse. I have moved in moneyed circles, and money has, as it were, touched me on the shoulder and glanced away again, every time. And it has never been otherwise, in so pointed a manner that I grew aware that I was not to have it, and that the Curse had decreed for me "Poverty in the midst of Plenty." A very light part of the Curse; I have always been at my happiest and most carefree when without money.

Today, of the "cursed" generation, none are left, except my cousin Joyce, my sister in our earlier life at Ditchling in 1500, then named Helena; and in the current life her second name is Helen; her brother Denys, who would have been Eric's contemporary and companion had the latter lived; and poor Joan, and her elder brother Phil, whom I liked, as a fellow-Sagittarian, but have not seen for many years. It's hard to believe we all played together as children.

Joy is the only one who corresponds with me, faithfully relaying the "news" at birthdays and Christmas of the remnant of the "family." There are some younger ones, but they are scattered over the globe, and I do not know them. If there were karmic links, I should, of course; but there are none.

Now the Curse reached down to the lower echelons, and laid its icy fingers on my son Ian. But, albeit bowled over at first, he seems strong enough to overcome it. He has an alert mind, and is wise and sensible in many ways, able to adapt and compromise and recognise advantages where they lie. In his generation, the Curse is diluted, and has, thank God, lost its initial virulence.

Everything in the early years was so prim and proper. Names meant a great deal, and had to be adhered to. Importance was attached to proper addressing, "Mr. and Mrs.," and so on. It isn't now. Anyone can write to anyone, using the "Christian" name. By all accounts, this must be "better." One of the few things that is "better." There isn't much warmth these days. There is tolerance, a form of indifference. But that betokens a measure of *freedom*. We can't have it both ways.

I have had so many *names* in this life. The consistent label bears the name "Mollie." I have never liked it. When people use it today it accentuates the coldness. My children use it, simply because I once mentioned that the name "Gran" adopted by their children, or worse, "Nanny," is reminiscent, after a lifetime of spiritual service, of a packet of sugar or a female goat. Parents and brother, uncles and aunts and cousins, long-dead, used to call me "Moll." That was sort of nice. But no one has done that for many decades. Joy is the only one left who does it. As for "darling," I would give a great deal to hear my Dad's voice calling me that! but I don't like it from other people. The absence of warmth is doleful. As English people, some of us are still very conscious of our island status; others have been content to be swallowed up by Europe. Now Mr. Major dreams of the "classless society." It's a horrid society, albeit doubtless "better." Who's to say? Once we were terribly snobbish, and had notices on our gates: "No Hawkers, No Circulars" "Tradesmen's Entrance" (round the back), while a lady engaging a maidservant stipulated that she must encourage "No Followers," which seems odious. Now the pendulum has swung too far in the other direction, mob rule is the order of the day, and criminals run amok, uncaught and unpunished.

Ouspensky stated that evolution is not necessarily improvement, just change. I didn't understand the statement when I first read it, but I do now. The high moral standards this country once had are inevitably bound to be productive of intolerance. The low-grade people predominating in England today are "tolerant" or apathetic, because they have no standards and do not care about anything or anyone.

Various "surnames" have come my way too, having blundered more than once into the matrimonial arena, but these are meaningless, a by-product of the "Patriarchal Society," which come into being under God knows what malign

10

aegis, from which we are barely now in process of extricating ourselves.

If I had had any sense, which I hadn't at the time, I would, for literary purposes, have retained my father's name of Kipling. It does pull strings. My father, as a regular commuter between England and America, on being informed the Cunard Line was fully booked, expostulated, "What? No cabin for Rudyard Kipling's nephew?" He was assigned a cabin forthwith. My father, like George Washington, never told a lie. He made no claim to be Rudyard Kipling's nephew, though doubtless there is a link somewhere, Kipling being an uncommon name, but the bluff worked the oracle. My second husband had a Kashmiri name, which I never adopted. It was Brahmin, meaning "an Astrologer." No one in England could spell or pronounce it, and it did not suit my son, even if it suited my daughter Mavis.

My first husband was Harold Lisle, a Somerset name, and I only use the name "Moncrieff"* inasmuch as at the height of the stormy interlude which terminated the partnership with Ian's father, he muttered sullenly, "and you can stop using my name, too!" Whereupon I riposted with unjustifiable triumph, "I shall use your name as often as I like, wherever and whenever I like, for as long as I like, in whatever mannner I like, irrespectively of anything you may have to say on the matter." A woman always has the last word, but whether or not it did me any good I really don't know. I saddled myself with the name, and just had to make the best of it. Perhaps it was just a part of the Curse of the O'Connors. But it suits Ian to a "T." ◆

* The name "Moncrieff" incidentally, means "the Hill of the Tribal Tree." They were an ancient Perthshire family, dating back to the fifteenth century. They were art and part in many battles, including the infamous Massacre of Glencoe. Captain Robert Moncrieff, Ian's direct ancestor, confronted by a MacDonald boy of seven, clinging to his knees and begging for his life, stabbed the child through the heart. No praiseworthy heritage, any more than was that of the Kings of Munster.

11

Queenie

Queenie was, if you recall, the second one, who reacted from her sister's alcoholism. She married my father, Ernest Kipling, and having secured a settled home, (a Capricorn subject must have a firm and reliable base), "took up" politics as a vocation.

She was fanatical, dynamic, dogmatic, a pioneer of the Socialist Movement, had been in her early years a suffragette, was the first woman Labour candidate for Streatham, at a time when it was not fashionable for females to "do" anything much. She was so capable and such a competent organiser that despite all the calls on her time, and all the pressing "outside interests" and extramural activities (as more stay-at-home relatives termed them), she kept everything running on oiled wheels, was a first-class cook, and we had in our domestic background all that we could desire: lovely holidays, a top-grade education, country-fresh food, and the housework done by a series of "helps," from our favourite "Emmy" onwards.

At age eighteen months, I caught polio, then diagnosed as "Infantile Paralysis." My brother Bernard brought it from Gorlestone on a holiday, and transferred it to me without himself being affected by it. Doctor Channing-Pierce of Harley Street, the most venerated consultant of his day, worried my mother to death by averring, "that child will never walk." My father paid the specialist handsomely for his erroneous diagnosis. I have had no faith in doctors ever since, although I really liked Dr. Lindsay, our family doctor at Purley.

No one has since walked further than I have—all over the British Isles, the Peak District, the Lake District, Scotland, Sussex and Kent and Devon and Surrey, Yorkshire and Northumbria and the Thames Valley, in all weather. At fifteen I could swim a mile, and once swam across the River Dart from side to side. It looks most dangerous now, but then it didn't.

So after that they took me to an osteopath. I can't recall the details, being still an infant. All I have is a faint recollection of his placing a piece of paper on my back and applying what looked like a lighted cigar. "Health experts" are more likely to be interested in the antique methods employed than I am, but the upshot of it was that I got better.

When I say I got better, I seem to have done so, with the exception of the right arm, (polio always leaves its visiting-card), which has been virtually useless ever since. Despite this, I appear to have "managed," regularly commuting from Brighton to Derby when the children were small, via the London Underground, with a pushchair, a large case, a typewriter, plus the two aforesaid children. In retrospect, I can't imagine how. Since then, I have had two broken wrists to add to the score, a damaged knee, and a dismal " condition" called "Hypoglycaemia," that causes one to freak out at untoward junctures.

Childhood, looking back, emerges as idyllic, in comparison with all that has come later, as systematically the pollen is dashed from the butterfly's wing, the rose-tinted spectacles lie cracked like the Lady of Shalott's mirror, *"the sedge is withered from the lake, and no birds sing."* *

My earliest recollections are of my mother's political meetings, of Ramsay MacDonald, Herbert Morrison, Fenner Brockway, Ellen Wilkinson, Margaret Bondfield, Lady Violet Bonham-Carter, lots of others. Sometimes they would stay the night, and I would vacate my little bedroom for them. Once there was a garden fête at the estate of Earl de la Warr at Withyham, where Ramsay MacDonald stood on the balcony to make a speech. He picked me up, as politicians are wont to do as a vote-catching ploy, and with me on his shoulder, turned to the earl and quipped, with his pronounced Scottish accent, "I don't know whether to address the masses, or the classes!" The masses, congregated on the lawn below, roared with approbation; the classes, in the shape of the aristocratic family on the balcony, beamed benevolently. I have never forgotten it; the feel of his hair as I stroked it, so soft and silky to my infant touch, and thought what a nice grandpa he was. Before he died he wrote a verse for me in my autograph book; all school-girls had autograph books, but not all of them embodied poems by the Prime Minister. What a shame that little red leather-bound volume got lost in one of the many moves; it would have been very valuable today, as well as a curiosity. The verse ran as follows:

To serve another's will, that's not for me.

La Belle Dame Sans Merci, Keats

My heart is not athrill for slavery.
To serve another's need, right heartily,
In thought and word and deed, that's liberty!

Well, it was lost, like so many things.

I remember throwing an omelette at Fenner Brockway's daughter. He had two daughters, Audrey, who was a little older than I, and Margaret, a little younger. Audrey was four years old at the time of the omelette episode. I remember not liking my mother's meetings very much, and my father getting fed up with them too and decamping to America. He always came back, but he was an Aquarian, a born traveller, and used travel as a bolt-hole as well as for business. His voyages back and forth were on the old Cunard Line, especially the *Mauretania.* Among the things he told me was the incidence of the migrating birds clustering on the masts of the ship, thumbing a lift, since the vessel was heading in the direction they wanted to travel in, and how in an Atlantic storm, the soup-plates would careen down the almost vertically slanting table, and disgorge their contents into the passengers' laps. I would listen awe-stricken, but much later, when I was writing the biography of General Oglethrope, I realised how greatly more awe-inspiring must have been the involvements of the sailing ships of his time, at sea for months, in cramped quarters with unappetising rations deteriorating daily, when John Wesley, venturing upon that daunting journey, recounted how *"the waves of the sea were mighty, and did rage horribly, They rose up to Heaven above, and clave down unto Hell beneath."* When I think of the miraculous ironmongery that whisks me back and forth to America in a matter of hours, drinking cups of coffee, with lunch served by immaculate decorative "air hostesses," my mind boggles; it just doesn't seem possible.

Now the dismantled *Mauretania* is in Bristol where I live, converted into a restaurant, with the same panels and timbers utilised to reconstruct its image; how strange, when I go there for a meal or a drink, to contemplate those very accoutrements that my Dad looked at . . . !

The happiest days of my life were spent at Ashurst, where Auntie Madge and Uncle Bert had a farm. They were not my aunt and uncle, they were just called that. They were Queenie's lifelong friends. They had two children, Toby and Ethel; she was named after Queenie. There was a whole brood of

14

country children too, with whom we played in our joy-filled, carefree holidays from school, although we were not encouraged to fraternise with the gypsies, who did not like us anyway. In Spring we would return from our long days in the fields and woods, laden with primroses, in Autumn with blackberries. It was exquisite country in those days, unsullied by cars and fumes and litter and endless people. Just rural. Auntie Madge had no "mod. cons.," an exciting novelty to me and my brother, coming from the comparatively civilised environment of Purley. There was a rain-water butt outside, and they had to wait till it was full before they could do the washing, an earth-closet, a cesspool at the bottom of the garden, to which the buckets had to be conveyed by hand. There was an antiquated, creaking pump from which drinking water could be coaxed up from the bowels of the earth, provided one was not deterred by the iron filings and taste of ink therein incorporated; candles to light us towards bed, and a while owl sitting on the windowsill, staring into our bedroom; an oil lamp on the table spread with its green chenille table cloth, round which Auntie Madge and the rest of us would gather in the evening to do the mending and chat spontaneously. We did not need the painful "music" or dreary football commentary which seems an indispensable adjunct to today's activities; though Uncle Bert would smoke his pipe in his quiet contemplative way, and tune in to a primitive "wireless-set."

In Auntie Madge's bedroom hung a picture of Bonnie Prince Charlie saying goodbye to Flora MacDonald.* I used to sneak in there breathlessly to gaze at it at every opportunity. Now it is reproduced on biscuit tins and looks rather tawdry, but then I regarded it as the epitome of high romance.

It was only possible to indulge in a bath once a week, in a tub, in front of the "Aga-cooker." Boots were discarded in the scullery, and stood in serried ranks, liberally plastered with Kentish clay. Sussex clay as well, for the cottage

---

* Years later, I held in my hand a lock of Bonnie Prince Charlie's hair. That would be impossible today; there are too many people. But in those days things were more accessible and humanity less prolific. It was in Sir Walter Scott's house at Abbotsford. The curator, noting my wistful expression, very kindly opened the glass case and took it out for me. *See photo of Sir Walter Scott's study.*

It was a faded strand, that might have belonged to anyone, it probably would not do much for my disillusioned eye today, but then it did, and it was with elation and reverence that I replaced it in the case.

It had been a bequest to sir Walter Scott from that sentimental lady, fervently loyal to the House of Stuart, who in the poem by Lady Nairne,

> *sheltered Scotland's heir,*
> *And clipt a lock wi' her ain hand*
> *Frae his lang yellow hair.*

was just on the county boundary.

I used to accompany Uncle Bert to the farm to feed the chickens. He was such a reserved, refined man; some might have considered him incongruous in a rustic setting, but I was given to understand that the doctor had sent him to the country for his health's sake. The baby chicks were enchanting, cheeping and tumbling in their incubators, graded as to size, with paraffin-lamps to keep them warm, corn to nourish them, drinking-water in upturned vessels which kept their little troughs full. No shadow yet of the horrendous "batteries" which render today's farming a nightmare, because predatory humanity will not, and consistently refuses to, moderate its obscene numbers.

Sometimes I would join Uncle Bert in the packing shed, not that he wanted my company I'm sure. He would be wiping mud and feathers from white and brown eggs with a damp cloth; but he always had a far-away look in his eyes as if he were thinking of something else . . .

We were never called upon to "dress up." It didn't matter what we wore, or how muddy we got, or whether we had dirty faces. There was no one to see us; only cows. They had five cows, Daisy, Daffodil, Trixie, who was unpredictable, and not above administering a few kicks, and two more whose names I have forgotten. But everything was "free-range;" anything else was undreamed of, "factory-farming" a future horror, like Hitler's concentration camps. Auntie Florrie, who worked in London and used to go down there for weekends, once said to me in the course of a walk to the primrose-woods, pointing to the men engaged in the country-crafts of ditching and hedging and splicing and thatching, "one day, before long, you won't see any of this. It will all be done by machine. There will be tractors to do the harvesting . . ." She was prophetic, a "natural" psychic, as opposed to her brother, Uncle Bert, who was erudite and intellectual. She added, "there will be too many people, and they will have too much leisure; they won't know what to do with themselves. And you will be told what to do by robots." She meant the traffic lights. I did not know then what she meant . . . there wasn't so much as a Belisha-beacon.*

But her words stayed with me, as words will in a child's mind. Thoroughly perturbed, I hastened to Auntie Madge, whose practical, down-to-earth commonsense was often reassuring. "Oh!" I told her, "Auntie Florrie says . . . Do you think she's right?" I'll never forget Auntie Madge's reply, "(people seemed to be so much more positive in those days, or do I imagine it?) "Well, if she is, I'm **very** glad I won't be here to see it!"

I *am* here to see it, and I don't like it one little bit.

---

*An amber coloured globe mounted on a black and white banded pole, the sign of a pedestrian crossing in Britain named after Leslie Hore-Belisha, Minister of Transport, 1934-7.

Meanwhile, where ignorance is bliss, 'tis folly to be wise, and we lived out our Summer days in bliss. We jumped off the haystacks into the warm, yielding, sweet-smelling hay beneath. We (or rather the boys) fashioned a boat, out of salvage of some sort, which proved seaworthy until it reached the centre of the pond, then sank, with all of us aboard. There were so many ponds. I marvelled that they were so prolifically stocked with fish. *How* did the fish get there, with no stream to bring them and no visible means of support? Roach and dace, and perch, all fat and well-fed, and in the brooks the swift-darting minnow and the voracious stickleback which we would catch in jars.

The incidence of the "Kent Ditch" at the foot of the hill below the cottage, accounted for so numerous a gypsy-pitch. It marked the boundary between Kent and Sussex. The gypsies were always stealing Uncle Bert's chickens. Then they forded the stream, overnight, into the adjacent county, where they could not be prosecuted for misdemeanours perpetrated on Sussex territory and vice versa. No one seemed to worry so much about such things in those days. Life moved at a measured tempo, and stress and strain were a rarity. Auntie Madge used to counsel, in her forthright way, "Never worry about things that don't matter." And that's how we were brought up. But there was so much more importance attached to things that *did* matter. Whereas today people have ceased to worry about things that *do matter*, and therein lies the alarming difference.

This chapter is called "Queenie" inasmuch as she was the king-pin (or rather, "Queen-pin") of our lives; but she did not like Ashurst, and seldom visited with us. She preferred Madge and Bert to come to Purley, where there were mod. cons. She found the cottage freezing and comfortless; the fire smoked. On the occasions when she did accompany us, they would arrange "concerts" in the front room. Auntie Madge played the piano and sang Highland songs. The front room overlooked the road and had a little "front garden," into which the cows would sometimes stray and eat the flowers and churn up the sod. Nobody minded at all.

Mr. Clarke's shop, the only "shop" in the village—Auntie Madge had to struggle to Tunbridge Wells each Friday for the week's groceries (two miles' walk to the "Forge," then the ramshackle 'bus that twice daily rattled over the nine bumpy miles!) was a curiosity out-rivalling the Dream of Gerontius. I used to look forward to my visits there on an errand for the odd item which hadn't been included in Friday's list. It was so dark, so old, its blackened beams resting on your head as you stooped to enter. Mr. Clarke and his wife were unbelievably old too. At the age of ten I was convinced that they were as old as the house. They couldn't have been, since it was Elizabethan. Everything round there is Tudor, all the farm-houses and cottages, and some of the buildings and barns and out-houses, are mediaeval. Today the region is "developed", but it wasn't then. Mr. Clarke was nearly blind. Peering through his antiquated steel-rimmed spectacles, he would penetrate, mole-like, into the dimmest recesses of the premises, to emerge an eternity later, bearing the item I had asked for, brushing dust and hay from it, which he had disentangled from the amorphous heap that constituted his wares. If he couldn't find it, he would call to his wife, engrossed in her knitting in some cobwebbed corner, "have we got any candles?" "Yes," she would volunteer, without looking up from her knitting, "they're with the butter." If it were a reel of cotton you required, or a yard of elastic, he would free it from the embrace of the bacon, and would take so long to measure it, and cut it, and unearth a minuscule scrap of paper to wrap it in, not deeming it worthy of a brown paper bag all to itself. I would often be late for lunch. But that signified nothing in those leisurely Halcyon days. And once the carrots got mixed up with the firelighters, and had not Auntie Madge been conversant, not only with the absorbent properties of carrots, but with the vagaries of Mr. Clarke as well, we should have sampled a very paraffinny dinner. It was no use asking for postage-stamps, for they would inevitably have been stuck to the boot-polish, and we did not write many letters from Ashurst.

Each season, the hop-pickers came down from London, just as Irishmen still came for the harvest, descending in their numbers upon farms and cottages for their accommodation, or camping out in the fields. One year my brother, being perennially short of pocket-money, joined the team. I couldn't do it, because of my arm. They only received a pittance for picking a lot. I would not have got anything; so I was content to watch, as the curiously-smelling plant was laid out on racks, and that unique Kentish feature, the oast house,* came into play. Today, several of these, quaintly enough, are converted into dwelling houses. In our dismally overcrowded island, it seems one can live anywhere, from a yellow submarine to a re-constituted stable, provided one has a roof over one's head.**

I did not "get on" well with my brother Bernard. In the early days we were continually at loggerheads. That was probably because I was a horrid

* A building containing a kiln for drying hops.
See photo.

**These people are the *"travellers;"* not gypsies, not anything, who have ten children apiece in some cases, and consider it the Government's duty to furnish them with a home, and social security benefits to live on for good measure. Where on earth have all these people come from who think that the world owes them a living?

18

pampered child, by reason of my disability. I was likewise sickly as one stage, with tubercular glands in my neck. My health was delicate, and the poor boy was doubtless instructed not to upset me. He would infuriate me by holding me at arms' length while I raged at the ends. I recall that he and his school-mates, all of whom I hated, used to taunt me by placing my dolls on top of an imaginary bonfire, imaginary, that is, insofar as they did not light it but kept pretending to.

After Bernard's death, I did briefly communicate with him, when he mentioned that he had been taken out because he wasn't "getting anywhere." That was true, and is often the case. People are held up in their spiritual development by other people, and in the case of Bernard, his wife Joan had had that effect on him. He was a Libra subject, not a strong character, but probably a nicer person that I was, while Joan was hard and materialistic, determined to get what she wanted. It was just that we did not gel. We might now. Perhaps we will, in the other dimension. Even now, years after his departure, I still see him as a remote person. That may find redress. Or we may pursue our separate ways, in that he evinced no interest in me or my work or what I thought about, either while he was on earth or greatly either in the alternative dimension, whatever area of it he occupied when I communicated with him. He declared aversion to his doorkeeper, a South Sea Islander, whom he referred to as "a savage." It may be that more recently he has become reconciled and effected spiritual progress, but I am out of touch for the time being, and as for Joan his wife, she re-married, and it being many years since I saw her; we would not know each other if we met

I outgrew my delicacies and have enjoyed good health, all my life, until now, when I assume inevitably it must revert to type. It has been said that people often end their lives in circumstances similar to those in which they began them.

We had a nice garden at Purley, terraced and sloping, with a hedge all the way round planted with a hawthorn tree and a hazelnut tree alternately, so that it was interesting both in Spring and in Autumn. Dad was a keen gardener, and in Summer was always cutting the grass (such a lot of grass!) while I would sit on my swing, swinging and dreaming, looking out across Densham's Woods. It was quite countrified in those days and we could walk all over the North Downs to Caterham and my school at Whyteleafe. I can't remember much about the house we had at Chipstead until I was four, except that it was called *Heron's Croft*, and was even more countrified. There were two summerhouses in the

Purley garden, in which my brother would indulge in a clandestine cigarette,*
enlisting my services to keep "cavie"** for him against the encroachments of the
adult world. I hated doing this, and when we had one of our frequent rows, would
decline to fill the role, whereupon he would dub me a miserable little cat, which
I have no doubt I was.

There was yet another non-relative called Auntie Minnie, who used to
get on my nerves. She would despatch me to the shops to execute her errands,
one of which, for St. Ivel cheese, was the epitome of embarrassment, in that she
insisted on my opening the packet to ascertain that the bacteria was still in
active form. I wanted to drop through the ground. On the other hand, she was an
inveterate theatre-goer, and would compensate for this by taking me with her, so
that at an earlier age than most, I had the run of the London theatres, and prided
myself on being quite a connoisseur of good acting. There were first-rate actors
too—Phyllis Neilson-Terry, Sybil Thorndike, Valentine Dyall, Malcolm Keen
and Jessica Tandy and John Gielgud. I was not allowed to go to the cinema until
I was fifteen—it was among Queenie's prejudices. My brother rashly volunteered
to take me for my initial introduction, when we went to a dark and stifling flea-
pit in South Croydon. It was unhygienic and horrid. I superciliously upbraided
Bernard for laughing at the antics of Laurel and Hardy, which I dismissed as
rubbish. He assessed me, again with perfect veracity, as an ungrateful little snob,
and vowed never to take me anywhere again, and never did. He was not at home
much now, having, after an adventurous but academically remiss school career,
found a job in Brighton, with the Parks and Gardens Department of the
Corporation, in which capacity he worked until his death in a car-accident.

It was the fifth of October. He was forty-nine. ◆

* Another recollection involves Bernard's cigarette-card collection. Such cards
were all the rage. Marvellous productions, quite unlike the shoddy paper
wrappings of today, but glossy and tastefully finished instead, just as Mr. Read's
artistic bill-heads were that we found in the attic at Brighton later on. They
depicted interesting features such as famous steam-trains, "Cries of London,"
reproductions of old masters, ships, birds, animals, "Dandies" like Beau Nash and
Topham Beauclerk, and politicians like Benjamin Disraeli. The would be worth a
fortune today, and collectors clamour for them, but Bernard's many sets were,
like so many treasures, lost in one or other of our "moves."

**Literally, "beware."In America, "keeping lookout."

III

Kathleen

But all that lay in the future, and we had not yet left behind the Halcyon days when Kath and I were regular "commuters" between Purley and Ashurst.

There is a *nostalgia* for steam-trains. Even the "telly" admits it! They don't know what it is, but they know *that* it is! The electric trains have no soul. And that sums up the entire trouble with today's people; everything is so sterile. We are living under the Pale Horse of the Apocalypse, that shadowy negative beast without substance, under whose sway no one is responsible for anything, everyone passes the buck, all is impersonal and unconnected, and each man is an island as never before. There cannot be any soul where all is achieved without human involvement; robots and computers are no warm substitute. Cars are no substitute for horses. Men who looked after horses and constructed carriages themselves by hand, not piece-meal, are bound to be more aware entities than those who merely check the workings of one portion of a machine.

We used to travel by ourselves to Ashurst. Children were safe in those days. Young women were safe. They could return from a dance late at night on the London Underground without fear of molestation; now even little girls cannot walk home from school in guaranteed safety. Old people were safe in their homes—incomprehensible in today's violent world. Sometimes a man would speak to you, but as soon as you intimated that you were not interested, that was the end of it. He would apologise, go back to his newspaper, or leave the train. Now, he would stick a knife in you. *Autres temps, autres moeurs!*

Leaving Purley seemed an adventure then, as suburbia was left behind, and the then unspoilt countryside unfolded itself before our wondering eyes:

21

Upper Warlingham, Woldingham, Oxted, Hurst Green Halt, Monks' Lane Halt, Edenbridge, Hever, (where Anne Boleyn lived), Cowden, Ashurst. Then we walked, all the way to the farm, past Blackham Forge, down the hill with Basset's Farm in view, where I lived for a brief span in mediaeval time (not "I," but *Marjorie Wollaston*) then, when we left, on that now extinct Tunbridge Wells line, the entire family, plus the "farm children," would clamber onto the fence that ran all along by the railway line, and wave and wave and wave until we were out of sight, until the next time, and the station-master at Ashurst station, with its gas lamp and cosy coal fire in the waiting room, would impress upon the engine-driver, "slow down past the farm, mate, won't you?" so that we could savour that delightful ritual to the full. Then Toby and Ethel would catch the train at Christmas and come to stay with us at Purley for the parties and pantomimes they could not enjoy in the rural seclusion of Blackham.

Our parties were the envy of the neighborhood. Homespun entertainment, certainly, with no pretention to the sophistication of the telly, but most people could "do" something, and there was quite a lot of talent about. Dad was an Aquarian, a born entertainer as well as traveller, generously endowed with the social graces and a love of socialisation, although paradoxically in old age he went to the other extreme and became very lonely. Aquarius is a dual personality. Someone made an apposite rhyme about the New Age Aquarian:

> *Who sits brooding all alone*
> *With a time-bomb on his mind?*
> *Who runs to help the crippled crone*
> *And find a pathway for the blind?*
> *If these are truly both Aquarius,*
> *His Age may prove a mite precarious!*

Dad sang songs, comic and "straight." Whatever became of all the *funny* songs? Vanished off the face of the earth, it would seem. In any case there would be no demand for them now; their funniness was of a simple brand which would not be rated funny now, even by children, who are no longer children in the sense that they used to be. We used to laugh heartily at *When Father Laid the Carpet on the Stairs,* and *The Brotherly Twins,* and *Lucky Jim.* Dad's favorite "straight" song was Masefield's *Sea Fever* set to music, because it reminded him of his sea voyages. Then there were the "serious" songs, maudlin, in fact, some of them, a residual legacy from the Victorian Parlour days. Goodness knows what happened to them either . . . *Alice where art Thou?* and *Come into the Garden, Maud?* which, rendered by visiting aunts, were admittedly rather excrutiating. But Dad played the piano brilliantly, he had taught himself, and all

22

would gather round the piano and sing, and what they may have lacked in professionalism they made up in gusto and enthusiasm.

I could sing, and knew all the Scots and Jacobite ballads by heart, all 347 of them, just as Uncle Bert knew all the wild flowers, and their names, that he found on Ashdown Forest, though I never solved the mystery of the fish-filled ponds, one of so many delectable mysteries. It does not apply today. The ponds are gone. There is no more mystery. I wonder if it is something today's children miss? Perhaps it is "better" that they have no illusions, nothing to unlearn, so painfully? Or perhaps they will have other things to unlearn. Who can say? What would Ouspensky say? People must speculate in other galaxies to find mystery today, another dead-end.

We wove discreet circles round the gypsy-encampments. They were *real* gypsies in those days, swarthy and mystical, surly and noncommittal, with their own code and life-style. We were fascinated by them and their highly-coloured "vardos," * and they were suspicious of us, eyeing us covertly whenever our paths intersected. They did not go to school as we did. Toby and Ethel and the village children had to walk three miles to their school outside the village, quite a chore in winter. Auntie Florrie told me of an older winter custom, out of practice by her time, but she recalled one incidence of it when a small boy accosted her, announcing proudly, "I've been sewn up." "Sewn up?" she echoed. Even she, accustomed as she was to country folk and their curious secrets. "Yes," he confirmed. "Sewn up for the winter." It would seem that in November, he and his contemporaries had grease rubbed all over them and were encased in their flannel underwear for the duration, being released in April. It really doesn't bear thinking about. Anyway, thank goodness it didn't happen to Toby and Ethel, who were not exactly country folk, but imported material, as it were.

On one occasion my brother had a serious fight with a gypsy. perhaps the innate antagonism towards a "Gorgio" was never far from the surface. I'll never forget it. He was considerably older than I, and at fifteen, slim and wiry, and had been taught at school to fight "professionally," whereas the gypsy youth was seventeen, heavily built and clumsy. The source of the conflict was that the gypsy had robbed a bird's next and killed the fledglings; the gypsies were not kind. I was only seven, and with the other children stared with bated breath as the two wrestled and pummelled each other all down the field to the stream in the valley. Then they were in the stream, locked in a deadly embrace, and Bernard was in the process of pushing his adversary's head under water, when a farmer arrived and separated them, clouting both, and Bernard repaired to Auntie Madge's cottage, (everyone did, sooner or later, as it was our "second home") with nose bleeding copiously. Strange how some memories persist intact forever, while others take their place in the limbo of temporarily forgotten things. Nothing is

*painted wagons

23

ever actually forgotten; all is faithfully inscribed on the etheric wax. The Akashic Record is eternally ours to refer to when the time is ripe. It's just that we can't hold everything all at once. So comforting to know that. We never *lose* consciousness; it is simply that we *are* where our consciousness *is*.

Kath used to go with me to Ashurst. She was my "best friend," to the extent of the proverbial "David-and-Jonathan" set-up. I did not of course realise until later that it was karmic, but right from the outset, when Fate cast our lines together, and we met in the same class, the Lower Third, we were inseparable, and remained so throughout our schooldays. A contrast attracts.

Kath came from a totally different background from mine. Not only a brilliant artist, she was clever in other ways too. She won a scholarship to the school I attended at Whyteleafe. There were only six places offered in those class-conscious days. She was the daughter of a butcher, and one of a family of ten, while I was the pampered product of a relatively well-to-do household. There were snobbish cliques in the school. I was often persecuted by reason of my mother's unpopular political attachments. I was not strong, and could not defend myself, and would climb a tree in the school playing-field to escape from Joan Farnish and Co., as the bullying girls were dubbed. Whereupon Kath, lithe and muscular, would take up her stance with folded arms at the foot of the tree, and challenge anyone to physical combat. There were never any offers, and unfailingly she established herself as my protector.

Once, swimming in the countrified pool at Upper Warlingham, some boys made off with our clothes. Kath raced after them, seized them in a vice-like grip, and cracked their heads together like a couple of walnuts. The impact lingers in my ears to this day! The incidence of five brothers represents the nursery for that skill! Such a resounding crack! It just epitomised Kath. But she could write too, and was studious.

Kath and I wrote a book together. At least, I wrote the book, Kath did the illustrations. The outcome was hilarious, but we were quite solemn about it. We were eleven years old, and our Magnum Opus was entitled *The Ghost of Garstleigh Grange*. It is still extant, but my son took possession of it as a curiosity.

Sometimes at weekends or during the holidays I would go to her home at Tatsfield, remote in those days. Kath could not go home each day, but had to stay in lodgings during the week, and we would wander the Surrey and Kent countryside, swim in the freezing River Darenth at Brasted, climb Crockham Hill to hear the ghostly hoof-beats of the headless highwayman as he galloped by, as the local folk averred he was wont to do, and walk through Marden Park to Godstone and Oxted and Tandridge, or take the train to Hever. It was not until later that I came closer to that home, in the course of an exorcism.*

---

*See *More Astral Rescues*

The River Mole, true to its name, travelled underground, (*"sullen Mole, that hides his diving head"*) and was dangerous for swimming; and there was another underground stream at Kenley near our school, called the "Woe Water" in that it was only known to appear when there was a national calamity *"time of travail and grete bataille."* It rose for the Great Plague of London, and the Fire, for the Great War, and all these appearances are on record.

To Kath and me, life seemed just one long exciting discovery.

Kath's mother cooked enormous H-bones of beef and vast piles of mashed potatoes, and Kath painted her lovely pictures and illustrated the books I wrote, (I was always writing books.) The flavour of that beef was out of this world! Today's people do not know what anything tastes like. Eggs don't taste of anything at all. The fresh large eggs we used to find beneath the hedge at the roadside had their own inimitable delicate flavour and fluffy texture; to describe it would not convey anything to anyone today.

Kath and I shared tastes at school too, and disliked the same things, and people. Inevitably Kath was less sentimental that I, more realistic. She had not been sheltered as I had. But she was strong, in every way, and clever, which I was not. Subsequently, people have called me clever, but they had got it wrong. I am wise, but that is entirely different.

I doted on English literature and its teacher. Kath nurtured no illusions and did not indulge in schoolgirl "crushes." Miss Mizen in my estimation was nothing short of godlike, and I continued to hold that view long after I left school. She was the most sensitive exponent of poetry I have ever known; she really made it live. It is, I am sure, due to the love for it that she inculcated in me that I can to this day recite a poem by heart just by reading it once. She had a profound influence on me too, not only throughout my schooldays, but in perpetuity. Far more than had my parents. It is strange, but the number of people who truly have any effect on one in a lifetime is minimal. In my case they can be counted on the fingers of one hand. Most people don't do anything for me at all, and "leave me cold," as the saying is—now I think it would be "turn me on." I am eternally grateful to her for her sensitivity and understanding and sense of humour. To other teachers too, in a lesser degree. All our teachers were cultivated ladies, some of whom had studied at Dorothea Beale's famous *Ladies' College at Cheltanham.* The standards and values they passed on to us were of sterling quality, and a source of lasting gratitude.

The headmistress was solemn and rather fuddy-duddy, but she was sincere and dedicated. Even Miss Keen, who was cantankerous and tyrannical, certainly knew how to bring history to life. She was nonplussed when I wrote an essay on the Duke of Monmouth. "It was as if you knew him," she observed, and did not contradict the statements I made which did not appear in the history books. "I did," I said simply.* But that was when I talked with her later, after leaving school, and she had ceased to be cantankerous or tyrannical, and was quite nice.

Queenie was adept at catering, knew how to organise a convivial "musical evening," with lavish refreshments, often after a long day out rambling in the country, for my parents gave the impression of possessing boundless energy. They never seemed tired, or depressed or discouraged. However, perhaps they were, sometimes, but were brought up to keep a stiff upper lip and not reveal it. I am in no position to assess that. I only saw them through the eyes of a child, and was without cognizance of any problems or difficulties that might have been theirs. Certainly their policy was not to let me see them. I was given everything, sheltered from all that was unpleasant, from thunderstorms, (Dad would put his hands over my eyes when they occurred), from unkind people.

Another of Dad's social acquisitions was that of ventriloquism. He had a funny "doll," in the guise of a mischievous boy, who sat on Dad's knee and "talked back" in a cheeky way when Dad cleverly "threw" his voice. This performance we found hilarious, and the naïve smaller ones convincing. Again, today's children would not be thus spellbound.

Our holidays were marvellous. Our "real" Summer holiday, apart from the excursions to Ashurst, were in Devon or Cornwall or the Isle of Wight. Fairly well-to-do families frequented those regions as today they fly to Teneriffe, and in fact anywhere and everywhere. People used to speak of the "Cornish Riviera!" It was to us children like going to another planet. During the Summer term at school we would cross off the days on the calendar looking forward to this annual event. In anticipatory excitement we boarded the train from Paddington, and the excitement escalated to fever pitch as we were informed by a placard in a field: "You are entering the Strong Country." All that sort of thing was just beginning and represented a novelty; now it is commonplace. And as the train wound its way along the coast via Dawlish, and we were within touching and smelling distance of the sea, then really by the sea, and actually in it, we had reached Mecca. We could all swim; we were taught at school, and at fifteen as mentioned I displayed prowess, but not at eleven, and I should not be sitting here had not Cousin Joy rescued me in the course of a forbidden midnight swim, when I was all but drowned in a bid to reach the lighthouse off Bembridge, weed-encrusted and sinister, and much further from the beach than we had calculated. I can feel to this day the slimy embrace of the floating tendrils tugging at my ankles. Spared for worse things, I sometimes reflect. But Fate is

*As *Jennifer Butler,* I knew Monmouth in 1685. See *True Tales of Reincarnation and Astral Rescue*

inexorable, and all is pre-ordained.

We usually stayed on a farm, or hired a cottage for the duration, i.e. of the school summer recess. Once at Ryde, our swimsuits and towels, draped over the fence to dry, were devoured by goats grazing in the field. So many wonders, so much laughter in Paradise, as it then seemed to be. One never-to-be-forgotten holiday I spent with Queenie at Colyton; just the two of us. *Bonehayne Farm*, the ancient house was called; presumably, "good hedge." Its thatch was so dense that little mice made nests in it. On the table were always huge jugs of home-brewed cider, and bowls of cream, supplies of which were limitless. Everything was so rich, so plentiful, uncontaminated by pesticides and chemicals and whatever other dilutants have subsequently imposed themselves, like the grass in the lush pastures where the plump brown cattle browsed. So beautiful; a dream-world long faded. It was £1 a week for Queenie, ten shillings for me!

The farmer came to meet us at the railway station; a little rustic branch line, now disused: Colyton, Colyford, Seaton. I stood amazed; his conveyance was a pony-and trap! Such an equipage would have drawn a crowd in the streets of Purley. There was a lamp affixed, and an adjustable step, and high seats. Queenie and I had to climb up into them. It was a six-mile drive to the farm, *"all-along-down-along-out-along-lea,"* * that is, Northlea and Southlea and then just winding lanes all the way. Narrow lanes with over-arching trees; nothing could pass. A young motorist tried to, hooting aggressively. The stolid Devonshire farmer did not bat an eyelid. "Thinks he's an airman," he commented to my mother. "Aw noa," he continued, and deliberately slowed down. "I pay rates for these roads all through the winter. I'll noan be chased into a gateway by a young whipper-snapper who's just bought a motor-car." *Neither was he.* Our farmer kept the motorist behind him, at a snail's pace, and after a while the hooting subsided.

Queenie and I walked miles over those bountiful hills and valleys. The September sunshine was mellow and warm, and one day, never before or since, there was a Purple Emperor butterfly, spread out full in the sun on a bulrush in a marshy place. Scarcely daring to breathe, I signalled to Queenie to come and look at it. She too was amazed at the beauty of those velvety wings, royal purple and luminous gold. The butterfly is obsolete now, like so much wild life and so many flowers. Man and beauty cannot live together; all that is green and lovely recedes before the onslaught of man. Once they could, but those days are over. . . thousands of years over.

The next summer we were on a farm at Compton Marldon in the hinterland of Paignton. Dad came too. That was wonderful too. The farm-folk were so friendly in those days, all was rural and unspoilt. "Farmer Dommit" as the villagers called him, showed me how to ride a horse, and proudly showed me

*From *Widecombe Fair,* an old Devon song

27

how his prize-bull could lift a gate that was closed, and answer to his call. If ever anyone tells me that they are unintelligent, I will give them the lie.

Ashurst was Paradise. No Paradise when World War II came. Toby,* was killed at age twenty, drowned when his ship was torpedoed. In 1990 I met Marc Lecordier, the Frenchman who is translating my books and negotiating a publisher in Europe. Marc is Toby.

When a karmic contact is renewed, the moment of realisation is overwhelming, and mutual. Then naturally after a while it becomes absorbed into one's everyday philosophy and is no longer surprising or even remarkable. Summaries are inadequate, and details of the karmic contact are set out in Marc Lecordier's File called *The Smiling Lady*.

Marc grasped the situation at once. Contacts are being renewed all the time, more and more with the colossal speeding-up of events, and the universal transport which permits us to go and find them, where a hundred years ago we could not have done so. There is nothing "strange" about them, neither are they "coincidences." They simply obey the Law of Synchronicity, and the sooner they are worked out, the better for all the individuals concerned.

Taking a late holiday, it always seemed rather melancholy coming home to an incipient Autumn. It would be raining, and Purley looked drab, and one would be going back to school straight away too, after the weekend, which was something of an anti-climax. Not that I minded school, or some aspects of it. . . my friend Kath, and Miss Mizen, and poetry, and history, and literature. . . the views and the trees in the playing field, and the countryside beyond, leading to our favorite leisure-time haunts.

*Auntie Madge's son and my playmate when we were seven years old.

28

The parts of it that I did not like, I blotted out, by the simple expedient of a "closing-off" process, so that there were certain subjects, such as mathematics, about which I learned nothing, and left school as wise about them as when I entered at age eleven in the Lower Third. The mathematics teacher solemnly declared that if I had not been good at other subjects she would verily have thought me mentally deficient. It is possible to be like that, developed on one side of the being only, and in my case I felt that the artistic, creative and psychic aspects of life were so important and all-embracing that there simply wasn't room for anything else.

Kathleen and I read voraciously: Keats and Shelley and Byron and Wordsworth and Alfred Noyes. I wanted to meet Mr. Noyes but Kath said it was best not; we'd only be disappointed; he'd have a bald head or something. Kath was so much more realistic than I was. A brilliant artist, Kath was the best I knew till I met my first husband who was an ARA.*

Kath and I devoured girls' school stories, written by Angela Brazil, and historical romances by Dorothea Moore, and each Saturday the *Schoolgirls' Own Library* came out, and we would rush to the newsagent to secure one before they ran out, the lurid fourpenny paperbacks about Betty Barton and Polly Linton and Paul Creel of Morecove School, and about Cliff House School by Hilda Richardson, and Billy Bunter and his sister Bessie, and "William," all the *William* books. Earlier, as recounted, I had been a sickly child, with glands in my neck and other complications, and was sometimes away from school for weeks at a stretch, during which interludes I laid the foundations of avid reading, mostly about seventeenth century England. I have always been overshadowed by my seventeenth century incarnation,** and have never really taken root in the current one.

The books in the school library, that were deemed suitable for our juvenile perusal, were with one accord voted "soppy"—meticulously expurgated editions of the classics, the insipid exploits of Little Lord Fauntleroy and Eric (or, "little-by-little"), while we unequivocally drew the line at *Little Women*. So at home we regaled ourselves on the stirring yarns of Henty and Ballantyne, and I found *Two Years before the Mast* and *Tom Brown's Schooldays* more stimulating than *What Katy Did*.

Pocket money was sixpence a week. For sixpence you could buy a veritable armful of sweets. Wonderful sweets. There were bulging sherbet-fountains for a half-penny, enormous peppermint humbugs and liquorice braids, and luscious chocolate, and on the railway stations were little slot-machines which for a penny yielded a small bar of Nestles' milk chocolate encased in silver foil. The machines were always empty, because there were so many

* Associate of the Royal Academy.
**i.e. the memory of *Jennifer Butler*.

schoolgirls, but they were never forced and vandalised as they would be today.

Coins of the realm had their playful nicknames. A shilling was a "bob," sixpence a "tanner" and the little silver threepenny piece a "Joey." No one calls the money anything now; probably because it goes out so fast that we don't have time to get to know it properly.

Easter would soon come round again, and it would be time for Ashurst and the primroses. Yet time does not go so fast when one is young. They say it goes much more quickly when one grows older. This is very popularly accepted; but the truth of the matter is that time *is* in fact going more quickly. And it will go progressively more quickly as the planetary incarnations supersede one another, until the final one, the Vulcan Period* as it is called, will literally skip round like a two-year old.

I thought Auntie Madge's mother was immeasureably old, like Mr. Clarke and his wife. She lived in the adjoining cottage by the railway line. She wore a black shawl and a little lace cap, completely out-dated even then, and never went out. She was Highland Scots, and spoke with an unintelligible Fraserburgh accent, so that I could only identify a word here and there. "And phwere are ye gooin'?" she would enquire, when I tiptoed in to greet her before embarking upon the enticing programme the day held out to me. "To the farm," I would reply, in the voice that indicated that I was living in a fairy-tale.

Sarita, the eldest of the "farm-children," grew up and married a Kentish farmer, whose Tudor house in the midst of fields had a floor composed of split oak trunks which soaked up literally gallons of linseed oil in preserving and keeping it polished, and a massive table of the same ilk, which was so heavy that I was convinced it had taken root in the floor! So many marvels! I knew I had lived there before,** long, long ago, though I did not *consciously* know it until appreciably later. All I knew then was that it was home, whereas Purley, which according to the Laws of the Medes and Persians should have been, *wasn't*, at least not nearly so much.

Sometimes we would organise a paper-chase, all across country. What an anachronism it seems now! You couldn't do it. Quite apart from the cars and motorways, there's so much litter that it would get all mixed up!

The Normans left their mark on this land, all the way from Pevensey Beach, Hasting and Robertsbridge, all across Sussex and Kent they built their castles, and enlarged the Saxon churches, all the way through Fordcombe, and Chiddingstone, and Withyham and Hartfield, and Leigh and Tonbridge and Tunbridge Wells and on to London.

Today, when I re-visit that magic world, (*magic* no longer), and pass what once was Mr. Clarke's shop, I have to rub my eyes to credit what it has

* see *Prisoners of Time.*
**As *Marjorie Wollaston*, in the fifteenth century

become. It has been "done up" in compliance with today's inexorable standards of hygiene and the Statutory Requirements of the Ministry of Something-or-Other. *WHERE ARE THEY*? Mr. Clark and his knitting wife? Figures of fantasy? Figments of my imagination? Perhaps they never existed, except in some mythical recess of time. Oh, but they did! And they are still there, somewhere on the Akashic Record, still groping for the oranges among the kippers. Or reincarnated perchance into "better" conditions, a nice clean Council-house for instance? *Nothing that has once lived ever dies.* That is the Law, an integral part of the Eternal Verities.

   Would Mr. Clarke and his wife have been happier in a nice clean Council-house? It's hard to say. Country folk did not always relish innovation or welcome "improvement." Mrs. Kemp, daily sweeping marsh-water out of the front door of her mediaeval cottage at the foot of Blackham Hill, was quite nostalgic (when she was compulsorily re-housed with mod. cons.), for the swamp blossoming with bright yellow marsh-irises that had been her lifelong home.
   Who can pass judgment as to what is "better" or "worse"? It was much the same with the Shambles of York. I saw it, exactly as it was; as it had been for centuries, just before it was "cleaned up." Now it displays smart fashionable boutiques and salons and antique-shops and cafes for a million tourists. Then it was dark and squalid, sinister and filthy, a ghetto for Negroes. Of course it's "better!" How could it have been anything but "worse" for those poor Negroes, tenants of the original mediaeval hovels, unchanged and untouched? The house of Margaret Clitheroe, just as she left it when she was pressed to death for harbouring a priest. She was belatedly canonised in 1970, and her house duly "done up." Yet all the "doing up" in the world does not detract from the macabre nature of the story for those who know about it.
   The Negroes did not seem unhappy, sitting placidly in their doorways. Now they are. Like their Western counterparts, well-dressed and affluent, driving the inevitable and ubiquitous car, they evince truculence, discontent, and like them, clamour for their "rights." Life has to go on. The new, the hygienic, secular and materialistic, is superimposed upon the old, the dirty, the mysterious and religious. The difference is superficial. But it is clear that man, collectively, can only do one thing at a time; he cannot achieve everything in the course of one lifetime, or even a chain of entries. Ouspensky observed that Evolution is not necessarily improvement; it is simply *CHANGE*. I could not subscribe to

31

the sentiment when I first read it, but I can now. "Good" conditions do not bring out the best in people, while "bad" conditions certainly do. Unkind treatment often produces heroes, kind treatment whining malcontents on strike for more and more, and the "Welfare State" breeds selfish uncaring attitudes and the shedding of individual responsibility. What *is* one to think?

However at twelve or fourteen years of age I was not thinking much at all. Kath and I were just "being." And when one is young, life is forever, stretching ahead in an unending vista, and always beckoning. So that one has a perpetual urge to press on, and see what lies over the next sunlit, windswept or rain-drenched hill.

Holidays were not confined to Devon. At the age of sixteen I went on a school expedition to Bruges. It made a profound impression on me. The only regret was that Kath was not included in the party, and that Miss Keen, instead of Miss Mizen, was in charge of it. Still, in this dimension, there's no rose without a thorn, and perfection is not for this world, at least, not for more than a split second. One may just touch upon it, but as Robert Burns observes:

> *Pleasures are like poppies spread.*
> *You pluck the flower, its bloom is shed.*
> *Or like the snowfall in the river,*
> *A moment white, then melts for ever.*

Our accomodation was in a convent—*Le Couvent du Sacre Coeur*. It was astonishing. Every item was in the shape of a crucifix, candlesticks, door-knockers, even match-holders. The soft-footed nuns waited on us at table, and all along the outside wall were closets with bars, where the cloistered nuns would reach out emaciated hands through the grill to receive their daily ration of food. This total focus on the other dimension is no more exaggerated than is today's exclusive focus on the physical dimension, and no more alarming, although at the time to my adolescent mind it seemed morbid and macabre.

The church, the centre of the town's activity, was dark and dirty, with cruets on the altar containing what looked like red ink but was affirmed to be the blood of Christ. People were genuflecting there all the time. To my childish mind it was rather nightmarish; the stealthy black-clad figures creeping in and out, seeming to have materialised out of nowhere, like spectres, and returning to nowhere. I had never seen anything like it before, and have not since. We climbed the dizzy height of the "beffroi." How low the parapet was! Broken too, and dangerous. (Shades of Beachy Head!) it made me feel ill, and I had to retreat. From this belfry tower we could see all over Bruges. We visited Rouen and the market-place where Joan of Arc died.

We were conducted to the Field of Waterloo, and I recalled how the Duke of Wellington, surveying the recruits allocated to him for the battle, turned to his aide and said, "I don't know what they'll do to the enemy, but they certainly frighten me!" I have often wondered about it since, in these latter days when we are hourly victimised by burglars and murderers, when louts and thugs are running amok, unchecked, uncaught and unpunished. This *element* has always existed, but our ancestors, for better or worse, knew how to utilise it, and channel it for their own ends and the maintenance of the "Establishment," worthy or unworthy. It won the Battle of Trafalgar, the Battle of Waterloo, it dragged through all Marlborough's Wars, it defeated the Spanish Armada. It was culled from taverns, victims of the press-gangs, prisons, the unhappy dregs of humanity whose sole other option was the gallows, and it made an invincible army.

How can it make sense?

Definitely ill-treatment brings out the best in people; kindness the worst. Only karma can account for it. It loved Nelson. History informs us that men who had fought like tigers wept like wenches when the great Admiral died. Today's scowling, snarling, mugging criminals have nothing to which anyone can appeal, yet they have Social Security disbursements to ensure them the strength to go on mugging. What are we expected to make of it? Which system should we condone? Is mob rule an improvement on judicial oppression? *And will there ever be a compromise?*

Later in our trip, we were taken to Ypres and the Menin Gate and St. Omer. O, that forest of graves and crosses! stretching as far as the eye could see, and *much* further! My young mind could contain no more emotion.

Almost I had no tears left for this horrid twentieth century of ours, during whose third decade my sheltered life slept, although I read of the Great War, and the loss of the *Titanic*, surely, on a small scale, the most poignant the said century had to offer! confronting individuals as it did with the most agonising impossible choice that could ever be made. Only two people made the choice. One was a boy of twelve who would not leave his father, the other an elderly woman who refused to leave her husband. There were only 19 lifeboats, which carried 712 women and children to safety, leaving their menfolk to die a horrific death in the icy sea.

God help me! The choice could have been mine! That is why the fate of the *Titanic* haunts me forever. It was too early for us, certainly; my father did not commence his travelling to America until the thirties, on the *Mauretania* and kindred vessels, but *then*, he might have had to take me with him, as I had no one else. And if *that* had happened to the *Mauretania*, that dreadful choice could have been mine. What would I have done? I wake up at night sweating with the nightmare. It's all very well *now* . . . I could not leave him, my darling Dad . . . I could not! But then, as a girl, with all life in front of me, pressurized and dragged to the lifeboats . . . It just does not bear thinking about . . .

Years ago in Brighton I met an old lady who with her sister had been a survivor of the *Titanic*, invincible and unsinkable as it was —she too was haunted for ever. She said that the doomed passengers were clinging to the iceberg with bleeding fingers, as the escapees pulled away in the lifeboats. I had to close my eyes and turn away, so powerful and terrible was the trauma of what *might* have been! Futile to torment oneself with a hypothesis! It *didn't* happen! And I must be thankful I am not among those "special" souls who are chosen for such appalling tests, and was spared the horror.

All that was in the nature of a digression. For the nonce, Dad was still in our midst, hale and hearty, and on a note of cheer, I will append what I can remember of the songs he sang at parties. One of them narrated how in the London he knew, it was viable to proceed from the Lord Mayor's House to the King's house without touching a street.

> *The coachman gave the Lord Mayor a curious kind of treat.*
> *He drove him from the Mansion House to Buckingham Palace*
> *And didn't go through a street.**

It could be done. The route was via the Mall and the Old Bailey and Drury Lane and Long Acre and St. Martin's Lane and Ludgate Hill, and included nothing named a "street." It was clever really, and had an exciting tune. To renew acquaintance with it, you would probably have to consult the *Musical Archives* or something. In our resourceful world, it is possible to find out anything you want, if you are prepared to do the necessary research. I have held the Duke of Monmouth's pocket-book in my hand, by dint of going, long ago, to the British Museum *Reading Room*, filling in numerous forms and waiting a long time. Worth it, though, for the evocative experience of communicating with that little, black, leather-bound volume with its näive entries.

*From *The Lord Major's Coachman*, circa 1890

There was the comic song about the seaside trunk that was packed with an endless inventory and the key lost with dire consequences, and my father's favourite one I can remember without the archives. *When Father laid the Carpet on the Stairs:*

We all stood round attentive father's orders for to take;
And not a word was whispered, such a fuss did father make;
Altho' with smothered chuckles all our little ribs did ache
When father laid the carpet on the stairs.

First one of us he sent away to purchase carpet-tacks,
Another one for carpet-thread and one to bring bees' wax,
And one to find the hammer, and the gimlet, and the axe
When father laid the carpet on the stairs.

After super-human struggles father got the carpet spread;
He tried to drive a tack in, but he hit his thumb instead.
He dropped the hammer with a grunt, and Oh! the things he said!
When father laid the carpet on the stairs.

Next father tried unrolling it and climbing bit by bit;
He got it right up to the top, and stooped to make it fit;
Then perhaps it was an accident, or perhaps to show his grit
He tobogganned on his waistcoat down the stairs.

Then father rubbed his funny-bone and father rubbed his knee,
And if anyone was laughing father flared around to see;
And tho' we were mearly throttled still we bottled up our glee
When father laid the carpet on the stairs.

We all of us enjoyed it; it was bliss without alloy,
Altho' to show our mirth we were naturally coy;
And mother went behind the pantry-door to hide her joy
When the carpet laid poor father on the stairs.

Then father used some language that is not in common use;
The hammer and the tacks and things he covered in abuse,
And father he consigned the stairs and carpet to the . . . !

So mother laid the carpet on the stairs.

I could sing that tune now. It is as fresh in my memory as if it were yesterday, as is the tribute to John the coachman by the Lord Mayor,

And when Trafalgar Square is reached, the Lord Mayor in a pet
Cries "Dash my wig and barnacles, I think he'll do it yet!"

In default of being able to travel to London to the archives where these childhood memories linger, I can only piece together scrappily the ones I can't remember so vividly. There was among many others the one about Uncle Jeff who was rather deaf.

No matter what to him you say,
Altho' you shout the words right out,
He'll turn them round some other way.

One night, after a Temperance meeting, the vicar proclaimed,
"Drink is a sin."
Said Uncle, "Hey? You'd like some gin?"

"Tut-tut, will you take it neat or no?
Oh, I've got some in.
Oh, you didn't say what?"
"Oh, drink is a sin. Oho!"

And deaf Uncle Jeff again . . .

When church was done,
The curate at our table sat.
We tried in vain with might and main
To carry on a friendly chat.
While Uncle carved, the curate starved,
As helpless as a newborn lamb.
Said Uncle, "Come now, do have some . . .
Shall we say a little beef or ham?"
The curate said, "I don't care for ham."
Said Uncle, "Hey? You don't care a WHAT?
Tut-tut, you mustn't swear, you know!
I'm surprised I am! Oh, you didn't say what?
Oh, you don't care for ham! Oho!"

Then there was the Magistrates' Court, where Uncle Jeff was a magistrate. The question was mooted as to the rectitude of kissing the Bible. . .

Then Green and Brown strolled round the town
And talked about it all the day;
To the court they went, and the argument
They put to Uncle in this way:

"What do you say, Jones? Should we kiss the Book?"
Said Uncle, "Hey? Should we kiss the WHAT?
Tut-tut, I do myself you know, as soon as look . . .
Oh, you didn't say what? Oh, should we kiss the Book?—Oho!"
Old Uncle Jeff is not so deaf at THAT, Tut-tut, Oh no!!

Uncle Jack's song was *Stone-Cracker John*. He couldn't sing, but he was good company. Dad could sing, and he sang *Gypsy John*. Where is Uncle Jack's one-and-only song now? Heaven only knows! But then Heaven *does* know! *Not a sparrow falls*, so 'tis said, and so far I've had reason to gainsay that. But it does not manifest in this world, for innumerable sparrows, and God does not stir a finger to preclude it. Thus the statement of Jesus is borne out, *My kingdom is not of this world*. Ah, I'm forgetting, it was not Uncle Jack's *only* song. For the sake of accuracy, he also sang *Chorus, gentlemen, just once more*, and *Marry old Marjories? No, no, no!* But I had a fellow-feeling for *Stone-Cracker John*, and liked the rousing chorus too:

I sits by the roadside with great regularity,
And I cracks up the stones for the highway authority.
With a Crack-fol-de-riddle-O and Whack-fol-de-ray,
I cracks 'em and whacks 'em for ninepence a day.
Yes I do, then so I do, then, all for ninepence a day.

When the grand folks go by in their wild-cat machinery,
They kicks up a dust and they spoils all the greenery.
With a Crack-fol-de-riddle-O and Whack-fol-de-ray,
I'd whack 'em and crack 'em and show 'em the way!
Yes I would, then, so I would, then, if I had my way!

Goodness knows what Stone-cracker John would make of today's motorways. It probably beggars description and is best left unsaid. They had rollicking tunes set to them, those old songs, and were coherent, which is more than can be said for the whining, snarling "pop-songs" of today, where no words are distinguishable or intelligable, and we are left wondering what in the name of Pete they are trying to express.

Queenie's largesse was not evenly distributed. She fell into the error common to politically orientated persons, that of restricting their friendships to those of like political persuasion. This sterile and unimaginative outlook condemns such persons to a narrow limited horizon and cuts out lots of very nice people from their coterie.

Queenie harboured positive likes and dislikes, and did not like Dad's family; he was the youngest of a too-numerous family, and consequently they seldom visited us, so that with one or two exceptions I did not know them. Probably they were quite nice. I have vague recollections of Auntie Emily, whom we dubbed "the two-shilling aunt", because she always gave us two shillings, a fortune to a child in those days. And speaking of fortunes, there is a fortune in Chancery* in the Kipling archives. Many members of the family in succession tried to run it to earth, but it eluded them. Thus "poverty in the midst of plenty" was always to be my co-keynote with "No Fixed Abode."

There is, or was, an extensive range of wealthy relatives in South Africa, whom I never met. Auntie Ivy came once to England, complained of grey skies and 'buses full of gloomy-faced people in drab raincoats, and never came again; and during the war, my brother, Bernard, on a ship bound for Egypt, met a fellow-soldier of the same name, and Kipling being an uncommon name, sought him out and introduced himself. He turned out to be one of the cousins from Africa.

All this because Uncle Herbert, at age twenty, (he was many years older than Dad, so it was a long time ago), was fed up and out of a job, and one morning decided to work his passage somewhere on a tramp steamer, and try his luck overseas.

His luck was in. He staked out a field in South Africa, (you could do that in those days; it was virgin territory and you could earmark it for yourself), built a shack in one corner and raised a few sheep and grew corn for basic sustenance. Then he secured a job in the diamond mines of Johannesburg and made his pile. He never looked back. But Dad still had to struggle, and was "self-

*The American equivalent of the Unclaimed Accounts Department at the banks.

made." By the end of his life he looked like an aristocrat, with his nice silver hair and stiff white collars and bow-ties, and had taught himself all manner of skills, although he left school at twelve and had to clean the shoes of all his brothers, whom, he declared jokingly, he hated. So the Curse of the O'Connors can be said to have touched Dad vicariously, "Curse-by-Marriage," it might be termed.

Dad's other brother, Uncle John, was the Mayor of Sutton and Cheam. He may have been a trifle pompous, a venial sin, but Queenie didn't like him either. It was his position which accounted for my being included in the welcome to Edward the Prince of Wales, before he became King Edward VIII and ceased to be so because of Mrs. Simpson. He was to cut a length of white ribbon stretched across the Thames officially to "open" Teddington Lock. I was seven years old, and among the handful of infants privileged to witness the spectacular event.

The Prince of Wales obviously did not esteem it a privilege. He was in an irritable mood. Uncle John, in plumed regalia and gold chair of office, was in process of delivering a portentous and long-winded peroration, and the prince muttered, with ill-concealed impatience, "Oh, give me the scissors!" It may well be that I was the only one who heard the injunction; it was *sotto voce*. Uncle John was still droning on; but I was within touching distance of this royal anti-Monarchist. A lifetime later I wrote about him in my most recent book, *The British Monarchy and The Divine Right of Kings*.

As a family, our annual treat was our visit to the Queen's Hall and the Glasgow Orpheus Choir under its famous conductor Sir Hugh Robertson. Their voices were so pure and sweet. Jean Hastings and Annie Tait singing *Bonnie Dundee* enchanted me; they strike chords in my heart to this day. Auntie Madge and Uncle Bert always came up for this, laden with primroses and brown eggs in a basket; it was always just at Easter. One memorable year, Miss Mizen accepted my parents' invitation, given for my sake, and my cup of happiness was full and could hold nor more.

Later, as Kath and I grew older, we would go up to London ourselves, and queue up, sometimes all night, for gallery seats at one-and-six at the Old Vic, to see John Gielgud step out of his taxi and go in by the side door of the theatre. All we saw of him would be his hat pulled down over his eyes, and his coat-collar pulled up to meet it as he rushed in out of the rain. Heavens! I would want paying to do that now, let alone pay one-and-six for it! I hate getting up early, and sitting in the rain, and still more I hate a howling wind. I was killed by a gale of wind in an earlier life and have been terrified of high winds ever since.

Other friends, close to Queenie, but only names to me, were Bernard Shaw and Beatrice and Sydney Webb, and the Pethick-Lawrences, some less well-known ones, and before my time, Emmeline Pankhurst, when Queenie was young. She would recount enthralling anecdotes of how the suffragettes climbed on the roofs of buildings and threw tiles down before the horses' feet, and of their sojourns in prison, and of Lady Constance Lowell's book on the need for prison reform. I have been a pioneer myself in the esoteric field, and whenever I apprehend myself feeling sorry for myself by reason of the thanklessness of the task and the absence or paucity of "feed-back," I recall the sacrifice and suffering of those brave women, without whose dedication I would not have enjoyed the freedom I have known. Because whatever I may have lacked, I have had *that*.

Subsequently I gave lectures on the suffragettes, and in America much interest was aroused.

Queenie's "constituency" or political arena was Bermondsey, where she worked with Dr. Alfred Salter, a champion of the poor. She waged strenuous battles with the Conservative Committee to get poplar trees planted along the streets of Bermondsey. The committee intimated that trees were not a necessity for slum-dwellers. This aroused her Irish ire; she kept on, and won, and the trees are there to this day, still "Queenie's Trees," though doubtless generations of Bermondsey residents would not know why.

Queenie's link with the district stemmed from an earlier life, circa 1480, when as the wife of a humble market-gardener, (my father 'Ernie' in the current entry), with my brother Bernard and Cousin Joy as they became), she would travel by barge past the marshes of Rotherhithe to sell vegetables to the convent at Bermondsey, where she observed Elizabeth Woodville, in whom she was greatly interested, being, then likewise, keenly alert to the politics of the day, and infiltrated a great deal of intelligence concerning that unhappy queen.

There was one outstandingly vivid childhood recollection which I think laid the foundations of all that I have thought or done during my entire life. I was only four or five years old, but it is etched on my mind in letters of fire . . .

My mother hated the Church, and all manner of humbug and hypocrisy. She was devastatingly and embarassingly outspoken. The name "Queenie" was an allusion to the kings and queens of Eire, and to her regal demeanour. Her actual names were Ethel Isabel. She used to take me to school daily on the top deck of the 'bus, whence I was monarch of all I surveyed. We used to pass a viaduct, which was plastered with advertisements extolling the merits of Cadbury's Milk Chocolate, and informing that Rowntrees' Cocoa was the best, and that Bovril Prevented That Sinking Feeling, and sandwiched in between them a statement from the "Religious Tract Society" that *"God is Love."* At four, I could just read short words, and knew that the cat sat on the mat. I asked, "Mummy, what does that mean? God is Love?"

I shall never forget my mother's reply, and the clipped iciness of the tone: "I haven't the slightest idea, and neither have the people who put it there!"

I was totally perplexed. Why did Mummy sound so angry? I knew I hadn't done anything. She was talking , not to me at all, but to herself. I think that even at that early stage, something began to stir in my soul. I believe that I formed a resolution, or began to, at the monadic level of course, which grew into a crusade, to find out. Now I have. And it doesn't mean anything like the Religious Tract Society thought it did.

My mother died.

Bald statements can embody more significance then a wealth of detail. I could not have given a detailed description, or any description at all, of the way it happened, or the sense of stunned confusion it engendered, which beset me at the time. The sense was in abeyance, then descended again like a pall, in later years when the full reaction set in. She was the healthiest person I have ever known. She always steered clear of doctors. She went on holiday, cut her foot on a rock while bathing, was dead within three weeks from Septicaemia. It was the year for her to go. I have always averred that we go when our work is done. To wit, William Wilberforce, who dedicated his life to freeing the black slaves, and died on the eve of his Bill at long last being passed through Parliament. *"The One who opens the Door never enters."* So it was with Queenie. So it has been with me, in the esoteric field. . . . . not that that is a "field"; it is all God's acres. But the principle is the same. The end of one's work should synchronise with the end of one's life. Where it does not, the evolutionary path is not being followed, and deviations are being allowed to retard progress, or else one is deliberately "cliff-hanging" for the sake of someone else, or is aware of some outstanding item of karma.

The ancients knew how to dispose of the physical form when it "dies." This is lost knowledge. They may not have known how things were done, but they knew what to do.* We know how things are done, but we don't know what to do. *Autres temps, autres abilities!*

A cremation represents trauma to the young. . .that is, the sort of "young" that we were, with the horrid black cars, the massed flowers,. . . gloves . . . I glanced down at my hands, helplessly folded in my lap. I never wore gloves. Queenie wouldn't have wanted me to wear them; she never bothered about such things. *She* never wore them. . . at least I don't think so. I never saw her with them. But I was in a daze, and could not think coherently.

The hastily contrived blue coffin stood on a platform. In a trance I was aware of Dr. Alfred Salter reading a poem,

Calmly, calmly lay her down;
She has fought a noble fight. . .

Then with a hideous swishing sound, a curtain—also blue—it's surprising how such details linger, was drawn across it, and it disappeared. Where? *Forever?* NO! I found myself almost shouting out loud. It wasn't possible! There was no logic in it, no sense! There must be something else! It was not so much that I had "loved" my mother. I hadn't had time to do that, It was the thought of that powerful, vibrant, dominating personality being snuffed out! Just like that! My undeveloped mind could not assimilate. It choked my already choking throat; my whole soul rose up in repudiation. And then, in a flash, I knew that it is only the *form* that disappears, not its more durable counterpart.

I threw myself assiduously into a hectic social whirl; partly to be in the swim, and partly no doubt to take my mind off what had transpired. I joined the Rambling Club and the Youth Club and the Swimming Club, went to dances in the Corn Exchange, and cultivated a succession of boyfriends.

It was not then fashionable to sleep with one's boyfriends on first sight, but a competitive spirit prevailed among adolescent females as to how many one could "go out with" in the shortest possible time. I counted twenty-two in as many weeks. One, at Lyme Regis, took me out in a rowing-boat and lost the oars, whereupon we drifted for hours before being rescued by a fisherman. That one I dismissed as the twit of the week and turned for solace to another. He introduced me to raw Devon cider straight from the barrel,

---

*I am not fully conversant with the ins and outs of this but I gather that it was related to the science of sonics, and had something to do with the middle ear. The ancients were trained from the outset to discover the sounded *note* which would result in the dissolution of their particular physical form, just as Joshua discovered the note that would bring down the walls of Jericho. The militating factor was the middle ear, the membrane referred to as the *tympanum*, which was the last portion of the last faculty to "die."

persuading me that it was a form of lemonade. I was dehydrated with thirst after hiking all day in the hot sun. I downed quarts, and disappeared beneath a hedge for half a day, and the Rambling Club had to wait till I regained my faculties. That one was written off as a cad and a deceiver and I never spoke to him again. None of them represented perfection in my rather fastidious estimation, though I was pretty and found little difficulty in attracting them.

There was one nice one, Robert Patchin (a true old Sussex name), but he grew too "serious," lapsed into melancholy and indited soulful (though really quite professional) poems to me, until the War absorbed him and hopefully he forgot me and my faithless ways. Others followed, but after a while the pastime palled. I registered the reflection, "Chaps of my own age are callow. Girls are more mature. I'll try my luck with older men." No need to go to extremes, but Sagittarians tend to be "all or nothing," and all my husbands and subsequent attachments were older men.

I half-heartedly took a few "jobs." Like the boyfriends, they seldom lasted more than a couple of weeks; they were so unutterably boring. It seemed to me that practically all "jobs" were negative. In a decent society, I thought, we shouldn't need a twentieth of the vocations or commodities that employ the populace; no police, no lawyers, because everyone would behave decently; no doctors or dentists, because no one would be ill; (to think that indeed in antiquity there had been civilisations like that, no cigarettes or alcohol, as no one would be under the stress and strain that needs these narcotics); no spare parts for motor-cars, as people would use the legs God had given them. I came to the conclusion that it was all a dead end and a waste of time, secretaries typing rubbish all day about things that didn't matter, business-firms making long-distance phone calls to Australia talking rubbish. I became a sort of refined drop-out. My academic qualifications would have secured me a "career." I had an Honours Degree in Matriculation, and had got as far as Inter-BA at Kings College in the Strand when my mother died and we moved to Brighton. But I was unambitious in that area. Dad could keep me, and I simply let him. I was still egregiously selfish, while he was generous to a fault. I made a concession to learn shorthand and typing, forgot the shorthand but can still type, after a fashion. Just as well, since I've had to do so much of it.

At one point I longed to be an actress. I was good at that, and had scored a number of triumphs in the school plays at Whyteleafe. In London I enquired at the main Drama School in Gowar Street, but the Curse of the O'Connors stepped in. I could not take the course because fencing was a compulsory aspect of it, and my arm would not permit.

I was versed in foreign languages and was bilingual as far as French was concerned—I could have got a "good" job as an interpreter or something. But why bother? I was lazy and unambitious, and content to drift and dream.

But not entirely content. I wanted to know what life was all about.

43

My father was seeking an answer too. Together we "took up" elementary spiritualism. In those days it took the form of "table rocking." How that table rocked! The "evidence" we received was so total, so incontrovertible that we could never doubt again. At the same time, it did not solve mundane problems. My father was a dear; but he could not cope. Our home broke up. He sold *Millerdene*, the Purley House, at a loss, and Queenie's full set of leather-bound volumes of all the famous poets was stolen, a great grief to me.

We drifted. We moved to Brighton. Dad purchased a house there, in Chatsworth Road, and Bernard and his fiancé Joan moved in with us. Kath came to stay, and we walked the many miles to Alfriston and Cuckmere Haven, and picked mushrooms and swam in the sea. For a while, briefly and in a shadowed way, we relived our happy childhood.

Meanwhile, Dad travelled to London each day. I know he used to get very tired doing that, and he was no longer young. But I was by no means fully aware of him, or of what his feelings and thoughts must have been, or how lonely he was. I was too much immersed in my own living. He did not marry again, albeit not for want of those who hoped he would team up with them. There would have been no substitute for Queenie. Again, I have no way of knowing whether he "loved" her. Their temperaments were diametrically opposed, but much may be ascribed to the fact that each was absorbed in his/her own pursuits, she in politics, he in travel, that even if they had not "got on" together as the saying is, they could have covered it up. Whatever their relationship had been, Dad still had twenty-two long years of loneliness to face before he won his freedom. I must have been quite useless to him as a companion. I truly loved him, but somehow could not "get through" to him, nor he to me. And I know that he loved me, more deeply and faithfully than I deserved. Parents and children often break each others' hearts. It is one of the inexplicable things that just happen. He and I would walk to Rottingdean along the cliff-path, or over the downs to Poynings and Edburton, but said little, and kept dumb about our sadness. We were tongue-tied, and to me it seemed as if a shutter had come down over my ability to communicate any kind of comfort to him.

My brother got married and moved to Southwick. The house was too large for Dad and me. We moved to a flat in Croydon. I never had a home after that.

But before we left Brighton, there was a letter. It was from Tatsfield, in an unformed, childish hand. It was from Kath's youngest sister, Ivy. The family were at breakfast, she said, when they heard a shot. They rushed out to the barn. Kath had shot herself. She had taken her father's gun, that he used to shoot rabbits, and shot herself through the head. No one knew why. I did not, then. *I do now*. But last year, 1993, I found her elder sister Gladys, after a lifetime, and reassured her that she would see Kath again. I gave her the pictures Kath had painted and given me, and her last letter to me, and Gladys, no longer sad, went back to her home in Australia with the hurt gone. She is a part of the Sandys Butler* network, and the *Sandys Butler File* is extant for Posterity if Posterity wants it.

For the nonce, however, none of that had entered my consciousness, and all I could do was to cast myself down on the stairs—I can recall the vaguely dusty smell of the carpet even now, and sob, "O Kath! Kath! Why? Why" *Why?*"

It was probably then that I began to grow up. O, Byron, how right you were when you said,

> *There's not a joy the world can give*
> *Like that it takes away,*
> *When the glow of early thought declines*
> *In feeling's long decay.*
>
> *It's not from youth's smooth cheek*
> *The blush alone that fades so fast,*
> *But the tender bloom of heart is gone*
> *Ere youth itself be past.*** ◆

* See Appendix.
**From *Stanzas for Music.*

I V

Dad

But it was not quite over, and youth is resilient. As intimated, a shutter had indeed come down for the time being, as a kind of defence-measure; and I know that the full impact of Queenie's death, and Kath's, hard on each others' heels, was deferred.

Moreover, the War supervened and claimed everyone's attention, no matter what their circumstances may have been. When that happened, I was all alone in London. Dad had gone to Switzerland when war was declared, staying in his favourite hotel, and eating his breakfast kipper, (kippers were the hotel's specialty). The manager rushed to warn him . . . "Oh, Mr. Kipling, pray leave! The last train for England is due to depart, and you will be interned for the duration!"

It is one of those strange truths that my father never missed a train in his life, and likewise that he never hurried. "These kippers are so nice," he declared, "It's a pity not to finish them." Rather like Drake's game of bowls.* Dad picked up his little case, (he was adept at travelling light; sometimes my mother had avowed he only packed a toothbrush; he was the tidiest man I ever knew), walked leisurely to the station, and stepped into the last carriage of that last train, just as it was moving out. What a blessing for me that he did, for I was all alone on Hampstead Heath when the first siren sounded and the whole world surged in a wild stampede for the Underground.

It was a weird experience. The September evening was heavy and gloomy. The heath where Keats roamed was as deserted as it was when he wrote his *Ode to a Nightingale* there in 1819. I expected a bomb to fall at any moment. But it didn't . . . And none fell for the rest of that year, till a lot of

---

*England's Sir Francis Drake anticipated the arrival of the Spanish Armada calmly. He trusted the tides to tell the time reliably, while he carried on with his game.

people were beginning to call it a "phoney war." But I couldn't face the claustrophobia of the Underground, and would rather die in the open air.

Then Dad was there again, and shortly after that we moved to Yorkshire.

Dad's company was affiliated to that of Sir Harold Macintosh. The famous firm was founded on tiny beginnings. An old lady invented a recipe for toffee. her humble cottage on the outskirts of Halifax was the cradle of world trade. Her grandson took some to school; someone tasted it who wielded "influence," and she was approached and persuaded to put her product on the market. Dad, at the age of 46, elected to change course in midstream, and created his own business in *chewing gum*! "Bubbly Gum," it was called. Horrid stuff, but it caught on like wildfire, first in America, then in England. The resultant company was amalgamated with Macintosh, and accordingly we transferred to Halifax, which was a relief from being bombed nightly in London.

We had a narrow escape from being bombed the night before we left, (only one of several, but everyone had to refrain from recounting "bomb stories" because they were such a common experience.) We were covering our heads in the basement of the Strand Palace Hotel.

We arrived at Halifax after a sleepless night and a train journey packed like sardines with the Army and the R.A.F. One poor young soldier was so exhausted that he leant against me, slumped into my lap and snored all night.

It may sound selfish, but in many ways the War years were the happiest of my life, except of course for the magic year when I was sixteen, before anything happened to me at all, before I knew what the world was like, when my horizon was bounded by school and Kath and Miss Mizen and Devon and Ashurst, every goose was a swan, every man a gentleman and every tree was green. Now everything had fallen apart. The family was decimated, Queenie, Uncle Ernie, Kath, Eric, Toby, all gone. Youth can put it together again, albeit only temporarily. For me, though not for my father, sorrow was in abeyance. It was not until much later that it came back with compound interest.

I had met an artist. In the Studio Club in Piccadilly just before it was bombed. His name was Harold Lisle, and he came from Taunton. He was a fine artist, and dressed for his ARA part, wearing a wide-brimmed black hat and a cloak instead of a coat, which was assumed to add kudos. He was twenty-seven years older than I. He painted my portrait which was exhibited in the Royal Academy. It was a miniature on ivory. Miniatures were Harold's specialty, and

he excelled at them. He was a nice person, if I recall aright, it was all so long ago, and had a genial sense of humour, which appealed to me. God knows we needed that during the War. Churchill was invaluable in that respect. His inimitable early morning chats to the nation were a tonic. Only five minutes, but they kept us going all day. It was literally the only entertainment we had; and if he were remembered for nothing else, he would be forever remembered for that wonderful capacity for making people laugh.

I decided to marry Harold. My father, almost on his knees, begged me not to. As mentioned, Harold was a nice enough man, but permanently impecunious, as is the wont of artists, was always borrowing money, no less from my doting and long-suffering father, and "No Fixed Abode" was his mode of existence, as indeed ours had become.

It was not that Dad did not like him, but he, unlike me, could foresee the consequences. Notwithstanding, when you are twenty, you know everything. There simply isn't anyone can tell you about anything, least of all your unfortunate parents. I, who knew all the answers, dismissed my father as senile, (he was fifty-six), and charged full-steam ahead in my resolution to marry Harold. To which end I tramped seventeen miles in deep snow to Bradford to find him lodgings and a job. I found both, "imported" him from London where he was eking out a miserable existence working in some office and being bombed nightly, and married him.

Poor Dad, lonelier than ever, remained in the same lodging without me. Loyal to me as ever, he made the best of Harold, and in many ways the two got on well.

I registered for employment and took a job tramping the moors interviewing sailors' wives and pensioners about their war allowances. It entailed being out in all weathers and walking miles. But I had always been out in all weathers and walking miles. Indeed I can't bear to do anything else. I grow claustrophobic indoors for any length of time. It was exhilarating. I was being paid for doing what I liked doing, and not many people are so lucky. We were not paid much, but that did not signify. It was a solitary vocation; I could think my own thoughts, make up stories and prepare newspaper articles as I went along, commune with Nature. There were no cars, no fumes, no crowds, no louts, no criminals. They were all away at war, under supervision, out of harm's way. We were safe. From each other, that is. Looking back, it is like contemplating another world.

But there were *bulls* in the beautiful countryside and on the moors. I wasn't safe from them. Once there was only a patch of stinging nettles between me and one of them. Bulls terrify me. I was killed by one in a former life. However, he only stared at me, swinging his tail.

Dogs abounded also. The memory of a singular incident is so vivid that I set it on record, since it does not come into the category of "bomb stories."

There was a surly farmer, living in a cottage at the foot of a steep slope near Luddendenfoot, who kept a collie-dog chained to a kennel all the time. It was angry, frustrated and ferocious accordingly, and would have killed anyone who came within reach. On the occasion when I encountered it, the slope was a sheet of ice. We were issued with what was euphemistically termed "Government Protective Clothing." In other words a hideous stiff shapeless garment which resembled a tent, and made no concession to the waistline. My foot slipped on the top of the slope, my protective clothing acted as a sledge, and I careered remorselessly toward the slavering jaws awaiting my descent. I calculated the distance and grew aware that I should land helplessly at the extremity of the dog's chain. I recount it in detail in that it is illustrative of the calmness and crystal clear thinking which comes when death is imminent. The dog would have torn my throat out, and I was simply calculating.

It was the same at Wimbleton when Dad and I had been in the cellar of the house we were lodged in after Croydon and before Hampstead and Kensington. A bomb had demolished the adjoining house which had been metamorphosed into a crater. The brick wall of the cellar caved in, literally folding up, (a phenomenon I have never witnessed since, but those versed in such technicalities explain as being caused by "shock waves"), then, miraculously it went back into place. My father's eyes and mine met, and said without a word being uttered, "This is it, Goodbye." And I had been as cool as a cucumber. It is the subsequent reaction that brings the fear.

It may well be a universal experience, whereby Spirit provides us with an extra quota of insight, or an access of adrenalin or something. Be that as it may, my headlong course terminated just one inch from the dog's teeth. Otherwise this would not have got written. One thing's certain; we cannot go till our time's up.

I helped the Billeting Officer find homes for evacuees. Another bald statement. I wrote a book about it.* It warranted a book all to itself. The book was in a light vein. That a lighter vein was needed if ever anything was! They say it was the English sense of humour, as epitomised by Churchill, that won the War. The Germans did not appreciate that indispensable asset. One hears from the younger generation of Germans that during the War their parents never laughed. They were entirely *literal*. They regarded English people as mad. *"How* can you hang washing on the Siegfried Line? This is stupid! Ridiculous! And why do they publish in their newspaper that their Prime Minister is allowed an extra egg because he has to get up before five o'clock in the morning? They are insane people, with their silly jokes!"

Anyone who wants to read *IMPACT* will find therein an expanded chronicle of our adventures and occasional hilarity. We were a threesome in the

*IMPACT, 1945.

Billeting Office. There was Mrs. Foster, little Joyce Pickles, and me. Mrs. Foster was "out of the Top Drawer," a true blue Englishwoman of the old school, with quality and culture and the proverbial stiff upper lip. After the War, she was invested by the Queen for her unfailing patriotic service. In 1990 I revisited her, (it was so strange to be in Yorkshire again, so very karmic), and renewed my awareness of that same indomitable spirit, keen blue eyes and ineradicable, indefinable "class." It has all but died out. *

I am always quoting poetry. Mrs. Foster noticed the habit, and suggested that I should gather together all the poetry I knew and compile an anthology. I did so that year, and sent her a copy at Christmas, and one each to my best friends in America. All my favourite poems, and there are so many! I can recite them all by heart. The anthology is in the trunk with the other papers and books for Ian to handle. In this respect I will not emulate my father, who cleared out and destroyed all papers and items relating to his life. It is not I who wants to be remembered, but my knowledge, amassed over the years. God knows I have been privileged to get it! I would not have got it had I not known what it is to be poor; it was during that phase of my life, when I and the children were poor, that I learned, once and for all, beyond cavil, that help is available. Had I been always as I am now, furnished with somewhat more of this world's goods, it is doubtful whether or not I should have got it. I never cease to thank God for that strange, and to me, *sweet* interlude, in a dip in the Sussex Downs, when we were all alone with Nature, and the angels, and the Source. Invaluable, precious, unrepeatable!

Mrs. Foster came from Wellington in Somerset. The cause of her being in Yorkshire was that her first husband, whose name was Ashplant had crashed as an RAF pilot during the war and had died there. The reason for her still being domiciled in Yorkshire was that she had remarried there. The first husband's ghost was there. I told her about it gently and tactfully. Conventional people do not understand at first, but later they do. And of course in the sleep state, and on the astral plane, they do all the time.

Halifax was ear-marked as a "Reception-Centre" for evacuees. It has been cleaned up now, but then it hadn't been. It reposed beneath a pall of smoke and industrial grime, and the aroma or rather effluvia from the bone-yard at Southowram defied description. If you wore a white collar, it was grimy by lunchtime, while an old man I met there declared that as a boy he had been under

---

* Mr. Major aims at a "classless society," and what a mediocre society it is! Systematically everything and everyone is trampled down into the common mud. Mediocrity is enthroned and extolled. The eternal trouble with the "levelling" process is that the levelling is always *down*, never *up*. Even very old people can scarcely remember what an English gentleman was like. It is an endangered species, if not extinct.

the impression that trees were black, because if you touched one, your hand would be covered with soot.

So Halifax nestled cosily under its blanket of smog, and the Germans could not find it, and it formed thereby the ideal reception area for refugees.

Yet long anterior to that, when the broad acres were pure and clean and cold, young Langdale Sunderland set out one sparkling October morning in the highest of spirits from that amazing home of his, High Sunderland, on it's windswept height overlooking Halifax, to join his uncle Sir Marmaduke Langdale at Skipton in the Civil War.

I know how he felt. I was out all day, braving the moors in all weathers, twenty miles a day sometimes. There was no transport; no *cars*; what bliss not to see them! Strings and strings of them, nose to tail, one silly face after another staring over a steering wheel, clamped into place by seatbelts, like a dreary contingent of convicts. At night it was uncanny; no lights; only the moon, and we have never beheld it to such advantage since. The Atlanteans would have marvelled; they knew no moon until the end was upon them. It must have been like that centuries ago, and the peace of the countryside and villages something we noise-racked, speed-frenzied moderns could not hope to comprehend in a month of Sundays.

It was here that I first became *consciously* aware of the mechanics of reincarnation. I had of course always known the truth of reincarnation as a fact of Nature, and in that sense everyone knows it. But people don't know they know it, until they attain to their individual moment of truth, or, technically, "the soul's awakening," or Liberation of Consciousness. The truth within all of us has to unfold; as Browning observed, *"Truth is within ourselves; it takes no rise from outward things."* And the tempo of that unfoldment varies with the individual and his/her degree of advancement.

I knew my way over earthly territory which in the current life I had never seen. I had only once been in Yorkshire before, and that was a long way from the West Riding, at Whitby, on one of our CHA* or HF** holidays, the year before Queenie died. I spontaneously recognised all the seventeenth-century landmarks. I had covered that terrain thoroughly in my life as *Jennifer Butler*. I wrote an article about the Shibden Valley*** which was published in *Country Life*. I wrote articles for the newspapers in the intervals of billeting evacuees. It was a wondrously stimulating phase, but not, probably, for my unfortunate husband, who was rather left to fend for himself.

This beautiful area near Halifax about which I wrote the article, I called *The Valley Time Forgot*. All the farms and cottages along its extensive length

---

* Co-operative Holidays Association
** Holiday Fellowship
***see photo

51

are at least three hundred years old, and I knew the names of all of them, and all the landmarks, and no one told me. The article marked the beginning of a series of contracts with newspapers, and I savoured the kudos of my status as part-time journalist. There wasn't much leisure however wherein to savour it. As the War entered its third year, pressures escalated and we were continually on call. Nevertheless it was enormous fun, as I recall it, in the intervals of our nerves getting a trifle frayed. I am convinced however that, despite being young and carefree, we should not have been so happy and even hilarious sometimes, had we known about the concentration camps and the horrors being enacted in Europe. We had no cognizance of it. Churchill did not tell us that. His task was to keep the morale up, and he certainly did so, with this wit and eloquence and understanding of the British people, as we then were but no longer are. There was only one-third of the number of people then; they were all English, and they were nice. Rarely does a monarch or statesman possess that gift of understanding. The first Queen Elizabeth had it, and Churchill had it. The English respond to inspired leadership, and to nothing else.

In default of that, they slow down and grow disenchanted, and when "little men" mess about with us, we are doomed. When bureaucrats take over, as has occurred in the last half-century, a nation such as we were does not adjust or adapt, or conform to alien types of "Government." It dies, as England has done. Without Queen Elizabeth, the Spanish Armada might have invaded; without Churchill, who knows? Rudyard Kipling, in his inimitable way, summed up the charisma in one concise verse:

> *When king and country understand each other, past a doubt*
> *It takes a foe, and more than a foe to knock that country out.*
> *For the one will do what the other requires,*
> *Whenever the need is shown*
> *And hand-in-hand they can make a stand*
> *That neither could make alone.*
>
> *This wisdom had Elizabeth, and all her subjects too;*
> *For she was theirs, and they were hers,.*
> *As well the Spaniard knew.*
>
> *So when his grim Armada came to conquer*
> *The nation and throne,*
> *Why, back-to-back they met an attack*
> *That neither could face alone.*

The dominating and most impressive feature of the Shibden Valley* which my spirit urged me to frequent, was *Scout Hall*, built by one John Mitchell in 1680, and I recognised it at once, and recalled John Mitchell too, for as *Jennifer Butler* I had seen him from a distance, when his house was new, and the stone a creamy colour instead of being smoke-grimed by the Yorkshire Woollen Industry. It boasted 365 windows, one for each day of the year, and over the portal was carved and depicted a fox-hunt, as being the favourite pastime of the owner. In my current life I communicated with John Mitchell, who lost his life at the age of thirty-seven, in trying out a flying machine of his own contriving, from the steep escarpment behind his house.

When I first saw Scout Hall in this life, the house was dilapidated, and occupied by war refugees, but it was occupied by John Mitchell's ghost as well, and his dark mysterious and somewhat sinister portrait was still inset in the wall. The evacuee families assigned to Scout Hall protested that they could not stay there another second, by reason of the said ghost, which walked up and down, up and down the panelled staircase all night, the footsteps echoing hollowly in the kitchen where they had their meals. Subsequently I exorcised it, and the circumstance is more fully dealt with in the *Sandys Butler* story.**

Now, my past lives were becoming revealed to me, in rapid succession and meticulous detail. Then the War ended, and we continued in the motley assortment of "furnished rooms" that had become second nature to us. Thankfully, however, Dad was vouchsafed a little luck at last, and moved in with Molly Mason, a kindly soul who genuinely cared for him. Harold and I, with our label "No Fixed Abode" now indetachably pinned on us, negotiated one furnished room after another, all awful, and he perforce toiled on in "Commercial Art," with me writing the captions. His artistic skill was utterly wasted, but that was a part of War, while journalism came readily to me, and somehow we eked out some sort of precarious livelihood, frankly, I shall never know how!

I was writing now. Articles no longer sufficed. I aimed at historical novels. I went to Scotland, followed faithfully in the steps of "Bonnie Dundee," John Grahame of Claverhouse, in whom I was passionately interested, partially as a legacy from my previous life as Jennifer Butler. I became entranced by that magical country. From Dundee's castle at Dudhope I travelled to Paisley and the home of his wife Jean Cochrane, and thence to Pitlochry and Killiekrankie. I shall never forget the uprush of emotion engendered by his lonely grave above Blair Atholl. I had climbed up there during my solitary peregrinations with a sandwich but not the ubiquitous tin of "Coke." You could drink from the streams in those days. It was like stepping back in time and into a different

* It means 'Sheep-dene' or valley
**See Appendix

53

world. The outcome was my book *The Devil and Dundee*, which the publisher Sir John Murray personally commended, but feared that while it would make a best seller in Scotland, it might not fare so well south of the Border. Disappointment is an integral part of publishing, and it was my first but not last salutory lesson in that.

Apart from work, Harold and I lived our separate lives. The Billeting Office closed down, but I carried on my tradition of walking about, encountering ghosts in the ancient halls of Yorkshire, and delving into my own past lives, recognising landmarks without consciousness, yet relating them to my own former identities. That did not supervene all at once. I took all my holidays and weekends apart from Harold. He was a bit of a stick-in-the-mud by my impatient standards at that time, and did not care to participate in the same strenuous programmes. But he did not begrudge them to me. He was content with his own measured pace, as a middle-aged Capricorn subject, would quietly smoke his pipe, do his painting, spend time with Dad, sit at home. All proceeded on very amicable lines, and indeed might have done so indefinitely, had I not met Robert Moncrieff. But there it was, I did. Nelson did not say, "Kiss me, Hardy"* as some chroniclers claim. He said, *"Kismet, Hardy!"* and that's what I had to say. **KARMA!** Lots of it!

I have always been "led," inexorably, to karmic contacts, major or minor. There is no escaping them. Such re-introductions are taking place all the time, all over the globe, though not everyone is able to recognise them when they present themselves; and of course with today's rapid universal transport, there has been a massive speeding-up of karma, since people, dashing here, there, and everywhere, are in a position to meet them, whereas a century ago they could not have done so.

But before the War ended, I went on several solitary walking tours. Solitary they were too! At night the moon was so bright, by reason of "the blackout." The peace of wartime can only be imagined by the most imaginative of subsequent generations! Except for the awesome raid on Coventry which lit up the sky for so many miles that we could see it from a hill above Leeds. It was not until peace "broke out" that internecine warfare began under the aegis of petty bureaucrats who had never enjoyed a monopoly in England before.

I elected to walk from Macclesfield to Buxton, (it must have been in repudiation of the strictures of Dr. Channing-Pierce) and become hopelessly lost. There wasn't a dwelling for miles on those heathery heights. I had finished my sandwiches and was ravenous. I had a tin of Nestle's milk and no tin-opener. I bashed that tin on every sharp rock and boulder I came upon. I jumped on it, stamped on it, threw it against cliff-faces, all to no avail. It was growing dark, and I was exhausted. A thunderstorm threatened and the sky lowered. I recollected

*while dying aboard his flagship *Victory*

reading that the last wild cat in England had been killed in this location in the nineteenth century. Perhaps it hadn't been! My heightened perceptions may have conjured up its phantom. What if it had had kittens? Perhaps one of these was crouching on that awful boulder, ready to pounce on me! Well, at least I could hurl my tin of Nestle's milk at it and go down fighting. That was, if I had the strength left to hurl anything. I sank down beneath a skeleton thorn-bush and waited to die.

After what seemed an eternity, a lorry hove into view. In my near-delirium it could have been a dinosaur. The driver stopped, leaned out, and demanded, "What the Hell are you doing here?" I could not articulate. "Jump in," he directed, jerking a thumb. For a split second I must have demurred, for he added with some irony, "Well, you've nothing to lose, have you?"

Too right I hadn't!

"There won't be another vehicle this way for a week," he pointed out. "and that'll be me!"

He was the sole traveller on that route, long-distance, overnight to Glossop.

I huddled on the elevated seat beside him, more dead than alive. Darkness had fallen. He halted at a wayside spring and took out a razor. For one ghastly moment my heart stood still. "Got to shave," he explained. "Got to deliver a few things in Glossop first thing."

Having performed his ablutions he produced hunky sandwiches and a rare bar of chocolate, his ration, which he shared with me. "We'll get breakfast at me mate's caff," he promised as we set off again. He was kindness itself, and I, fortified by the refreshments, was able to appreciate the magnificent scenery we passed as dawn broke.

"Now I'll show you some *real* scenery," he said, and took a detour so that I could see the beauty of the Great Snake Pass. He showed me where they had "drowned" a village to make a reservoir. A calm, untroubled enough stretch of water it seemed. "But they say you can hear the church bells at the bottom," he said. Strange. A miniature Atlantis, or Lyonnesse. He treated me to strong hot tea and wartime sausages (mostly oatmeal) at his mate's "caff," and wouldn't accept payment. His name was Arnold Blood, "Bloody" for short, among his mates.

Bloody drove me all the way back to Halifax, from door to door. I never forgot him. He came to see me once thereafter at the Billeting Office. Ships that pass in the night. They are not always ships. Sometimes they are lorries, and to some of them we owe our lives.

Those were wonderful days; except for that "sixteen" year. You couldn't have parallel adventures now, in England at any event; there are too many louts and criminals about.

Ranging the moors in all weathers, with the wind in my hair, and no responsibilities (that I was prepared to shoulder), I was as fancy-free and carefree as a curlew. It was not that I had erased the memory of my mother's death and Kath's death from my thoughts; far from it; but the full backwash of that lay in the future.

Although the War was over and the mass rejoicings in London had subsided a little, we still had to register for work. I wanted a part-time job, so I could be free to walk about. There was only one. It was for a secretary to the Research Chemist at Patons and Baldwins. I did not fancy it, and turned it down repeatedly. But it was always the only one, every time I went back to the Employment Agency. At last, inevitably, to terminate the War of Attrition with the Powers That Be, I capitulated and took the line of least resistence as I was destined to do.

Robert Moncrieff succeeded in wrecking my life, at least temporarily. I believe, after much soul-searching, that there *is* something special about Sagittarians, in that they can go down to suicidal depths, for a long time, but come up again at last, where another would have been submerged beyond all redemption. He wrecked his own life too, and that of his wife only for good measure. He also contributed to my son Ian's bewilderment.

He was a brilliant man. He once observed with perfect veracity, "I think everything about me is bad, except my mind." He was the best Research Chemist the famous firm ever had, the managing Director readily admitted, but because of his total inability or unwillingness to get on with his fellow-man, he was asked to leave, an unprecedented circumstance in a business concern noted for its tolerance and broad-mindedness.

Matrimonial impasses, as mentioned, are adequately dealt with in the tabloid press. Most people at some stage of their lives seem to become embroiled in such fraught and emotionally charged passages, even to the extent of rendering their own and others' lives a misery. In our current society, this truth is exemplified by the curious exploits of the 'Royal Family,' which is alleged to represent all of us. Looking back, it all seems so unnecessary, and you wonder whether, if you had your time over again, you would have bothered at all about anything or anyone. As far as husbands are concerned, you probably wouldn't have exerted yourself to cross the road to speak to them. Yet you produce children with them. That would be frightening indeed if you did not know what the process was all about, and then too, that these children knew it too, *at the monadic level,* before they appeared to commit so egregious an error of judgement. We are all only ships that pass in the night, and we are all one in the end. But karma is terrifyingly compulsive, and a great deal of turmoil can be stirred up in the passing of the ships, especially if they happen to be battleships. All part of the Great Illusion, and while we are here, unavoidable. Where children are involved, there is an eternal outcry, and the children appear to be victims of their parents' apparent mistakes and misadventures. But children choose it

56

themselves, or at the behest of their oversoul, which is always mature and wise. We choose our parents; they don't choose us. And we choose them because they are going to prove conducive to our speedier evolution, however painful the experience may seem to be. All is semblance, and at the monadic level where the choice is made, wisdom dictates the choice, be it that the child's father is a drunkard or an imbecile, his mother a criminal, whether he is an orphan or a foundling who never knows or meets his parents or whether he is conceived in a test-tube and has to all intents and purposes no parents. As for "families," they are merely inconvenient "karmic clusters," a grim encumbrance while the illusion holds sway, meaningless in the ultimate analysis.

Thus to gloss over the tedious details, I left my impecunious artist, Harold Lisle, who despite being quite nice, and assuredly in retrospect the best of the bunch, was proving rather dull to my energetic spirit, in favour of this brilliantly clever but impossible scientist, Robert Moncrieff, and the manner of it was a karmic sequence which is recorded in my incarnascope.*

Seldom is anything *all* one person's "fault," (as the popular but unthinking saying is). A wealth of factors play a part. Robert was an alcoholic. The only times he was pleasant was when he was under its influence. The Irish say, "when the drink's in, the truth's out," so it may well have been that he wasn't all bad, only warped, perchance by disillusionment or frustration at the stupidity he saw all round him. Who is to judge? Otherwise he could be morose and ill-tempered, and while he could find someone to put up with him the way he was, made no effort whatever to remedy the position. He was insanely jealous, and capable of making statements that took one's breath away, being not only unreasonable but positively devastating in respect of blatant defamation of character and bare-faced lies, all delivered with a bland blue-eyed stare seemingly impervious to challenge. Yet it could not be denied that he was, in his better moods, livelier than Harold, and better informed. His conversation was more stimulating, and he could walk. Harold never wanted to do anything but sit and contemplate the Universe in his own quiet way. Later, when I was a little better endowed with wisdom, I wrote to him and told him how sorry I was for all that had happened, albeit too late to have any application in the current existence. But he understood, and I was able to communicate with him afterwards too.

It would intimate that there is something radically wrong with the marriage arrangement as currently applied, and that its obvious imperfection may

*See Appendix

be due to man's ineradicable propensity for reducing all concepts to the physical level and the lowest common denominator. There can be no true "marriage" until the opposite polarities merge.* We are truly ships passing in the night, and all one in the end. Yet karma is most compelling, and will not be assuaged until it is paid to the uttermost farthing.

Robert was the only male of my acquaintance who could walk level with me, (maugre the prognostications of Dr. Channing-Pierce) except for *Ted Smith*, who did not come into the picture until later.

Robert was immensely energetic, and he knew how to organise things. Harold didn't. If Robert and I were going anywhere, he would arrange everything. I had absolutely nothing to do, a novelty which appealed to me. Harold never had any money, and never took the initiative about anything, and that had grown a little tedious. He never attempted to find a home for us. He couldn't have paid for it if he had. Robert was different; he got a move on. He owned a car, an additional novelty in those days of post-war austerity, and liked to go about. He was older than I by fourteen years.

We wrote a book together; at least I wrote it, and Robert took the photographs. It was about the River Aire. Ian has the book. Ian was born on March 18, 1947, an unlucky birthday. He was scheduled to arrive on the 17th, Saint Patrick's Day, and that would have been more propitious, but it was not to be.

Ian travelled with us in his "karricot," while we explored the region, and at eighteen months old, loved to dip his feet in the cold streams we came upon in our peregrinations. He still thrives on the sea and has since taken up surfing.

Lovely country—that reach of the Broad Acres, its starting point at Malham Tarn. Harold had already painted a scenic picture of Malham Cove where the River Aire has its source. Swimming in the tarn was the coldest experience I ever had (at the physical level . . . the world can be a cold place at other levels!) The water looked black; just a trick of the light. Robert was a Stoic, breaking the ice in January to swim.

Our book was very good. The Dalesman Publishing Company applauded it, but there was a jinx on my work, part of the Curse of the O'Connors, and they could not handle it by reason of the post-War paper shortage. There was not a scrap of paper to wrap any commodity, even fish, and the fishmonger, if he had any fish, which he seldom had, would hold out two herrings by their tails, and if you had no paper, you had to carry them home that way. Today, so much paper is wasted that the mind boggles. I find it almost obscene, especially as so much of it ends up on the streets in the form of litter. I deplore likewise the wanton wastage of food that is one of the many shameful

* See *Prisoners of Time*

features of our affluent society.

Robert purchased a house at Keighley, and from there we explored the Brontë Country, and High Sunderland, and kindred fascinating locations. From High Sunderland a secret passage goes underground to Halifax Church, and through its mile-length the organ can be heard when it is played on Sundays.

Robert made no attempt to curb his drinking, Harold agreed to a divorce. He was most generous, I realised after, though at that time I was still taking others' kindly gestures for granted, conceding that he was "too old for me," and that I should be "free" (whatever that might denote!) I suppose I have always been "free", as far as anyone can be in this restrictive dimension. Freedom and independence are of paramount importance to a Sagittarian, to whom few other things are important at all. But, to cut a long story short, my association with Robert met its explosive Waterloo; interfering relatives played a part, certainly, but his total unreasonableness and insane jealously did the rest. I left, with Ian in his karricot, myself clad only in a swimming costume from bathing in the Aire which flowed at the end of our garden at Keighley, and descended upon Brighton, and Robert went back to his wife, who after the fashion of some long-suffering and misguided wives, had been waiting for him.

It is a common enough story. More common today than it was then, since people no longer put up with each other. Matrimonial entanglements arise, and falter, not from the "fault" of individuals, but from mankind's unending compulsion towards reducing every concept to the Lowest Common Denominator, and dragging it down to the physical level. There can be no "marriage" until the semi-monads fuse, but humanity *will* not understand the true nature of man, as an ensouling principle. As Jesus Christ pointed out, with what must have been some form of celestial exasperation, "YOU WILL HEAR, AND HEAR, BUT *NEVER* UNDERSTAND!" And it, the obtuseness, goes on, and on, and on, seemingly *ad infinitum.*

Harold eventually found lodgings, and true to Capricorn, married his landlady, who was not without modest substance, and moved to Settle, where the latter owned a house. At least he was provided for, and I think he was incapable of providing for himself. Capricorn subjects first and foremost need security, the saucer of milk on the kitchen floor to come home to. I was glad for him, and partly glad, no doubt, to salve my own conscience.

For me and Ian, furnished rooms again; I did not want to be beholden to relatives. Fate stepped in again, as it always does. Waiting one wintry night at a bus-stop, my eye fell upon a fragment of dirty newspaper, floating in a puddle under the murky lamp-light. I bent down and picked it up. It advertised the requirement of a Consulting Mining Engineer for an educated secretary conversant with Oxford English, capable of correcting the syntax of a book by an Indian author. I applied for the job, got it, wrote the book for him, and married him. His name was Lambodhar Zutshi, a Brahmin name which means "an Astrologer," and he came from Kashmir.

I did not particularly like him. I wanted a home for Ian. That, baldly, is the truth of it. To do myself justice, I don't think I fully realised that at the time. I realise it now. The scales are off, the barriers down. In later life, we see clearly. Halfway through, we don't. We vindicate our actions and reconcile them with our elastic consciences by all manner of plausible imaginings. Again, it is a common enough story. It always has been, in one guise or another, and it is not intended to fill these pages.

Ian and I led an erratic life, alternating between Brighton and Bayswater, where Lambodhar owned properties which he let to tenants. His cousin Balbadhar, whom we liked and called "Val," Lambodhar's somewhat down-trodden henchman, married Margot who hailed from Germany, and collectively we comprised a curiously-assorted household, at intervals being joined by my husband's two sons Derek and Trevor, who were half English. Lambodhar used to speak a lot about his wife Eileen, who was a native of Birmingham and unfortunately died from typhoid on a visit to India.

There was plenty of money. They wasted and mismanaged it horrifically. Indian visitors converged in an unending stream. My daughter has inherited this unbelievable thirst for entertaining and being dreadfully gregarious, while I have become the proverbial "loner," out of self-defence, not by intrinsic nature. Among the guests were Mrs. Pandit the Indian Ambassador, and her brother Mr. Nehru the Prime Minister of India. I had met Indira Gandhi many years earlier, when my mother was a member of the "Friends of India League" and I was a child. There were innumerable Kashmiri students too, who would sit around making no attempt to help with the refreshments or anything else, not even bringing their cups and saucers to the kitchen, until Margot in her forthright German way chased them out, reminding them that chairs did not carry themselves and they could stop lounging about.

Lambodhar was twenty years older than I, with two previous marriages to his credit, or discredit, according to where one is standing. It was not until years after his death in 1964 that I was apprised of his first marriage. He was ashamed of having married an illiterate Indian woman, and declined to recognise his eldest son Nandlal on that score. At the time I met him he was nurturing delusions of grandeur and considered it a source of gratification to exhibit an attractive English wife, preferably one with academic attainments, to act as hostess to the "dignitaries" to whom he aspired to open his home. He would buy up Oxford Street to purchase elaborate unsuitable clothing and jewellery to adorn my person, which I found highly embarassing, as I have never been addicted to dressing-up.

He would commute back and forth to India. Thus I spent the early Summer of 1949 in Derbyshire with just Ian for company. He was good company. A happy two-year-old, content to bowl along the country roads in his pushchair, chewing a bun or an apple, or gnawing the end of a French loaf, and drinking lemonade out of the bottle. It was an idyllic Summer, blue and cloudless, with wild roses on the hedgerows and larks in the sky. We traversed miles of countryside, bathing in the streams, picnicking in the fields, exploring the historic houses. We visited Dethick, where the young Anthony Babington and his friend Chideock Tichborne tried to dig an underground passage to Wingfield Manor to rescue Mary Queen of Scots, and Wingfield too, where the queen languished for part of her imprisonment. I wrote an article about her, which was called *A Derbyshire Paradise, But Prison to a Queen*, which was published in The Derby Evening Telegraph.

Lambodhar's daughter Mavis was born at the end of that Summer, and he returned from India, so we took up the threads again, in July, this time in a very large house in Perivale near Ealing. It boasted twenty-two rooms and an extensive garden. He named it *Gulmarg,* after the Kashmiri "Valley of Flowers." We enjoyed scant comfort in it, because he was never content with anything as it was, but was continually having "alterations" effected, so that the pretentious mansion was always full of workmen hammering and banging and rubbish and rubble widespread, and the wide branching staircase being transplanted, for no viable or visible reason, to the other extremity of the hall, and strip-lighting installed because ordinary lighting was insufficiently ostentatious.

There was so much of interest in Yorkshire and Derbyshire. We attended the annual well-dressing ceremony at Tissington, where the villagers weave garlands of flowers and blossom in praise and propitiation of the water sprites who preside over the water, water being credited with magic life-giving* properties. There were sulpher wells at Ayrton,** considered beneficial to health in the seventeenth century, and wishing wells, and wells where Edward I hung bronze cups for travellers.*** It was said at this time that such was the peace of the realm that if a woman with a new-born babe had wished to walk across England from sea to sea, she could do so in perfect safety. She could not do it today. There was the grave of Robin Hood in Kirklees, where he shot the arrow from the window of the priory to indicate his choice of resting place, and the seven-foot grave of 'Little John' at Hathersage. And we visited the Plague village of Eyam, where the rector, Mr. Mompesson, succeeded in containing the plague of 1665, which had been conveyed from London in a bundle of clothing, by placing bowls of vinegar all round the village, and by preventing all and sundry from entering or leaving.

And once, on the road from Nottingham to Mansfield, through the remnants of Sherwood Forest, I saw clairvoyantly a white hart, from the top of

---

* These are the ondines and nereids, Builders of the Universe.
** See *The River Aire*
***See *The British Monarchy and the Divine Right of Kings*

the 'bus. The driver could not see it crossing the road, and I feared it would get run over, until it dawned upon me that it was a ghost.

Lambodhar and I did not sort well together. His thoughts were very muddled, and he could not align them. I think he genuinely desired to help India, to which end he would sit for hours at a stretch, smoking and laboriously inscribing long-winded diatribes. His involvement seemed to be more by "remote control" than by working "in among" the indigenous natives, yet I believe his intentions were sincere and well-meant.

He was a Scorpio subject, not evolved. An advanced Scorpio can be clever, and at that level they make congenial companions, though probably not all the time, while an unevolved Scorpio is trying and tedious, in that he cannot grasp any point of view other than his own, and he will entrench himself behind that viewpoint against all comers, no matter how hopelessly in error he may be.

Lambodhar was the head of the "tribe" or joint-family in India, a position which conferred a sense of one-up-man-ship, or made a person conceited. He was likewise very materialistic, and could not understand anyone who was not impressed by wealth and ostentation. I once took charge of one of his tenant-houses in Derby, and took the children with me. It was Ian who got the brunt of the muddles we made. There were too many changes of school for him; he did not know where he belonged, and grew bewildered. This was a source of sorrow to me later, though at the time I was pre-occupied with pressing worries of my own. Accordingly more of Ian anon.

Mavis suffered less; she always has. Hers is a more robust and tough temperament, with (as an elderly gentleman, Rear Admiral Oldham, who painted her portrait at sixteen, remarked), "a ruthless streak." She inherited some of her father's character, while Ian does not noticeably exhibit much of his father's disposition, except that he can be impatient and bad-tempered. Insensitivity forms a part of Mavis's current "personality" or *mask*, whereas as a small child she was wholly different, both sympathetic and spiritually disposed to the point of possessing clairvoyance. The total metamorphosis that she underwent was until then outside my experience. In any case we do not enter into our "personality" until we are seven years old. Prior to that, we are employing our soul-forces. With Mavis, the marked spirituality was present until she was fifteen. After that, at seventeen, *she went away,* in every sense of the word. Yet these apparent regressions are necessary for an entity's progress. Nothing can be forced or hurried, and if that happens, it only means that the entity lapses back, further than ever, and has to wait to catch up when its true "time" is ripe, and not a minute earlier. But if entity deliberately sheds its quota of spirituality for the "wrong" reason, to flout or spite another, as Mavis did later, that is a more serious matter, and retards evolution, which situation has its explanation in the words, *"To him that hath, it shall be given, but to him that hath not, it shall be taken away even that which he hath."*

62

I asked Dad if he wanted to come to live in the big house at Ealing, where he would have plenty of space and could cultivate the garden, instead of his cramped quarters in Bernard's and Joan's house near Brighton. He was lonely and comfortless, but always so loyal; he would not leave.

Lambodhar and I disagreed fundamentally over the children. He had theories as to their learning to stand on their own feet. Derek and Trevor had a Spartan childhood. Lambodhar would readily go to the cinema and leave infants alone in a house, I would not go, and he remonstrated that it was no use having a wife if they did everything separately. He did prevail upon me against my better judgement to take a holiday with him in the South of France and Rome and Monte Carlo and Paris, leaving Ian and Mavis in the dubious care of a stranger who was paid to look after them. I could not enjoy the holiday, being anxious all the time and wanting to get back. When we did, it was to find Ian disturbed and grieved, and Mavis reproachful (she was only two), and refusing to speak to me. I felt guilty and ashamed and miserable, and vowed never to leave them again; and I never did. However poor we were, I was always at home for them.

Lambodhar and I drifted further apart. The children were ill-at-ease with him. The house was frequently full of women, the wives of Lambodhar's "dignitaries." Dignitaries they may have been, but they were supremely bereft of conversation, and I was expected to entertain them. They sat in serried ranks in the large withdrawing room, wearing colourful saris, bovinely placid and looking as if nothing could move them. At mid-day with one accord they would go upstairs to their respective rooms and re-emerge clad in different saris, to sit again, complacently ignoring my desperate efforts at conversation, until quite late in the evening, when they would charge in a concerted rush to the kitchen, to prepare a monstrous curry, whose ingredients were so varied and complicated that it was not ready to be served until eleven o'clock at night. Exercise played no part in their agenda, while for me it was a pressing necessity. I gave up sitting with them, since I felt completely *de trop*, and went for walks. In fact I was beginning to wonder what earthly purpose I could possibly be serving there. Lambodhar had paid the fees for Ian and Mavis to attend private schools. This can in conventional circles be construed into an "advantage," but it was giving him a hold on them, and on me. I have never been beholden to anyone in my life, either before or since, and I was growing aware that the only terms on which we could live under Lambodhar's roof would be by effacing ourselves and our own identity one hundred-percent.

I thought about the undoubtedly invidious prospect, and the more I thought about it, the less desirable it seemed. I told Lambodhar that he must accord the children breathing-space, and cease to impose his un-English ideas upon them. I pointed out that when in Rome, you do as Rome does, that he had of his own choice made his home in England, and should not seek to import alien lifestyles into a country which had a proud lifestyle of its own.

I consulted the children as to whether they would prefer to stay at Ealing or go with me to Brighton and take their chances. The opted for the latter proposition. Ian was nine, Mavis seven.

I issued an ultimatum to Lambodhar: if he had not changed his ways within six weeks, I would leave, and take the children. He did not think I would, because he could not assimilate the fact of anyone's being willing to live without "things." He did not change.

One can only do what seems "right" at the time, employing the wisdom one has acquired at that time. I have never regretted the decision I made to go to Brighton with nothing, and take our chances.

Ian had had an accident while playing football at school. He was in hospital, the result of the injury being diagnosed as "Osteomylitis." He looked so pathetic, tied by his neck to the bedpost. I hate hospitals, although I suppose they are indispensable to today's people, and the practitioners do their best, but such places always send a shiver down my spine. I waited till he was better, then left for Brighton, which I regarded as "home," if anywhere was, in that we had lived in so many locations. We found accommodation of a sort, and made the best of the material at our disposal. It was threadbare, and yes, we were poor. My husband essayed to starve us out, by only furnishing £3 a week. But I reasoned for better or worse that children are less victimised with one parent than with two who are continually at loggerheads or pulling in opposite directions. Mature wisdom does not supervene until much later in life, and then it is no longer valid for the situation in question, in that one would not have embarked upon the situation in the first instance! Surely life's supreme irony!, or part of the gigantic hoax that passes for "life," an integral part of the Great Illusion.

Lambodhar instigated a court case over the custody of Mavis. I won. The reason I won it was that I am not influenced by money, and never allow it to sway my judgement. The ploy was to separate Mavis from Ian, and send her to the famous boarding school for girls at Roedean. An unsound proposition. Such discrimination would have damaged Ian still more, and he was already damaged enough. I said 'No' and found that five lawyers, in full (and ridiculous) judicial regalia, are no match for a determined woman. Ian and Mavis stayed together, and apart from a very occasional tiff, they always got on well. Thus from the wreck of my fortunes I salvaged two children; that was all. I left with one child in each pocket, and made no claim whatever on any possession— chairs, tables, wine glasses, the sordid details which normally figure in court cases; I even left the dresses and jewellery, and resumed my gypsy-like apparel. It was better so. No one could accuse you of asking for anything, no one could gainsay you, there was no scope for litigation or argument or hair-splitting. I was free. My only regrets were for the unwise way I handled some of the subsidiary aspects of the major decision, which were detrimental to Ian.

Harold died. I heard of it from Molly Mason. I had written to him, once, to tell him that I was sorry. But he understood before he transferred to the alternative dimension.

My father died.

He died as he had lived: self-effacing and generous. He died in the Sussex General Hospital where my sister-in-law had sent him. The hospital had a bad reputation. It was cleaned up later, but too late for Dad. He had sustained a heart attack alone in the tiny room Joan had allocated to him, rather than disturb the household by ceding spaciousness. Dad had equipped that household with virtually all it had, to his own impoverishment. My brother Bernard was weak, my sister-in-law greedy, and Dad was caught in the crossfire. No "feed-back" was forthcoming, no love, not even appreciation. My sister-in-law appropriated every last item of the family "possessions," even down to Harold's pictures and miniatures on ivory of myself and my mother, which latter he had interpreted from a photograph, Dad's piano and the fine delicate china which had belonged to Queenie, and every perquisite of the original Purley home. I did not bother. It did not seem to matter. I have never been moved to contest such issues. I just continued to wear Queenie's engagement ring which Dad had given her, as I had from the time of her death. It is the only item of jewellery I have; all temporary acquisitions in that direction have been lost or stolen by burglars. As to anything my father may have left, he did not leave it! Never in my life have I witnessed such a clean sweep! It was as if he had never existed. He cleared out everything, every drawer and cupboard in his tiny room, even rooms he had always given up when they had "friends" to stay, were starkly empty.

Tidy in death as in life, he left not a paper, not a letter, no trace. He knew, in 1957 that it was his final year, and that he was not coming out of the hospital. He did not want anything of himself to remain for others to mull over and violate. He had been so hurt, so cheated and exploited by those to whom he had given so much, who gave him nothing. When I asked him, while still at Ealing, if he wished to join us there, since I sensed a lack of love, it was too late. He could not trust me either, I had been so selfish in my early years; he did not know where to turn. I am convinced that he died of a broken heart. I did too, nearly, in the remorse I felt for all of us, for long thereafter. I have always vowed that he had been reading *The Mayor of Casterbridge* just before he fell asleep: "AND LET NO MAN REMEMBER ME!" ◆

V

Angels

The angels keep their ancient places;
Turn but a stone and start a wing;
Tis you, with your estrangèd faces
That miss the many-splendoured thing.

—Francis Thompson

But I remember Dad. And now, in our spirit-communications, we share the close and loving rapport we were unable to achieve in the physical dimension. And soon we shall be together on *his* side of the coin, a time that I increasingly look forward to. Yet I would not be able to leave with a free mind unless I were fully satisfied that Ian was all right. And by "all right," I don't mean in point of money or a "job," people always "get by" in that area, even if they are, like Ian, victims of today's dismal "recession." I mean in possession of the esoteric knowledge which alone can enable him to ride out the storm. He did not want to listen to me while I was "alive," or rather he was influenced by Mavis, who of policy had made up her mind to discredit me through the medium of my work, a terrible mistake which she will live bitterly to rue. I can only hope and pray that Ian will recognise his need for it when I am "dead," and to that end I have done all that he would allow me to do, namely by leaving him a legacy worth more than any sum of money; *my tape-recordings*, outlining and explaining the vital "process" from start to finish. God knows, he will not meet anyone, anywhere, who supplies it as concisely as I have done, inasmuch as my life has been dedicated to the rendering of ancient truths into colloquial language for "everyman," such units of "everyman" as will consent to wake up and absorb them. The Theosophical Society headquarters in London presented me years ago with a "Certificate of Appreciation" for my service in "clothing these esoteric truths in modern language to be palatable to the Man-in-the-Street." Thus at the time I felt I had not lived in vain, even if on occasion subsequently the vast majority of mankind has given me cause to question it!

The marital upheaval accomplished, there was now ample opportunity to sit back and do some stock-taking. The penny had dropped, and I had reached the tardy conclusion that marriage was not for me. Even "affairs" took their place in limbo, the very last being with Colonel Stewart and that could be designated a sort of "the Gypsy and the Gentleman" arrangement, since he had no intention of breaking up his marriage, nor would I have wished him to. I realised that "he travels fastest who travels alone," and I have travelled alone ever since, and am glad to do so.

Once again, in due compliance with the Curse of the O'Connors, money touched me on the shoulder and glanced away again. The £35,000 set aside for me all the time I was "married," was transferred to the two stepsons instead, and as soon as I ceased to be "married," I was cut off with, or rather without, a shilling. Stepsons Derek and Trevor promptly squandered the windfall on sauna baths and trips to Europe, and did not appear to derive a great deal of pleasure therefrom, as they were always anxious about something or other and thereby were prevented from savouring life to the full, as their financial advantages might have been assumed to do. I, on the other hand, was footloose and fancy-free, and addressed myself to the task of bringing up Mavis and Ian on a shoestring.

So, alone in the world now, just the three of us, the children and I, moved on into the next phase of our chequered career.

It is when you are poor, (indeed I would go further, and aver that at this stage of human evolution it is *only* when you are poor), that you can appreciate the meaning of "spiritual help," divine intervention, angelic protection, and so on. It really works. I know that the Law applied totally in my case. When you are only concerned with basic needs, they are unfailingly met and catered for. Had I even been as well-off as I am now, modest though that criterion may be, I would not have won the priceless guerdon of true knowledge. So I never cease to be thankful for that interlude of truly basic living. The protection and provision were absolute. It conferred upon me the faith in Providence which has never left me.

"Seek first the Kingdom of Heaven and its righteousness, and all these things shall be added unto you" is absolutely true, provided you use "righteousness" in its correct connotation, and not the sanctimonious substitute

superimposed by the Church. It simply mean, "TRUTH." "These things" *were* added to us, unfailingly, as far as basic necessities were concerned. If only people had not grossly misused words over the centuries, what a lot of misunderstanding and misery would have been obviated. Outstandingly, *"Love!"* How glibly that has been bandied about! It just means "Wisdom," that's all! Not cheap sex or sloppy sentiment, nor even affection.

It's odd, but such simple truths do not seem to occur to people. If you mention them, some sort of penny drops, and then they do understand.

For a while I worked in Kensington for Jasmine Chatterton. She was a Literary Agent, conducting her agency solo. I had to read the MSS and do the typing. Another ship that passed in the night; but a ship-in-full-sail, a courageous lady for her generation. Yet I think there were many courageous ladies in that generation. She told me that I had a profound influence on her life, and asked many questions about my esoteric studies and communications. And when I come to count them, I realise that over the years lots of others have done the same.

Summaries are inadequate. But if my *Memoirs* are to be of interest to more evolved people, matrimonial squabbles will not loom so large as they do in the tabloid press. Suffice it to say that the emotional content of a situation diminishes with advancing years, and involvement therewith grows increasingly dispassionate. Humanity, collectively, can no longer afford to exist at the "personal" level, and the fact that so many still do, is not conducive to speedier evolution. It is a mistake that Mavis made, reverting to the personal level for the wrong reason, when she had virtually passed it.

Lambodhar Zutshi died from lung-cancer in January, 1964, aggravated, I think, by repressed emotion as much as by heavy smoking. I contacted him in spirit afterwards, and again it was endorsed how much more quickly they learn "over there," where in this dimension they would be bogged down by a really obtuse "fixation." Once released from the trammels of the physical form and its demanding "personality-surround," they are in a position to grasp the point and view things objectively. I was able to explain matters to him, where before any kind of explanation had fallen on stony ground. I was sorry it had to be that way, but so often, as in our case, we are used as instruments in each others' advancement. Had he lived longer, that opportunity would not have been vouchsafed. It was a classic example of the Bahai axiom, *"No man is your friend, no man is your enemy; all are alike your teachers."*

I used to walk to and from work to save 'bus fares, over the South Downs. Whenever I was very tired, often quite late in the evening, I would invariably find a sixpence lying in the white chalk road and that would exactly get me home. "Home," after the series of furnished apartments, which could only be described as rat-holes, was within a pleasant dip in the South Downs. Not that I am anything but grateful to Ted Smith, who was a "friend in need," allowing me and Ian and Mavis to occupy one of his rat-holes for very little rent. Indeed I am eternally thankful to that kind man, and will have more to say about him in a while.

The children were growing older. They went to Middle Street School, the oldest school in Brighton. Now, along with other historic landmarks, such as the magnificent coaching in the "Clarence" in North Street, it has been inartistically demolished, and these buildings are irreplaceable. The children attending the school in 1805 were conducted to the beach to see Nelson's *Victory* go by, very close inshore, bringing the admiral's body home. It must have been a memorable occasion for them.

The original fishing village of Brighthelmstone consisted of four thoroughfares, East Street, West Street, North Street and Middle Street, not of course forgetting the Lanes, thankfully left intact by the predatory demolition-squad.

I joined the Theosophical Society. It was precisely what I had been waiting for. Its members were elderly and fuddy-duddy, but they were nice people. Knowledgeable too. The Society has since forfeited a great deal. Current members are of an altogether different calibre, have lost touch with the Masters, never discuss the devic kingdom or the Builders of the Universe, and indeed appear to have become entirely secular. But perhaps this is simply a part of today's phenomenon, a trend that has seeped into everything.

The Society had a fine library, and the reading I did there bore out to the letter the discoveries I had already made, and the impressive spirit-communications I had received. It began in Ealing, in 1956, before we resumed residence in what I suppose could be termed our "hometown," if anywhere could, inasmuch as "No Fixed Abode" was our inheritance, as the Curse of the O'Connors decreed for some of us. I used to attend Spiritualist meetings in London, and belonged to a succession of "psychic groups" which were all more or less tarred with the same brush. Here I learnt to perform physchometry to augment the card-readings I had given while working with Margaret and Professor Cullen, the well-known Brighton Palmists. The programme grew monotonous and unedifying. The messages were of the trivial nature typical of the Spiritualist Movement, and the members seemed content with that elementary level. I was contemplating resigning, when the never-to-be-forgotten incident arose that was to change the whole course of my work. One afternoon while the ladies were out of the room preparing the inevitable cups of tea and little cakes which form an indispensable adjunct to all proceedings, and I was alone for a few minutes, I was so fed up that I put my hand randomly on the glass and besought, "for Pete's sake tell me something worth hearing!" The response was electrifying, as was the force and velocity of the glass's movement, the spelling distinctive, if quaint, "BE OF GOOD CHEER. YOU SHALL PRECEEDE EYES WITH TRUE KNOWLEDGE." The glass leapt from my hand and splintered on the floor.

I was "over the moon," as the saying is. In my immaturity and its accompanying effrontery, I began to clamour for "proof," little knowing the futility, fatuity and fatality of such a demonstration of ignorance. The guide's name, he volunteered, was *Zeus*, a Grecian entity attached to my father, (not his doorkeeper, who was a Japanese female entity named "VILY".) "Give me a sign!" I implored, as foolish people have bleated for centuries. "O certainly," conceded the guide with disarming amiability, "I will give you a quotation from one of your famous authors which you can 'check in your library.'" Followed a passage from Charles Dickens, "and this you will find on Page 377 of his book" added the guide. Hotfoot I headed for the library, feverishly routed out the requisite volume and excitedly turned over the pages. The book had 376 pages!

It was a salutory lesson that so many people need and few get. I'm glad I got it. It left me sober, deflated and wiser. All dreams of being hailed as the world's top medium dispersed like gossamer. Years and years of hard, unrewarding slog ensued, with neither recognition nor encouragement, but only apathy, indifference, cynicism and that odious combination of ignorance and insolence which passes for "scepticism" and rouses me to fury. All these I encountered within my own family. I came face to face with the unpalatable truth that, as one writer puts it, *"he who desires to help humanity must be prepared for opposition, hostility, and that perversity which always upholds the opposite of what is said."* *

Perhaps more importantly for the work I was to do, I learnt never to test the guides, never to demand "proof." I learned that the Eternal Verities are not infiltrated except with an approach of the utmost humility, on one's hands and knees if one wants to be practical, and that the arrogance and argumentativeness that some of today's people see fit to bring to it are a sure recipe for abysmal and very long-term failure. "Permanent" failure to all intents and purposes for the relevant lifetime. Everyone has to assimilate them in the end, for they are our spiritual food, and the acquisition is mandatory, and by no means optional, as, again, some hopelessly off-course people like to assume. *When the pupil is ready, the teacher is waiting.* That is the Law. And some teachers have to wait an unconscionably long time. But offer the truth before the

*George MacKay

70

pupil is ready, and there is Hell to pay, for he/she will trample the pearls underfoot and turn again and rend you, as the timely warning intimated.

All this I learnt, and never forgot the lesson, and now I know exactly when to speak and when to keep my mouth firmly shut. And as far as my own family is concerned, it has been shut for many years, and will continue so to be, albeit I was rendered very sad in the process. But that, again, is the Law, and one that I could not alter if I would. You do not apply for the same job twice, and those who have repudiated your services, must seek a different teacher, but then it will be *their* turn to wait, often with heartbreaking frustration, and in a future life.

From that moment, I was performing automatic writing, daily and for half a year. Each time I put pen to paper my hand was seized in a vice-like grip and the pen flew across the pages, telling me every detail and incident of my past lives and the karmic contacts I had effected therein. I was introduced to my doorkeeper *Artimus*, a Syrian who was an artist and a maker of coloured glass, again to my father's guide Zeus, and then to **ELIA**, who soul-wise is an offshoot of my opposite polarity, with whom I was on earth eight thousand years B.C., in what is now Africa and was then *Moelanta*. He has acted as my guide to this day, and it is from him that all my esoteric knowledge has been derived. It was he who taught me to cast incarnascopes for others as well as my own, and the numbers of these I have compiled now totals thousands. Today the demand is more urgent than ever, the workload impossible, so that I have been forced to scale it down. After that prescribed period, the faculty of automatic writing with such intensity was withdrawn, and my service took a different form.

I acquired a measure of patience, and the awareness that, as George MacKay wrote, *"Men think in herds, go mad in herds, but they only recover their senses one at a time"* and that there is a deep-seated hatred and fear of the truth, doubtless inculcated by the Church, that forcing-house for spiritual destitution, and dwelling even within those who nowadays have nothing to do with the Church. It is astounding how these strangleholds die hard, even though they may have forfeited all but the theoretical death-grip. Lucifer and his faithful henchman Ahriman still stand should to shoulder, barricading the door to enlightenment, keeping the populace at large stupid, unreceptive and prone to undislodgable fixations.

Psychic "gifts" come and go, or, perhaps more correctly, are bestowed and withdrawn as and when they are needed or cease to be needed. Neither are they "gifts," but developments of innate faculties which we all possess but only a proportion recognise and employ. My psychism became, rather, a series of impressions and a process of infiltration.

71

We were tired of furnished rooms. Ian was now at school at Hove Manor and Mavis at Varndean School for Girls. But that did not mean parting from Ted Smith, of whom we still saw a great deal, and his friend Richard Gardener, who was Irish and a writer. In 1959, when Ian was twelve, a member of the Theosophical Society offered us a refuge. It was a "chalet" in the large picturesque neglected garden of her bungalow at Woodingdean. Alfred Noyes wrote poetry about Woodingdean, and although it was not quite the mystic abode it may have been in his time, it was nevertheless attractive and more secluded than it is today. Mrs. Lonergan was eccentric and a "loner," elderly, dowdy and countrified. I liked her. She did her best for us, and the chalet reminded me of Ashurst. It might indeed have been in the heart of the Sussex countryside. We used paraffin-lamps and a sort of "haybox oven" on the cooking-stove. Water we fetched from a tap in the garden, and rain-water we collected in rough-and-ready vessels. I consulted Ian as to his opinion of the place, and it seemed to find favour, for we took it, at the peppercorn "rent" of 25 shillings a week.

I loved it. It was the nearest approach to a "home" humble though it was, that I had known since our original home at Purley broke up when Queenie died. Dappled thrushes came in at the door, there was a fragrant May-tree just outside the window; we had total privacy, and were never without a cat, for a stray invariably found its way to us. As for the children, there was nothing to indicate that they were anything but happy. Our neighbour declared that they were lovely high-spirited children, always heralding their approach by calling out all the way down the garden path when they returned from school. I used to sing there, as I had not sung since girlhood, confident that I was alone, and it was a wonderful outlet and means of self-expression, and my neighbor Mrs. Futers enjoyed it, and continually asked me for more, and since I had a very extensive repertoire, that presented no problem. Mrs. Lonergan left us in peace and never bothered us, and we reciprocated in like manner for her. She would sit in the garden in the sun, brushing her long grey hair, and the little wrens made their nests out of it. I can still see in my mind's eye the lining of green moss and Mrs. Lonergan's hair that went to the exquisite workmanship of their tiny nests. Then one day workmen arrived with bulldozers and laid waste the copse where they dwelt. How hateful our society is! In a decent world they would at least have waited till the diminutive eggs were hatched and the fledglings gone. But no, everything must be sacrificed on the altar of commercialism, and soon unsightly buildings took the place of the woodland to accommodate more and more humans, a desperately poor substitute for primrose and wild life. If is a disconcerting truth that man and nature cannot live side by side, everything green and beautiful recedes before the onslaught of man.

All that however was not until we were about to leave. We were there for three years, which seemed to pass like a dream. Ian had to go to school, all the way to Hove. Sometimes if he got up late, he would dash off in the morning cramming a piece of toast into his mouth, to catch the 'bus. It was carefree in a way that somehow would not be possible today.

I used to walk to the village and carry the paraffin home, and on my visits to the Post Office and "General Store," the shopkeeper Mr. Goodenough would remind me, a tiny bit, of Mr. Clarke, in the way he would potter about, shamble to the back of the shop looking for a requested item, and transact the Post Office business with such maddening deliberation that even the queue of patient country-folk began to shuffle its feet. But there was no real similarity—compared with Mr. Clarke he was Speedy Gonzalez! And there was a vast enamel jug loaned to us by Mrs. Lonergan, beneath which, when Ian was old enough to come home and let himself in if I were out, I would conceal the old-fashioned key to the chalet door. The outstanding feature of our life there was the sense of perfect safety that we felt. I am very nervous, and cannot bear to be left alone in a house. But here, isolated as we were in the delightfully wild secluded garden, I knew the utmost serenity. Anyone, absolutely anyone, could have pushed the door or window in with one hand, flimsy as they were, but I knew that no one would. Mrs. Lonergan likewise used to sleep in her bungalow with the window open all night. There were angels there, and I used to talk to the trees. Prince Charles was ridiculed for doing so, but it is the people who call you a fool who are the fools. Poor fools, if only they knew it! But they know nothing, and don't want to know anything, hence the abysmal state of this unhappy world. I talked to the trees when we really needed something: shoes, gloves, any kind of necessity. Invariably within the hour, my neighbour would come to the fence with the item in question, and a tentative, "I hope you won't be offended, but these are too big, or too small, or too something, or my husband doesn't like me in them," etc., etc. Barbara Futers was our nearest neighbour, separated by another large garden. Before we came to the chalet, a medium had told her, "you will meet a lady, just over the fence, just over there, like that! She is rather like a gypsy. She will be the means of helping you a great deal."

Surely enough, in gratitude for these timely offerings, I told Mrs. Futers many things she would not otherwise have had the chance to hear about; and she recounted in amazement what the medium had predicted.

Richard Gardener came to the chalet to do some repair work on Mrs. Lonergan's rather decrepit bungalow, and made some suggestions to augment my book *A Bribe for Judge Jefferies*, a copy of which I gave him many years later. Life has not been kind to him, any more than it has to me in some ways, but some of us are better equipped than others to parry the slings and arrows of outrageous fortune.

Ian did not like being at school. Mavis did, and was doing well at Varndean. He left at fifteen-and-a-half, and took "jobs" in shops and similar situations. Ian did not really know what he wanted, and in his adverse circumstances he could not be expected to. He passed through a phase of feeling bitter and resentful, which was understandable. It is not until we are much older, and then only if we have acquired wisdom, that we recognise the fact that we choose our own circumstances. He ended by joining the Marines. But before that happened we moved back to Brighton. That was due to the intervention of relatives, for better or worse, and inevitably for worse, since no one can or should attempt to interfere with others' karma. But again this is something that today's comatose people do not know. For society grows progressively secular, materialistic and bereft of spiritual understanding. Probably we have never been so clever collectively as we are now, with our science and technology, but wisdom plays no part in our assesments or legislation, and even commonsense is at a discount. Relatives are congenitally incapable of minding their own business. In their untutored book, blood relations represent "fair game," and thus in their uninformed estimation Mrs. Lonergan's accommodation was "unsuitable" now that the children were growing up.

The upshot was that we resumed the "furnished rooms" syndrome under the kindly and benevolent but possibly equally "unsuitable" aegis of Ted Smith. He was a karmic contact too, dating from Egyptian times, and persistently recurred. Ian left for the Marines, and was not affected, except for brief visits, but Mavis was.

24, Dyke Road, Brighton, was another of Ted's rat-holes. The main one, it might be said, dating from 1850. Dyke Road leads up to the Devil's Dyke, that historic landmark carved out by his Satanic Majesty, and subsequently furnishing an escape-route for another sardonic king, Charles II. Anyone so-minded can read about that, so I need not dilate upon it. It is a very long road. Its upper end, bordering upon the South Downs, is flanked by the opulent homes of retired solicitors and others of that ilk; but its lower end claims no such pretentions, and can perhaps be tactfully described as "run-down."

No. 24 was definitely run-down. It had a chequered history. How Ted came by it is another story, and since this is a biography of "me," rather than of Ted, it may be prudent to throw a veil over the varied details. Suffice it to say that Ted, being endowed with a blend of kindliness, tolerance and indolence, was ingloriously exploited. Drug-addicts, dogs, defaulters-with-the-rent, and kindred weavers of chicanery comprised his tenantry. But I was from time to time among them, and am grateful for the asylum the strange house afforded me. His sister Ethel likewise was a standby, and I could always count on sharing her room if the worst came to the worst.

Ted was artistic, in a Taurian sort of way, and painted his pictures in surroundings faintly reminiscent of Mr. Clarke's shop at Ashurst, with carrots and butter and cups of tea and pots of paint in curious proximity. He could construct and convert rooms into cupboards and vice-versa, and we used to comment that so often the best work came out of the worst places. And so it does, because artists usually live in squalor, and the fabulous craftsmen who created the Sistine Chapel and similar marvels, were not venerated, were only paid a pittance, and probably slept on a heap of straw in a recess of the cathedral before resuming their unremitting toil to produce the wonders gazed at by today's heedless tourists.

The greatest sufferer was our dear black cat who had adopted us at Woodingdean. He faithfully followed us into the alien town conditions, and miraculously did not run away, for he was no urban cat, and found it difficult to adapt. But he loved me, and demonstrated loyalty. That is why I have never forgiven myself for what happened to him, and never will. Had it been today, with the added wisdom I have acquired, God knows it would not have happened. But I was, as once before in Derbyshire, when Robert was defaulting with his payments for Ian, I allowed an incident to occur concerning the infant Ian which I would not have dreamed of allowing today, when he was deprived of a cherished toy, and he had so few, I was between the devil and the deep sea.

I had been offered a flat in the Old Steine, a chance in a million. "No Animals" was a stricture. Again, had I known, Mr. Braybon, our landlord, of Braybons old-established building firm, would not have enforced it. But I did not know it, or him. I had not met him. Margaret and Professor Cullen with whom I worked, were moving out of it, and paved the way for me. It was ideal, and the rent unbelievably cheap. Nice accommodation was hard to come by at the rent I could pay. Although it would break my heart to part with the cat, I had the two children to think of, and had, or thought I had, no alternative but to try to find another home for him. Offers were few, but one of the tenants in Ted's house promised to look after him. But I learnt that on the first night after our departure, he was left to cry all night on the window sill. It was *his* heart that was broken. He had been used to sleeping on my bed, safe and secure and loved . . . there had been an ample featherbed at Mrs. Lonergan's chalet and he had shared it. I knew that I could not trust the person who had promised to care for him. I advertised again; there were no replies. To my eternal self-condemnation, I let him go to the Animals' Home. I had betrayed him; his eyes told me so. I was his only friend, and he could not trust *me*. Even now I wake up in the night and see his eyes again. He was such a dear cat. There are some things we cannot forgive ourselves. But the after-life is the same for animals; what we have loved we see again, and what they have loved they see again. In this dimension I have subsequently tried to make amends to other cats, but it isn't the same. Had it been now, I would have risked violating the contract, and when I finally met Mr. Braybon, I knew that he would not have minded. He was, to employ an old-fashioned or obsolete term, a "gentleman," a brief Roman contact, in an earlier life of mine, when his name had been *Orlinus,* and he had saved me from a horrible death at the hands of slave-dealers.*

Later, when Mavis went to Newcastle University after her year of VSO** in India, she brought another cat all the way by train in a basket. He was grey and beautiful. He was stolen for his fur. I am desperately sorry for animals world-wide. They have a dreadful time at our hands. As a humanity, we have abysmally failed in our most important mission of all, namely to help, develop, educate and cherish the next kingdom which supersedes us.

*Grim**** too, had become my friend and companion when I was alone in the flat, and I wrote the poem below from my heart. It was published in the Brighton *Argus* at the time. But I am certain it was more for the Woodingdean cat.

He Went With The Summer

He had travelled a long way
To find a home, for he was a stray.
He found one at last; it was a top flat,
But there was a garden, and he could climb.

He knew where his food was, where his box was, but he
preferred to sleep
On someone's lap, or on
The best bedspread.

He had endearing ways—on rainy days
Instead of climbing down the stackpipe for his morning walk,
He would chase a pine cone madly up and down the passage.

Then one day he slipped out as usual and never came back.
We knew that he was stolen for his coat.
Thieves get thirty shillings for a coat.
Thirty pieces of silver.

What did he care, the lout who sold him,
The Accessory Before the Fact,

---

* See Appendix
** Voluntary Service Overseas
****Grimalkin.* Gave rise to "Moggie."

That he had violated a home and left a lonely woman weeping,
Not knowing where the little creature was?
It paid a week's rent, didn't it? for his sordid room.

And he, the furry one, who was evolved, and chose it,
Reclines, and infiltrates,
Till he in turn is human.
But being Pussy still, he takes time out
To purr on someone's lap, or plague
His celestial pine-cone.

While he, the murderer, who filched the little coat,
Stumbles with blood-stained hands into the night,
Wondering in sick dismay why he should go blind,
His firm go bankrupt, his rabbits die?

But Whosoever Shall Hide Himself that I shall not see later?
Saith the Lord. ◆

VI

Communicants: Incarnate and Discarnate

However, I was not alone straight away, for Ian and Mavis shared the flat for the first year or two, at intervals. Ian was not happy in the Marines. He broke his leg, and it was wrongly set by their doctors. He had aimed to be a swimmer-canoeist. He excelled at both activities. A broken wrist precluded his participating in the Westminster-Devizes Canoe race. The broken leg further disqualified him, and he was desolated. But they wouldn't let him out. It was manifestly unfair. But in those days a recruit signed on for twelve years, a colossal demand to make on a sixteen-year-old. I determined to get him out. Another bald statement with a wealth of significance! But I make it without any sense of exaggeration or dramatisation. The statement may be simple, but the task wasn't. I don't think anyone else could have done it, certainly no one of my acquaintance. No recruit ever got out of the Marines. And that was a hard and fast rule. It may not be now.

I travelled to Deal on a bleak grey day in February to see the commanding officer. I was primed with one invincible asset, but even that would not have worked the oracle, had not Major Darby been interested in the mechanics of reincarnation. But he was. Very. I had to play my cards carefully till I discovered that. Thereafter it was a walkover. Fate! It had to be. I did not mention the question of Ian's leg at all. I played upon the fatiguing length of the journey, the raw cold of the weather, my own exhaustion and the distressing circumstance that I was recently a widow, the month before, and needed Ian's help and support. Blatant hypocrisy, since I had been separated from my husband for some time, and Ian was neither helpful nor supportive. He is now, but he wasn't then. "Oh!" exclaimed Major Darby apologetically and in palpable relief . . . "have some tea!" It was abundantly clear that he had been dreading the interview, as he had been expecting the advent of the average Marine-parent who would be truculent, aggressive, and would plunge straight into the delicate issue which had brought me there, namely the inefficiency of the military doctors, and demand the release of their son. Such tactics would undoubtedly have lost the day. The last person he had anticipated appearing was the pathetic little widow I successfully impersonated, especially one with the knowledge he was eager to gain. A juvenile soldier was dispatched to bring the tea, (and little cakes!), and we talked again, and charmed each other thereby. I led him through labyrinths of abstract thought, and answered his questions, only right at the end recalling him to immediate matters by the most casual, "Oh, about Ian's leg . . . " It could not have been more propitious. And here, again, as with the court case over Mavis, I was so acutely aware of being helped by Spirit.

It was, in a way, the same story. Men, collectively, of whatever calling, are too susceptible to be able to prevail against a determined woman. It is just that the brand of diplomacy differs. With lawyers, you tell them they are wasting their time; with soldiers, you appeal to their honour and chivalry as Officers and Gentlemen. Lawyers are not gullible; soldiers are. To cut a long (and fascinatingly psychological) story short, Ian was home within the week, with a gracious and gallant missive from the Colonel, hoping that he would be a comfort to me! I indited a grateful, flattering letter thanking them for their sympathy, kindness and understanding. Ian's reaction was to explode "Mum! You don't know! They're horrible! It's just that they never see any women, and they're trying to make an impression!"

A miracle, and a happy release for all and sundry. For one of the officers was heard to declare categorically that if he had to suffer any more cups of tea made by Ian, (who was on semi-invalid duty making tea for officers), he was going to resign his commission. While Ian would have had to brave a horrendous "assault course" which was looming, but for this timely rescue. He is not cut out for it. Lemurians are hedonists at heart, and need peace wherein to look around them and savour leisure and feed their intuition.

Speaking of soldiers, I have always liked them. As a class of men, they represent a nice type. Intelligent too, strangely enough, in a spiritual way, I've discovered. Not cynical or analytical. If they were, they could not effectively be soldiers. *"Theirs not to reason why; theirs but to do and die"* * is the attitude they instinctively adopt. In later life they frequently become interested in Esoterics. That would be accounted for by the fact that, seeing so much of death, and its continuity after physical dissolution, they naturally want to know more about life, and that the military profession is under the auspices of Saturn, which makes a man thoughtful in later life. Thus Colonel Olcott of the Theosophical founders, Colonel Chodewisc, the Polish lecturer at the Theosophical Society's meetings, Francis Carr, Mr. Braybon, Montrose, Claverhouse, the Duke of

* From *The Charge of the Light Brigade*, Tennyson

Monmouth . . . many of them.

It was in 1966 that I met Colonel Stewart, who with his wife Lady Daphne Hay, lived near Lauder in the Tweed country. He was a karmic connection, and in casting his incarnascope, I discovered that one of his former lives had touched mine. We became close friends, and I visited their home frequently. It was so remote, twenty-seven miles from Edinburgh, that one had to stay several days.

Lady Daphne was the daughter of the Marquis of Tweed-dale, while Colonel Stewart was descended lineally from James III of Scotland. The Scottish aristocrats customarily have no money, but they have a vast store-house of pride, and are romantic, and I valued the friendship.

In the same context I "met" Montrose, the soldier poet whose was the motto I adopted when I was adventurous and every-ready to take chances:

He either fears his fate too much
Or his deserts are small,
Who dares not put it to the touch
To win or lose it all.

Montrose was probably a Sagittarian. His fate was dire, and to all intents and purposes, he lost everything.

I had a friend, Iris, at Iver Heath, who died several years ago, and another at Uxbridge, Kath. They introduced me to their "Direct Voice" group at Gerrards Cross where my Uncle Jack lived, and he likewise was interested. The woman president of it "discovered" a powerful trance and transfiguration medium, albeit illiterate, a feature that made her demonstrations the more impressive for she had never heard of Montrose. I had spent the day in Uxbridge, much of it in the *Treaty House* where the fateful treaty was drawn up which sealed the doom of Montrose.* I was profoundly conscious of the presence of Montrose in my auric-surround, and suddenly the medium put her hand to her throat with a gesture indicative of acute discomfort. "Oh!", she exclaimed, "I've got a gentleman here whose collar is too tight. It's choking him . . . Oh, dear . . . !" Her distress was very apparent as for one whole minute the face of Montrose was superimposed upon hers in the half-light. For that whole minute I sat transfixed as Montrose

---

*There were three contacts with Montrose, afterwards. He was a kinsman of Claverhouse, about whom I wrote my novel *The Devil and Dundee*. And in my book *Where Do We Go From Here?* I established links in the past lives of Henry II, "Fair Rosamund," Eleanor of Aquitane and Montrose, and Archibald Campbell, the Marquis of Argyll who engineered Montrose's execution. The sequence is set forth in my trilogy.

and I looked full at each other. The lineaments were clear-cut, the portrait by Honthurst* delineated them faithfully. Then he was gone, and the medium's guide brought another communicant forward for someone else in the room. But the experience was unforgettable, one of many.

Lady Daphne and I exorcised a ghost at Ashietiel which had been mistaken by searching soldiers for Montrose. Details of this are in my book *More Astral Rescues*, in the chapter devoted to "Old, Unhappy, Far-Off Things, and Battles Long Ago." It speaks of Ashtiel, the ancient, mysterious house in the Border Country, where Sir Walter Scott lived before he bought Abbotsford. Owning it when I had occasion to go there were Admiral Abel-Smith and Lady Mary. They were elderly and gracious, and living in a bygone era, as did Lady Lauderdale of Thirleston Castle. They are impecunious, these aristocrats of Scottish lineage, yet as proud as kings, and patronising to "Sassenachs."** Lady Lauderdale's son was trying to eke out a living in London by selling vacuum-cleaners, the venerable lady herself held court in one wing of the derelict castle, and was served tea on a tripod by an eighteenth century lacquey who was ninety years old and clad in a threadbare uniform consisting of a green waistcoat and doublet. She extended her hand to me to kiss. I have never experienced anything quite like it before or since.

Admiral Abel-Smith was in charge of the Royal Yacht Brittania when Prince Charles and Princess Anne were children. His wife, Lady Mary, was a descendant of Montrose. She showed me a ring Montrose had given to his wife, Magdalen Carnegie. She had been offered a lot of money for it by dealers, but would not part with it. The story of how Lady Daphne and I exorcised the ghost in the fifteenth-century wing of Ashiestiel is recounted in my book *More Astral Rescues*.

However, that was in the nature of a digression. Lady Daphne had been in a past life a monkish companion of James IV, who, as the author A.J. Stewart would tell you, cultivated such companions, and had accompanied the king in that capacity to the Battle of Flodden. A.J. Stewart carried a "lifted memory" of it and always spoke of it as if it were yesterday. Lady Daphne was a gifted but absent-minded lady, as much at home in long-ago history as in her current existence, if not a great deal more so, and drove her husband 'round the bend by interminably holding up the supper while she dilated upon the mistaken tactics of James IV, "If *only* he'd held that position on the hill! It was such a strategic position! he would certainly have won the battle!" All this while she poised the spoon in the air instead of serving the food. "O Daphne!" plaintively expostulated the Colonel, "For God's sake! It *was* five hundred years ago, and we're all bloody starving!" All the waiting guests laughed . . . it was hilariously

---

* Part of the *National Portrait Gallery*'s collection
**The Scots' name for their southern neighbors.

funny, except to the colonel, who had suffered from it so often.

The history of 12, Old Steine, in Brighton is recounted in my book *True Tales of Reincarnation and Astral Rescue*, so I need not dwell upon it here. Suffice it to say that Mr. Read the dentist, whose offices were beneath my flat, was my constant companion for two years, along with his aged "general man," Simon, who could not win clear of the house because he had for so long known no other home. There was, too, the phenomenon of "deep breathing," which can be most disconcerting when one is alone with it. *I was*, in my lonely bed in the little room at the back, and it emanated from beneath the buttress under the window where, I understand, two women were killed by the storm of 1848. I was able to placate and dispose of all these ghosts, though it took time. There was even the ghost of a dog, *Nelson* (after the admiral, of course, since his name was on everyone's lips at the time.) "Ordinary" dogs in fleshly form would not enter the building, and nothing could make them.

Sandys Butler came into a different category. He was not a ghost, but a spirit communicant, who initially had come to me at Woodingdean, and now followed me into my "haunted" flat. He is dealt with in a separate file, labelled *The Sandys Butler Story* which is extant if the family or friends in America want it, for it embraces the American network as well. The Sandys Butler story has many ramifications, even extending to Kathleen and her mother and sister Gladys who I contacted again in 1993.

A ghost and a spirit *are*, as Charles I said about himself and his subjects, "clean different things." A ghost has a "fixation," and is chained to one location, one specific house or district, not knowing that he/she is "dead," and consequently performing the identical ritual and routine that was all he/she understood, in perpetuity, until rescued by a medium who understands the nature of the predicament. Whereas a spirit is to some extent free, and can communicate according to the measure of his/her awareness. These "touch down" into the physical vibration for the purposes of communication, and to some extent bring their own empire with them. Again, in accordance with their degree of infiltration as to what has happened to them. Thus with Sandys Butler I was able to explain step by step, often laboriously, (since he was a Roman Catholic), what had happened to him since he quitted the physical dimension in the seventeenth century.

No. 12, Old Steine had been empty for many years before I arrived. It was a Regency house, built during the period when "Prinny"* accomplished the journey from London in a record eight hours, and came down to Brighton to occupy his newly built *Pavilion*, about which a contemporary observed, *it was as if St. Pauls had come to Brighton and had pups.*

Apart from the onerous task of exorcising ghosts, I had to face total

*George IV, the Prince Regent.

solitude for the first time in my life. The children had been my sole, but constant companions and their departure left a strange sense of bereavement. Sometimes I would repair to Ted's house at night, since it was no longer safe to be in the flat alone. The lower floors were office premises, deserted after five o'clock, and thieves were breaking in to steal the copper piping and fittings.

One night, the last night I ever spent there alone, I had the psychic experience which was to be the deciding factor in the ensuing phase of my life. I was in bed, frightened, apprehensive and disquietingly aware of my loneliness, when I heard, or thought I heard, Ian's familiar step in the passage.

Thankfully, I sat bolt upright. "Thank God you've come!" I exclaimed fervently. But there was no one. It was not Ian. It could only have been a strong astral projection on his part, which builds up into an actual physical semblance of the person concerned. The only historically vouched-for instance of this is "modern" times was the appearance of Lord Dundee to the Earl of Balcarres in prison in the Edinburgh Tolbooth, at the moment of his death at Killiekrankie. It is a most striking phenomenon, which, when it fades, creates a sense of incredulity, so very "physical" it had been.

Notwithstanding, it taught me a lesson. "Never again," I told myself, "are you to rely or depend on anyone, *anyone at all*, for your wellbeing, safety or comfort. You are on your own, and *don't you forget it!*"

I never did forget it, and substituted over my bed for Montrose's brave "He either fears his fate too much," the maxim, *"Put not your trust in princes, nor any child of man, for there is no help in them."*

It is wholly true. And why should there be? There may sometimes be help *through* them, in minor ways, but never *in* them. In the final analysis we have to do everything ourselves, and the sooner we recognise it, the better, in our own interests.

I acted on my own stricture, and started afresh. I was still young enough to do it. I went out and made friends. I convened meetings in my little flat and built up a circle of acquaintances. I could cram thirty-five people into the front room, and in a series of lectures promulgated the Ancient Wisdom. I found there was a great need and as an outcome of these meetings, my friend Joan at Portsmouth founded a group which has been a flourishing going-concern for twenty-five years, and I have lectured there regularly. Thus "great oaks from little acorns grow." Almost without exception, all the friends I have made have been by reason of "the work."* It has taken me anywhere and everywhere, even to America.

*Win and Barry and their daughter Philippa were among them; all nice people, not bosom-friends perhaps, but they used to come to the meetings. I continued to visit them long after I left Brighton, and still do so when I re-visit there, not very often now, unfortunately.

One such interesting friend was Ron Cunningham, known as *The Great Omani*. He was an escapologist, who modelled himself on Houdini. His was the first incarnascope I made outside of my own, and the one which convinced me that I possessed the links necessary to make them for other people. I knew nothing about him and had no point of reference beyond an item of clothing. I told him that he had been a convict deported to Australia in 1800 for a felony he may or may not have committed.

The prisoners were chained to a stockade at night. There was a ring of fire round the stockade, then the impossible swim which led to no escape. He resolved to escape. He devised a method of freeing himself from his fetters. Somehow he negotiated the ring of fire; he began to swim the bay. But he was shot before he could make any headway.

A *resolution* must be implemented, and he came back this time equipped with the skill to exert mind over matter. His chief stunt was to dive from the end of the West Pier in Brighton, chained and shackled, subjected to the scrutiny of an audience to ensure that there was no trick involved. Paraffin was thrown on the surface of the sea and ignited. He dived through the ring of fire, into the water, swam to the surface and came up free. Thus he had performed in reverse all that I had recounted in his former life.

Further "turns" of his were to sit relaxed and smoking a cigarette in a bath of boiling water, perform a hand-stand on the precipice of Beachy Head, travel on a bed of nails, devour electric lightbulbs, be buried six feet below ground in a coffin for a prolonged period. He still flourishes in Brighton and hazards the occasional TV appearance.

Another friend contacted through my work was Guilivia Crystal, the famous astrologer who works for *The Sunday Mirror* and other papers; she attended the meetings regularly. An enthusiastic supporter was Iris Bryson-White, the dynamic editor and single-handed manager of *The Brighton Herald*. She was avidly interested in my incarnascopes, and in her autocratic way demanded more and more of them. Under her aegis I cast them for Barbara Cartland, who, I discovered without surprise, had been a gendarme in Paris, and Margaret Thatcher, whose first really positive entry was the current one, and Flora Robson, about whom I quoted, *"Some are born great, some achieve greatness, and some have greatness thrust upon them."* This modest, unassuming actress came into the latter category. She lived at Brighton and always smiled at me when we crossed paths on the promenade. Nicholas Parsons too, and other celebrities.

Iris was endowed with the "multiplicity of gifts," painting, writing, composing music, was a Country Councillor, looked after an invalid parent and ran a house. She was responsible for cleaning up the notorious Sussex General Hospital, which institution I know helped to hasten my father's death. Today it is a model of well-conducted efficiency. It had been converted from the original historic workhouse. Iris likewise died prematurely while I was living in Newcastle.

As mentioned, my work takes me into company I would not otherwise consort with. I corresponded with the Duke of Bedford and the Marquis of Tavistock and the Marquis of Bath, and with Lady Drage, the wealthy widow of that Sir Benjamin Drage who made "Hire Purchase" respectable. In *spirit* of course too, with the Duke of Monmouth, for years at a stretch, until he had imbibed the Ancient Wisdom and recounted his experiences in the "Summerland"* before he learnt that it all is illusion; with Charles I and his little daughter Elizabeth, details of which communication (some might think of it as an 'exorcism,' but it wasn't that), are in my file on *Fragmented Communications* with Charles II and James II and Edward II, with Queen Elizabeth and Mary Fitton and Francis Bacon. There is nothing remarkable about this. They cease to be "important" when they find themselves on the "other side," and anyone can speak to anyone. Spirit communication is the simplest operation in the world, except that today's people make such a fuss about it, as they do about everything, building up mountains of words and knocking them down again with tedious insistence. It is exactly equated with our telephone system. "Down here," provided you dial the correct number and pay for the call, you can speak to anyone in the world you want to. "Over there," the method tallies completely, the "Exchange" being the guides. Only the prerequisite differs. Instead of an inserted coin, it is **LOVE** (applied in its true connotation, as **WISDOM**), and a sincere desire for the other party's welfare. Thus having the full run of the Akashic Record, a medium is in touch with all his/her linked souls or offshoots, from all incarnations, high and low, rich and poor, great and small, though these terms only signify "down here," and with animals too.

Now, in the mid-nineteen sixties, I had Ian on my hands for a while. He was restless, fed up and raring to be on his way again. He soon was, his clarion-cry being, "I don't want to spend the rest of my life with you . . ." So flattering, but inevitable; and Mavis hastened to leave too. It seemed as if they could not get far enough away from me nor cut off from me quickly enough. Doubtless it is the customary procedure; I had deserted my father when he needed me most, and now must pay the debt in turn.

It was painful in the extreme, and a severe testing-time for me. It was, nevertheless, something that had to happen, in order that, presumably, I should be alone in the flat for the purpose for which I had been led there, and could not be released until I made it possible.

So much of my life has been integrated with my *work*, and yet the two are separate. That is where so many people fall into a fatal trap. They are unable to rise above the "personal" level, and assess everything from that illusory

*See *True Tales of Reincarnation and Astral Rescue*, Chapter XII.

standpoint. It was done with Lord Byron and Shelley, and Mozart, and Beethoven, to cite but a few, and with all pioneers in the esoteric field. And that is where my son and daughter have consistently, persistently and wholly, broken my heart. ◆

VII

Sussex Days

But that was later. I was still living in Brighton, and Ian and Mavis came to see me from time to time. Mavis, like myself before her, entertained a succession of boyfriends. Some of them were a pain in the neck. She outgrew them in turn, and was about to settle for Ian Gates, had not karma intervened and brought her into contact with an offshoot of her opposite polarity, the female principle in the shape of her current partner.*

As they go, Ian Gates was no worse than any of the others; today's society is not renowned for heroic males. And I liked his parents. They were simple countryfolk, with no pretention to be anything else, and we got on well together. "If only Ian and Mavis had stayed together," his mother once remarked, "we should have had nice friends." But that wasn't to be. I couldn't relate to the parents of her existing partner, who get on my nerves more than anyone I have know. But I kept up with Lily and Tom "in my own right," so to speak, after Mavis and Ian had gone their separate ways. Lily likewise lamented the fact that Ian had gone to the University. "He used to be so nice until he went there. It has ruined him!"

There's much to be said for the point of view. They certainly don't learn any manners, and often grow unprepossessingly above themselves. It has been too quick, too much too soon. Humanity is incapable of moderation. An old gate-keeper at Oxford was heard to observe, with a lugubrious shake of the head, "the people who used to come through these doors were gentlemen. Now they're just students." It speaks volumes.

Ian and Mavis and I, and sometimes "our Ian" and his friends, used to

*Chris Miller.

87

walk over to Hurstpierpoint via Wolstenbury Hill and have tea with Ian's parents. Lily always produced a sumptuous repast, and Tom would invariably send us back laden with garden produce and a lovely bunch of flowers. "Old Tom," as I called him, took immense pride in his garden. On Mavis's and incidentally Ian's twenty-first birthday, we celebrated in their pleasant garden. They only had a "Council House," but they kept it immaculately. Tom died in 1990; Lily is nearly blind. Buses are few and far between; I cannot get there now.

They were good days, as days go in today's world. Not, naturally, comparable with the very old days with Kath and Miss Mizen and Auntie Madge, but in comparison with what has followed, with the exception of America, yes, good. En route from Hurstpierpoint via Muddles Wood, we used to gather primroses and cowslips, and sometimes, when the young people were absent, I would gather them by myself, or with Sandys Butler for company. He was learning. Sometimes he would be in his own seventeenth century environment, sometimes translated into my vibration; then he would exclaim, quaintly, "It is you, yet not you!"

Yes good days, because, at that time, it was still safe to be out on the downs by yourself, gathering cowslips and the delicious white violets that Alfred Noyes wrote about. Now it is not. Criminality has spread to rural areas, and all unsavoury characters who at one time were under guard or deflected into constructive channels or detained at her Majesty's pleasure, are with one accord in possession of cars, and out and about everywhere, mugging, murdering, assaulting, and no one, no matter of what age group, is safe, either in his/her home or out of it, in town or city or the English countryside. As Montrose said on the gallows, "God help this poor country!" Thus all things being relative, good days.

I only salvaged one friend among the parents of Varndean School, Joyce Field, the mother of Mavis's classmate Pat, the rest were suburban, dull and conventional. Joyce lived at Lewes, and we would walk together over the downs. Inevitably she died. I am never suffered to enjoy protracted friendships. This has been so pointed, and so repetitive that I long ago accepted it, perhaps as a by-product of the Curse of the O'Connors. There has been no continuity in my life, *"this time, you walk alone."* The medium in London had been emphatic about that. No one at all has known me *all* my life. Uncle Jack was the nearest approach to that, and he died in the nineteen seventies.

While passing my days domestically in the manner outlined, I appear to have become "well-known." That is to say, people had exchanged intelligence concerning my clairvoyant faculty and the fact that I could cast incarnascopes. I had not fully realised it. One doesn't. One is so absorbed in the details of getting a living and the welfare of one's children, as far as they will let one be. It was not until I was approached by the television networks that I realised it.

The television in the '60s was, and still is, the very worst medium for promulgating the truth. Again, although I had an idea that this was the case, I was not conversant with the full extent of the ignorance and prejudice that characterised it, nor the calamitous stranglehold exerted by the Church, theoretical, possibly, but none the less virulent for that.

The telephone rang frequently, and journalists came to see me; articles began to appear in *Prediction* and the Sunday *Times*; there were telegrams from *Weekend Television* and the *Independent Television* at Southampton. Fame and fortune beckoned, and I had all the requisite ingredients, the looks, the eloquence, the inclination and enthusiasm, and the knowledge. Then, because of the Curse of the O'Connors, the tempting bait receded again, time after time. The words of the medium years anterior came back to me: *"You were born to be in the public eye, but there will always be something to prevent it."* And that accompanied the prediction *"You will walk alone."* Not that it matters. But it is not until much later in life that one can build that into one's philosophy. I had not attained to that degree of wisdom. At the time it was as if Fate were striking blow after cruel blow. Who knows? The Curse may ultimately have proved to be a blessing. It was not as though I had been conceited or egotistical, to deserve the robbing and cheating and despoilment of which I was the victim, even from "High Places," where integrity might have been expected, even from Court Circles, even the entourage of the Prince of Wales. It was probably in order that I should be more sympathetic and in a better position to assist others as a modest "back-bencher" than if I had been mixing in so-called elite circles where the humble aspirants I have since aided, would not have come my way at all.

Be that as it may, my first television assignment was with Kenneth Kendall. That was in 1966, when the media was tentatively tangling with what it and the world, sedulously copying The Beatles, was pleased to dub "the occult." What a silly word! It means "hidden," and God knows it is time the truth was no longer hidden from the people, whose birthright it is. However, the choice is theirs. While they all with one accord have to come to it in the end, they are in control of the time-factor, and can postpone the acquisition of this mandatory knowledge as long as they want to. Supremely and complacently incognizant of its compulsory nature, and its "sooner or later" option, so many of them stupidly and wantonly opt for "later." No one can hurry them; you can lead a horse to the water, but you can't make it drink.

The public interview with Kenneth Kendall was inoffensive but discreetly inconclusive. The Church still jealously exercised its stranglehold. Whether this is loosening now I do not know; I am out of touch and prefer to remain that way, since anything else is so exacerbating. No information was suffered to escape that the Church did not know about, and as that was virtually everything, nothing got through the net. Much the same applied to my interview with Dave Allen, but as a sequel to that, I received a telegram from the Beatles, who informed me that in their (then much-deferred-to) estimation I was "out of this world," and would I down tools pronto and commute to London where they had put a suite of rooms at my disposal. I was about to comply, because at that time I thought it a good idea to court fame and fortune which I seemed all set to enjoy. Within the hour, another telegram, to state that the Beatles had been whisked away to India in the wake of the Maharishi Mahesh Yogi and would contact me again. I wrote them to promise that if ever I could help them, they should let me know.

Next The Beach Boys asked me out to supper. They needed, they said, to enrich themselves knowledge-wise. They escorted me to English's Restaurant in the Lanes at Brighton. The price was exorbitant by my ultra-moderate standards and the one thing I recall about it was the distasteful vogue of bringing a tank of live fish round and inviting each guest to select one. Within ten minutes the unhappy creature would be served to him on a dish. I couldn't face it, and settled for something more civilised, but it is all so long ago that I forget what it was. I remember answering questions with my mouth full and being glad to get home. These harmless but loutish guitar players are so much a part of the prevalent cult of mediocrity.

My promising TV career was finally thwarted by David Frost, whose shallow "scepticism," ignorance and silly egoism typified the media of the day. Again, whether it has modified I simply would not know, nor particularly care, knowing as I do that nothing can be hurried, but that all is under control, and cannot manifest until the time is ripe. Suffice it to say that he, being still very much at the personal level, could not envision the wider canvas, and took umbrage because I was getting the better of him in point of repartee; I can always do this if I have to, but in this case it simply wasn't the object of the exercise, and constituted a consummate waste of time.

Floods of letters poured in from the public, demanding to know why "that woman was not allowed to finish what she was saying; she obviously had something to say." David Frost, however, either afraid of the Church's stranglehold, or of the defeat of his own ego, or a bit of both, had in fact succeeded in curtailing my flow of information. A friend in Fulham, who had seen the programme, told me that the only interpretation she could put on it was that the "vibes" at this period embodied so much antagonism, that had I been allowed to broadcast regularly as many people wanted me to, I might have met with the fate of John Lennon. As with so many things, devastating as they are at the time, indeed rightly termed "the Temptation of the Angels," in that one feels as if one had been taken to the top of a mountain and shown the promised land, then brusquely thrown down into an abyss. The episode has faded into obscurity, but I have to confess that it was not until the last ten years that it began to do so, and I thought that it was to haunt me forever with its injustice and futility.

Dave Allen was the only awakened interviewer I encountered, and he, finding that the esoteric path did not pay, took to one that did, the comic entertainer's path. I wrote to him in 1993, and received a warm and touching reply. The rich and famous are no better off than we are. It is exactly as Rudolf Steiner predicted. Now at the end of the century we all need the knowledge, and so many are tragically without it. Centuries ago, Plato exhorted us, *"MAN, KNOW THYSELF"* and *"THE PROPER STUDY OF MANKIND IS MAN."* But no one took any notice, and still they take no notice!

Investigating the reason for the extraordinary recession of interest in the so-called "occult" of the nineteen-sixties, it was because much of the upsurge of interest was among the youthful "New Age" types, who were not quite ready for it and took drugs in a mistaken effort to open chakras prematurely, "by force," as it were. There are no short cuts, and to endeavour to hasten a natural process is to attract forces which do not communicate the truth, but side-track and confuse, as well as being deleterious to the physical form. Accordingly the hopeful opening was closed down again, and subsequently the pendulum swung crazily as always, too far in the opposite direction, till we had a parallel upsurge of materialism which reached a horrific level in the nineteen-eighties. The nineties likewise are secular and cynical, with criminality rampant and no standards or values for the unfortunate populace to hold on to. Five years to go, and Steiner's end-of-century prediction bids fair to be borne out in a frightening degree: *"By the end of the century, those who are not spiritually orientated will become ill, either physically or mentally or both."*

It's hard to tell what became of those "Flower-People" and "Hippies" of the early seventies who emulated The Beatles and tried to develop spirituality as they saw it, i.e. in the ethic of sharing, and of näively liking everybody, etc., etc. Into what can their next phase have led them? They are in early middle-age now, and must presumably have become absorbed into the society from which they dropped out, or in some way come to terms with defeat and submitted to integration. It is not easy to succeed as a drop-out, in that we are all interdependent, and if you accept Social Security handouts, you are not a successful dropout. It is still unfortunately the same with the theoretically praiseworthy ethic of sharing, because our society is so orientated that those who want to share have nothing to share, while those they want to share with are not willing to share. Will Mr. Major's "classless society" come up with the answer? Shall we ever get it right?

Their successors, the "travellers," are not the same at all. It would not be safe to spend a night with them on Glastonbury Tor, as Mavis and I did, with the "Flower-People," before she drifted away from me. That adventure is related fully in my book *Call Joshua*. It was memorable, and highly significant. It was while Mavis was in a "No-Man's-Land" position, after Ian Gates and before taking up with Chris Miller.

We didn't know we were going to Glastonbury. I had been lecturing the night before in Southampton. We walked all the way from there. We got a lift on a cement mixer; I'll never know how I clambered up on to that elevated vehicle; it was like getting into Colonel Stewart's Land Rover, when I split my skirt from stem to stern. The residents of Glastonbury took us for hippies and would not serve us a cup of tea, let alone a bed for the night. So we opted for spending the Solstice Night on the Tor along with that motley but amiable company.

In striking contrast to that orderly and friendly scene, in what seems an age ago, I have tonight, October 16, 1994, made a point of watching on the television the "Glastonbury Festival." I have turned the sound down; otherwise it would be insupportable. There is a sea of faces in the green countryside, a surging entanglement of waving arms and legs, a celebration, a demonstration of ecstasy. It is doubtful if any of the participants would *consciously* be able to define the cause of the celebration or the ecstasy, any more than in Northern Ireland or Bosnia or Iraq they would be able to pinpoint the cause of the fighting. It has to be conceded that some of them take their ecstasy seriously, with set faces and grim expressions, but the performers in the marquee gyrate and contort their bodies into grotesque configurations as they scream into the microphone. Some of them bite the microphone, draw it into their octave-stretched mouths, and half-swallow it in their frenzy.

I drew up a collective incarnascope for the massive crowd. Its units are all young. The are the fore-runners of the New Age, the veritable First-Footers. All they understand is Freedom, the password for the New Age. For the first time in their chain of lives they have it. At last. All through the Age of Pisces they were repressed to the point of extinction. Chimney sweeps, children in factories and coal mines who never grew up. Now, their clarion-cry is, "Let me live! Let me breathe! Let me do what I like, go where I like, have what I want, scream and shout and clamour, make my voice heard!" Their movements are diametrically opposed to those of the juvenile Lemurians who go in for the Olympic Games. The movements of the Lemurians are rigorously disciplined, coordinated, and geared to demonstrate the total subservience of the physical form. The gesticulations of the Glastonbury throng are disconnected, chaotic and confused. They are a kindergarten, and Glastonbury has been ordained as their learning-ground. The farmers do not like it, the residents lock their doors, draw their blinds and refuse admittance to all and sundry. Bligh Bond* may not have approved of it, the phantom monks of the Abbey may cover their ears and flee for sanctuary, but it is an inescapable part of Evolution. Glastonbury is the cradle of the New Age, no matter how clumsy and embryonic the preliminary manifestation may be.

When the New Age actually dawns, these protagonists will be mature

---

*See *True Tales of Reincarnation and Astral Rescue*, Chapter XIV.

citizens, provided they have survived the drugs and live. God knows what it will be like. the mind boggles. But God always knows, and somehow the world goes on!

As the programme draws to its cacophonous conclusion, and the stroboscopic (is that the right word?) lighting fades, I give thanks to God that I am not in fact *there*, in my beautiful Glastonbury, but safely and cosily ensconced in my chair before the "telly." How very easy and comfortable everything is made for us today! Really, we ought to be working wonders, with the multifarious facilities accruing from our incarnation at this juncture! Yet here I am, lounging about gawping at rubbish.

I shared other adventures with Mavis, before she elected to chart a separate course. Our Irish holiday was amusing, though possibly we should not find it so now. This was organised for us by my Irish friend Mary MacCay, who lives at Woking. She had a friend who, she promised, would drive us all over the Emerald Isle. He did, but was always in such a hurry that we were not vouchsafed the opportunity to do justice to that extensive canvas. Furthermore the season was winter. Notwithstanding, there were some delightful interludes.

Our headquarters were with Mrs. Bridget Guiry, who owned a little shop in Garrick-on-Suir in County Tipperary. Her cottage at the back of the shop was on a road called "Mass Road," so named because at the time her house was built, in 1540, the Catholics had to celebrate Mass clandestinely on that site for fear of persecution. The country round was little changed since their day, and neither were Mrs. Guiry's mod. coms. There was no bathroom; all ablutions had to be performed in a cracked enamel basin in the stone sink in the kitchen. As soon as these were completed, with carbolic soap, she would throw cabbage leaves and mud-encrusted potatoes into the bowl, then cook them along with the fat bacon that comprised our dinner. Doubtless it was nourishing, but gritty, as the potato skins were left intact, and faintly redolent of carbolic.

It was a mystic land. There were only two trains a day to Limerick Junction, and the diminutive station was in the midst of fields. Otherwise just miles of countryside with an eerie atmosphere about it that was hard to define. Certainly in my solitary walks in other parts of Britain I had never experienced it; not altogether friendly, or did I imagine it? I don't think so, for I heard two retired head-mistresses, very down-to-earth types with sensible shoes and tweed skirts, confessing to the proprietor of their hotel that having reached a certain point in their post-prandial stroll, they were quite forcefully impelled to turn back. "Oh, well," he replied, "no one goes to that wood at dusk." I learnt afterwards that a Hibernian Mystery School had occupied that spot in antiquity, whose members had thrown out a magnetic field or "ring-pass-not" that repelled investigators. Until a medium happened along who was powerful enough to dismantle it, it would remain there.

Castle Ormonde is in Carrick, where Anne Boleyn was born. So much to discover, but Mary's driver who had been all over the world, was fed up with everywhere and simply would not pause long enough anywhere to permit of exploration, albeit we visited, hurriedly, every county. Neither was the weather conducive to lingering, so the quaint little wayside shrines and the one-floor cottages and the fairies beckoned in vain. Mrs. Guiry could "see" the fairies. "Just elementals in the wind and the rain," she explained, and even hard-headed business men would own that they heard the Banshee calling the night before a person died. I'm glad I went there when I did, as now I'm told it is spoilt and modernised like most other places. Mary prefers living in England. Even Dublin to her felt a bit antiquated; we spent a day there, and the lift in the hotel obstinately refused to stop at the destined floor, but always just a few inches below or above it. Not that we cared; we were still carefree. Mary delighted to put whisky in my glass, then top it up with strong cider, perchance in the hope of proving her favourite adage, "when the drink's in, the truth's out." She is no longer carefree; so much has happened since, much of it sad. But she was kind and helpful, and supervised the publication of *Call Joshua*, and I dedicated that book to her—*To Mary, who took a loving interest.* We seldom meet now; Bristol and Woking are miles apart, and we are both wedged in our circumstances.

We did spend some time at Bunratty Castle where they hold the mediaeval banquets, and saw the famous pub, "Dirty Nellie's," which is preserved in its erstwhile rough uncouth seventeenth-century state with straw on the floor and clay pipes and pewter tankards. The one place I regret being constrained to hurry through was the Valley of the Boyne, where Sandys Butler fought for King James and became an exile thereby. It was a most scenic location too. Never mind. I can see it in the other dimension. Sometimes we forget that there is plenty of "time" (we have all Eternity) for us to use as we please, and that the Akashic Record is at our disposal. But I know I am as guilty as the next person of getting impatient in this slow-moving dimension.

The psychic powers of the villagers in Carrick and the astonishing church-services held there are recounted in the Sandys Butler File. They were breath-takingly impressive, they must have been, to get me out of bed at six o'clock in the morning to attend "Mass," I only did it to please Mrs. Guiry. Impressive likewise was the (as I thought at the time) trivial and ridiculous prognostication by a friend in Brighton that I was going to Waterford. "Tipperary, Winnie," I corrected. "No," said Winnie, "Waterford." Fruitless for me to reiterate 'Tipperary,' so, thinking she was simply trying to be funny, I shrugged and was silent. Sitting one day in Mrs. Guiry's kitchen, apropos of nothing, the latter volunteered, "You know, I'm sitting in Tipperary, you're in Waterford. The county boundary line runs right through my kitchen." Yes, there's no doubt some people can read the Akasha, back and forward . . .

At this phase I was seeing a lot of Ted, and sometimes Richard. We used to laugh so much! That is what I chiefly remember about the association. People don't seem to laugh much now, and you never hear anyone singing. Once errand-boys used to sing and whistle cheerfully as they passed by on their bicycles. Perhaps they still do. Or perhaps it's just me. Or perhaps Rudolf Steiner was right, he usually was, in stating that before long it would be impossible to be happy while others (and animals) were suffering. Whatever the truth, although we were not "young" in the recognised sense, we were light-hearted. Relatively, that is, from the way we are (or at least *I* am) today. We can only legislate for ourselves. Maybe today's people laugh. My daughter holds many parties, but the noisy hilarity seems to echo a different ring, one which lacks joy and spontaneity. I just don't know.

All I do know is that, looking back, our shared adventures had every semblance of those of irresponsible teenagers. But it was all such fun.

Ted possessed a ramshackle vehicle which made no pretention to being a "car." Ted and I were never pretentious. He had an incurable proclivity for breaking down in the most obscure and highly inexpedient places. We went to Ireland again, all three of us, (Richard is Irish) by way of Festiniog, then a rendezvous for the hippies or drop-outs of the day. There was a coterie of them inhabiting an old derelict mansion on the Welsh border. They were amiable, intelligent, not very clean. They sat at Richard's feet while he held forth, an activity at which he was to the manner born. We spent the night there, in makeshift beds, then pushed on to Ireland on the ferry. There we parted company, Richard and Ted to Dublin, to engage in I never knew what, I to Tipperary and Mrs. Guiry again. Ted saw me off at the station. O! that song is so true! *"It's a long, long way to Tipperary."* I thought the train was never going to get there! I thought of the story my mother had told me long before of her railway journey to Killarney, where the stations had read: "Killmary, Killmartin, Killpatrick, Kill MacThomas, Kill MacBridge, Killemall." Then we met up again for home journey, through the Welsh Mountains, where Ted duly broke down for want of petrol, and he and I had to proceed on foot, goodness knows how many miles into Chester for the requisite fuel to enable us to re-start. Richard, meanwhile, one hundred percent self-centred and selfish, (there was a nice side to him and miraculously you could forgive him), curled up in the rear of the non-car, purloined all the blankets, ours as well as his own, lit a revolting cigar, hermetically-sealed all the windows, filled the vehicle with 'flu-germs and cigar smoke, and promptly fell asleep, greeting us as we returned, after hours of trudging through frost-spangled grass, the month being unequivocally February: "You've been a bloody long time! I've got an awful cold!"

How we laughed! I'm sure I wouldn't find the incident so humorous now! and Richard to this day is unrepentant, "It was his own fault," he chuckles. "He shouldn't have been so bloody stupid!"

Ted and I were always having adventures. Once, at Otford near Lewes, we met the most enormous bulls that could possibly exist. They were too heavy and clumsy to be fierce. They just stood there, knee-deep in mud, with faces devoid of any expression at all. One was in a shed with a half-door. Ted scratched his massive forehead, whereat he, in token of gratitude, licked all round Ted's face, like an application of sandpaper, it was, then, with one gargantuan slurp, manoeuvred his tongue round Ted's ear, nearly tearing that organ loose from its moorings.

A further spate of publicity came my way. As a result of a leading article with my photograph in the Sunday *Times*. I was re-contacted by Mildred Sharpe, who had been the Billeting Officer for Huddersfield during the war. She was eager for me to visit her in Yorkshire. A minor karmic contact, she had, as the blacksmith in Dewsbury in the seventeenth century, made the shoes for Jennifer Butler's horse for its rambles about the country, and had gleaned some items of interest from the conversation that always ensued in a smithy, the much sought-after venue for exchange of news and gossip.

I stayed a few days in her eccentric caravan-like abode in Magdale. She owned an eighteenth century weavers' cottage in the vicinity which she had no use for. She offered it to me for the peppercorn price of £300. It needed a great deal of repair. I roped in the faithful Ted. He was a Taurus subject, very handy as well as being an artist, and constructive by nature, and he and Richard could have done the repairs. Ted and I went up to view it, his decrepit equipage miraculously discharging the transport. It was like most things in those days, great fun. On the way up, we camped out in a ploughed field. I can still feel that furrow sticking into my neck. As chronicled, Ted had a genius for discomfort.

The field was fringed by a copse, and I lay there listening to the strange nocturnal summer sounds that emanated from it, rustlings and scufflings, squeaks and scratchings, of little unidentified woodland creatures, and the eerie muted pipings of night-birds. I think it was somewhere near Cirencester. We washed in the stream, and arrived at the cottage, somehow contrived to put together a make-shift bed of planks and car rugs. Astounding, how one's tastes change! I could do *anything* then! Now the deprivation of a full night's sleep makes a cretinous wreck out of me. That bed slanted horribly, and was as hard as . . . well, it *was* a plank, so that was hardly surprising.

After all that, it was reluctantly decided that the site of the cottage was too isolated. No 'bus stop, no jobs, no shops, no use. I had nurtured grandiose plans for it. I was going to christen it *Whittakers,* from Ian's name in his eighteenth-century life as Johnstone Whittaker; (the family, Whittaker's brewers of Luddenfoot, is still extant.) I had planned to present the cottage to Ian. Sadly, I wrote it off as a white elephant.

However, Ted and I compensated ourselves by breaking down on the motorway from Yorkshire in a howling gale. He had to trudge to the telephone box for succour while I crouched in the non-car, rocking perilously in the tempestuous climatic inclemency. Then, having battled our way to London, we broke down again on Vauxhall Bridge during the rush hour. That was the last straw, and how it culminated I shall never know, for I let Ted extricate us and "closed off" conveniently from all embarrassment. I have subsequently brought my innate "closing-off" propensity to a fine art.

Similar occasions enlivened our passage. Ted and I visited Glastonbury, before it became a regular haunt of mine, and he managed to drive into a bog. It was positively the only one of its kind in the entire environment. Ted was just guided into it. I spent most the night collecting straw and cow droppings to ease under the wheel, and after superhuman struggles on a par with those of the father who laid the carpet on the stairs, we got it free, and spent what was left of the night cramped in the back of the vehicle like two sardines, unable to move hand or foot, still less turn 'round. Today it might possibly wear the guise of a horrid endurance test, as indeed were most of my "holidays." I invariably needed a week's rest after them, but *then* we savoured it as a hilarious variation in the lifestyle. There was a vociferous white owl circling 'round that field. I could have sworn it was laughing at us.

Now Ted and Richard and I have gone our separate ways, and seldom cross each others' paths, except on my ever-decreasing visits to Brighton; no one ever comes to Bristol where I live now. It is too far off the map. Ted's sister Ethel is now dead. She and I were good friends. She always had a place for me to stay when I needed it. So many things and people have faded into the limbo of memory. Yet the memories themselves are vivid and alive.

This oppressive malaise I feel now . . . is it *just me?* Is it wholly brought about by the dismal piling up of years? Or *is* there something else that has silenced and stilled the laughter? Some X-factor that is unexplained? Or has life in England *in fact* degenerated into an over-populated, charmless, crime-ridden, litter-strewn shambles? At worst a nightmare, at best a dreary wilderness? I think I will never truly get the answer. ◆

VIII

Decisions: For Better or Worse

I now come to a fork in the road. We all have them, often more than one in a lifetime. Fruitless to speculate as to what would have happened if you had taken "the other one." You didn't, and it did not become a reality. Therefore, as far as this dimension is concerned, it is not inscribed on the Akashic Record but it *is* inscribed in the astral and in the sleep-state, and that happens after you have made your choice and begin to detect flaws in the choice you have made. Rather like the chela who petitioned his guru, *"Master, shall I get married or stay single?" The reply was, "Whichever you do you'll regret it."*

Nevertheless, since the choice is made by your semi-monad or higher self, it is likely to be the right one, even if you don't enjoy the working out of it, in that it will lead you more expeditiously to your karma, and escalate your evolution and that of the karmic contacts involved. Whereas had the choice been made at the "personal" level, you would not have liked the look of it, and would have opted for the facile, more pleasurable programme, or fallen for what appeared to be the "soft" option.

Accordingly I cannot hazard a guess as to what would have happened when it became imperative for me to leave my little flat in the Old Steine, if I had accepted the "alternative accommodation" in Brighton that Mr. Braybon at that time was obliged by law to find for me. Presumably I should have gone to America in any case, but it was still necessary to establish a base in England.

The alternative was to live with Mavis and Chris at Newcastle.

It is the greatest mistake any parent can make, although many make it. It killed my father, and I had made a vow never to fall into the same error. Notwithstanding, two factors operated. One, that I was planning to go to

America, and my home base seemed of secondary importance, and two, that Mavis had stated categorically that she would have no children; a statement made in the ultra-positive manner of a Leo/Buffalo subject. These two points decided me on the issue. I would never, in any circumstances, have consented to throw in my lot with a nuclear family.

But Mavis changed her mind, and it was too late. When I came back from America the first time, it was to find myself living in Newcastle-upon-Tyne. Mavis and Chris are excellent organisers, and had arranged the entire removal and transport for the remnant of my home and furniture.

I was reluctant to part with my unique little flat, and with Brighton, although possibly I did not fully realise it till later, and I was still obsessed by America and its wondrous stimulus. I used to swim in the sea, just opposite, straight from the flat, sometimes right into the winter, December 5th in 1959. Then Brighton was so central, so convenient—'buses at the door to the country, and as a visitor once observed about Brighton "so wonderfully get-aboutable-from."

My landlord, Mr. Braybon, was the principal of the long-standing firm of builders in Sussex. I really liked him. He was keenly interested in esoteric issues. But the relationship between landlord and tenant is never a happy or relaxed one. I had met him twice in earlier incarnations, and he was cautiously aware of it, but we always kept at arms' length, since his wife did not approve, either of his tentative partisanship, or of any association with me, no matter how formal and remote. Thus formal and remote it remained, and unspoken thoughts may well be registered on the Akasha in the time to come, in that unsatisfied curiosity must always be implemented, either in the alternative dimension or in a future incarnation. I no longer permit it to worry me. There is plenty of time in Eternity, and all things come out in the wash, if you want them to. And if you don't, it doesn't matter. So we are in the clear either way. It's just the waiting that grows so *grotty*, as The Beatles would have expressed it.

In 1978 Meg was born to Mavis. I realised that I had broken my vow through no fault of my own, and the realisation served to reinforce the conviction that it was pre-destined, and I could not have taken the other fork even had I wished to. So I adjusted to a situation I had not been prepared for, the first of many. Meg was born exactly between Scorpio and Sagittarius on November 22nd. Thus even if she is on the Scorpio border, she will not join the Buffalo stampede. She is a Horse. Mavis, Chris, and the younger girl, Laurie, who is the reincarnation of Auntie Doris, are all Buffaloes, and comprise a high-powered household.

That year I was very ill. At one point I expected to die. It was nothing more than a savage and prolonged attack of 'flu and bronchitis. In the Spring we had a week's holiday in the Lake District. I was still very ill. The weather was dreadful, and Meg cried most of the time. Wordsworth would turn in his grave, he probably has several times, if he could see today the terrain where he wandered lonely as a cloud. You literally have to queue up to take a walk. Hordes of tourists, with anoraks and haversacks and plastic dinghies and dogs and children, swarm up the hills nose-to-tail, treading on each others' heels, packing the streets of Grasmere and pouring into the pub in Keswick where Wordsworth and Dorothy found Coleridge prostrate in the straw, *"drows'd with the fume of poppies,"* or, more crudely, under the influence of opium. The place has simply become a "lung" for the overspill of our teeming urban sprawls.

I looked forward avidly to my trips to America and what I aimed to accomplish there, and the place where I lived and the adjustment to a lifestyle I had not included in my calculations, took second place. It was not until much later that its full import was borne in upon me, while now, in 1994, it is all 'round me, and there is no hiding-place. Thus, if I did not know what the "process" is, and pre-ordination, I could entertain bitter regrets that I took the line of least resistance and allowed myself to be overtaken by events, instead of exercising control of them, and considering the "alternative accommodation" that my kindly landlord offered me all those years ago.

We had two cats, Smudge and Grubby. They were good at moving. Just as well, for the family moved frequently. At first, we shared a house with Annie and Alistair. Annie was a minor karmic contact, having been with me in my mediaeval life, when there had been rats in the house in Pisa. Whenever Annie and I went anywhere together, we encountered rats. There was the farm called *Rattenraw,* on a freezing winter walk to Otterburn, when my ankles and toes were rubbed raw in the snow. I must have been really tough in those days. On another rugged ramble, there was a rubbish-tip swarming with rats; there was the inn named *The Rat,* with a sinister sign outside, where we paused for a drink. Even trifles will assert themselves when it is a question of karma. The repeated incidence of rats made an impression on Annie. I am beyond being impressed and I have not set eyes on a rat since.

The family fell out with Annie and Alistair, and we moved to another part of Newcastle, Seaton Burn. The new "friends" were certainly no improvement on Annie and Alistair, but there's no accounting for taste. I have seldom liked any of Mavis and Chris's circle. Like my mother's, their tastes are based on politics, and politics deteriorate, if that were possible.

During the (appalling) winter of 1979, I taught an evening class at Whitley Bay. It was a notable "breakthrough" for the Education Authority to countenance an esoteric course of study. It proved immensely popular, and drew the highest enrollment of all the subjects offered. When the caretakers of the college went on strike, a faithful nucleus met in a private house, being so dedicated that they commuted long distance through all weathers, (and *what* weather we get in Northumberland!), rather than miss an attendance. It was a great success. At that time, I went to Florida, and my students gave me a wonderful "send-off" in the shape of a party. Such sincere warm-hearted people the "Geordies;" * they amply compensate for their inclement climate with their warmth and hospitality.

Each time I returned from America, it was to find the family in situ in a new setting. There was never time to settle anywhere, but we always made a point of exploring the surroundings, and that has contributed much to my extensive familiarity with the English countryside. (I was, by now, curiously, a "dual personality." America had become my "alter-home" if one may coin a term.)

Still, while in England, there were strenuous tramps over the moors, excursions to Alnwick and Bamborough and Dunstanburgh and Lindisfarne and north to Redesdale and nearly to Scotland. We breasted the head-on gales on Hadrian's Wall,** which snatched the breath from our lungs before we could inhale, and we swam in the icy River Tyne and the North Sea at Whitley Bay and grim Marsden Rock too, wherein the temperature never rises above thirty degrees. Deceptively beautiful, these beaches; one minute you will be treading on firm sand, admiring the misty pearly distances, the next, aware of the sea swirling round your ankles, having with malice aforethought converged from all directions at once.

Some say that Bamborough Castle was Sir Lancelot's retreat, *Joyous Garde*. Others claim the distinction for Alnwick in its scenic water meadows, with its magnificent facade dominating the High Street.

There are some places in Northumberland that you never get to. One of them is Craster. When the signpost says six miles, you are still looking for it after another twelve. Of old, seekers on horseback must have abandoned the quest in their numbers, by reason of the howling winds and lashing rain, and turned back, to throw themselves on the hospitality of the monks of Tynemouth. If you do get to it, Craster is exactly like its name, crustaceans everywhere, and the herring-catch fighting its way in over the choppy waves. At Craster I found kippers and roses. Succulent kippers and beautiful roses. Roses because the month was July, kippers because they form the local industry, and you can smell their enticing aroma a mile off.

Then if you can brave the wind, Dunstanburgh Castle, the epitome of grimness, sinister with the waves creaming on the rocks far below, a fortress which in John of Gaunt's time took up its lofty stance there as a deterrent to the Scandinavian marauder who might venture upon that knife blue, steel cold sea. Then Lindisfarne, that watery wilderness that can only be approached when the tide sees fit. Determined American tourists succeed in beating the hurrying

* Northumbrians.
**Nearly 73 miles long. Built by order of the Roman Emperor Hadrian.

ripples. I was buttonholed by one once because I could answer questions about St. Cuthbert. The American was obsessed by that saint and the stark austerity of the régime he imposed on himself. "Surely he couldn't have lived in there without a fire," he marvelled, referring to the stone cell on that bleak shore where he conducted his orisons. "Didn't he have any windows either?" "Nor central heating," I replied. "Gee!" murmured the tourist. "Isn't that just something?" We were then steered towards the manufactory of the famous Lindisfarne mead, which the monks have produced since mediaeval times. We were given a little glass and invited to sample the product before placing our orders. The American sampled three little glasses and placed a lot of orders. Suddenly he snapped his fingers in the air. "Got it!" he affirmed triumphantly. "Stoned drunk out of his mind the whole time! Couldn't have done it otherwise!" I hadn't the heart to point out that the Lindisfarne Mead was not procurable by St. Cuthbert.

The next time I returned from America, the family had moved again, this time to Reading, where Mavis had obtained a job in the university. I quitted the frozen north with only a modicum of sentiment. No more rugged moorland walks; no more sawing up logs in the snow to fortify the "city farm;" no more giving lectures in Carlisle or the Pennines; no more excavations to convert a derelict fortified farmhouse into something that could be lived in; no more glacial immersions; nor was it any longer easy to slip across the border into Scotland, and I lost touch with Colonel Stewart.

All this time, Ian was again in Brighton, going from pillar to post, job to job, until he was offered a post at Gatwick Airport. He had a girlfriend, Mary Peters, who subsequently married someone else. Sometimes he would visit us, but I was out of touch with him, and he seemed remote.

It is difficult to assess what constitutes a "good" parent; where minding one's own business ends and "interference" begins. One can't win anyway. I had never been a parent before, in any of my incarnations. The first ones were all curtailed, and I had seldom lived beyond the age of 17 or 18. Jennifer Butler had no children. Ian would have been born to Marjorie Wollaston in 1518, but changed his mind, or rather, his oversoul changed it for him. So he was only nephew to Jennifer Butler, and this time, like Meg, came a step nearer. On many occasions as he grew up, I would surprise him looking at me really quizzically, clearly at a loss to understand what manner of person I could be. He no longer does that, and grows progressively more at peace with himself, I believe.

In Reading, we lived for a while at Caversham, and I traversed the area where Charles I spent time in captivity as a "house prisoner," as did his grandmother Mary Queen of Scots in her various prisons in the north. I began to think excitedly about my new book, *The British Monarchy and the Divine Right of Kings* though I did not start writing it at once.

I also began to get to know Meg. I had taken her out in her pushchair from time to time when we lived at Seaton Burn, all along the brook to the shops, and across the brook; I'll never know how I did that, with the pushchair, but somehow one contrives these things. The first time I went to America I stayed five months, thus missing that part of her babyhood, and that was an omission. Now she was nearly three, and I would look after her at night when Mavis and Chris went out to parties or meetings. Small children hate their parents going out, leaving them in bed, especially when it is an only child. It gives them a sense of insecurity. A grandmother is not the same. Yet I contrived it, and Meg did not dislike me. Laurie is the reincarnation of Auntie Doris and Sarah Whittaker. The animosity and jealousy has gone, but the antagonism was still there until Laurie was seven. *

Laurie is nine now, and a nice little girl, a Gemini Buffalo, so she will fit in happily with the gregarious lifestyle favoured by her parents. She no longer dislikes me, nor does she like me; she accepts me, since as far as she is concerned I have always been there, an integral portion of the background equipment—part of the furniture, as it were.

I looked after Meg a lot when she was small. At the crawling stage she would exhaust herself by far-reaching peregrinations on all fours, and I would collect all the cushions I could find, and pile them on the floor, then manoeuvre her towards them, when she would collapse on to them and fall asleep, whereupon I would cover her with a blanket and she would sleep for hours, permitting me a breathing-space. Looking after an infant is a full-time job; you cannot take your eyes off it, nor let your mind stray one iota. Little wonder that over the centuries men have boasted that it is only they who can do things, women can't do anything. This is the greatest fallacy of all time.

In today's desperately overpopulated world, the penny has still not dropped. Everyone but *everyone* must reproduce themselves. That is a cardinal rule. But equally they must all with one accord be *out* all day, endlessly grubbing for money. Once the Mecca of self-reproduction has been attained to and the resultant complacency established, there is a wild scramble to get

---

* Children do not inherit their new "personality" until the seventh year. Prior to that they are expressing themselves via the soul-forces, bringing over emotions and sentiments from the previous involvement, and thus the metamorphosis at seven can often be startling.

someone else to look after the two numerous progeny, grandparents, foster-mothers, play groups, nursery schools, neighbors, anyone but themselves. Curious phenomenon. And it must be two children, never one, frequently more. Totally unnecessary. Little Tommy no longer **must have** a brother or sister, because there are millions of kids to play with and everyone goes to school. The reproducing generation is determined to keep the population at the existing level, and the planet is doomed. It is futile to chide the preceding generation for having reproduced itself, for that generation had to face a different problem. Each generation has its own problem. The preceding one had the war, with no alternative; the current generation's problem is overpopulation, fairly and squarely it sits on their shoulders; they have the alternative, but will not apply it. A world-wide resolution to produce one child per family would solve our problems overnight. Nothing else can. And they cannot or will not see; as the old proverb affirms, *"None so blind as he who* will *not see."*

When Meg was three, I took her to the Day Nursery in the morning, brought her home for lunch and read to her about *Brer Rabbit* and *Winnie the Pooh,* and took her back in the afternoon. Then the same routine to and from school, but most of all comforting her at night when the house was empty, and she came to trust me, and solicited my reassurance by earnestly demanding, *"you* wouldn't leave me, would you?"

There was just one karmic incident with Meg. In 1943, standing outside the *Locked Gates of Traquair* in the Border country,* I heard the sound of a motorcyle, an unusual sound in that war-time year. It was "Jim," a dispatch rider. Pausing, he registered the thought, "she'd look good on a horse." Meg, being a Horse-year subject, has an interest in them, and learnt to ride at the age of six. Well, in 1943, I *would* have looked good on a horse! That was all. Just enough to register a mild interest. The young dispatch rider was bound for Poland. He met his death there; Meg this time 'round has a Polish grandfather; she will have met him there, the same lifetime for him, i.e. *JAN,* Chris's father: a new lifetime for Jim, as *Meg.* So Meg had come in again, to get one step closer to me for a second casual glance, just as Ian did, when as Johnstone Whittaker, his curiosity was aroused by his eccentric aunt, Jennifer Butler.

Now Meg is sixteen, far removed from me, not in the least interested. I maintain a wholly casual relationship, simply exchanging "hullo's" and "goodbye's" in our respective comings and goings. And it is better that way. Doting grandparents can be a menace.

*The gates are locked because the laird in 1745, heart-broken at the defeat of Bonnie Prince Charlie, locked them and threw the key into the Tweed, declaring that they should not be opened again until a Stewart held the throne of Britain. You can trace the overgrown drive by its straight row of very old trees on either side.

In 1980 I spent a couple of weeks in Majorca, exorcising ghosts. I have never experienced such a location before or since. All the houses in Deya are at least 500 years old, carved out of the rock. It is all described in my book *More Astral Rescues*, in the chapter.headed, "A Haunted Island." Here also I met Robert Graves, and that meeting is recounted in the same book.

Before ceasing to visit Scotland, I stayed for a few days with A.J. Stewart at her home on the Isle of Bute. I have never felt so cold in my life. It was just like staying with James IV. She is exactly like him—the same ginger hair, melancholy disposition, born under Pisces, even physical stigmata are evident, from the chain he wore round his waist as a form of penance. She was ill-at-ease in any garments other than his mediaeval robes, which adorn her tall figure and are at odds with her fairly modern bungalow. The latter was dismally cold. She did not get up till mid-day, and I sat and froze, not liking to turn on the meagre electric fire, and read from cover to cover her autobiography called *Falcon*, that of her alter-ego James IV of Scotland. It was arrestingly authentic, but in getting it published she was up against that devastatingly obtuse attitude that characterises today's people when confronted with anything they cannot see, hear, feel or touch. In negotiating her manuscript, she was exasperated by the publisher's demanding "proof." When any individual belongs to the dreadful "prove-it" brigade, there is no doing anything with him. "You'll have to call it an "historical novel," he told her, "as there's no proof."

A deadlock would have ensued, but she had no intention of enduring such a stalemate. She recalled one incident that might conceivably pass for the "proof" that would satisfy him. James IV had been ahead of his time in matters of hygiene; he had taken exception to the conduit of filth, offal and sewage that coursed through the banqueting-hall at Linlithgow Palace, and ordered it to be bricked in. Experts were sent to examine the stones, and pronounced them to be of a later date. "Yes, that will do," conceded the publisher. "How silly," she registered. "It doesn't *prove* that I was James IV; I might have been one of the workmen employed to do the job." How fatuous and ineffective the "proof" demanded by today's people! No proof at all, of the kind they crave, the kind you get in a court of law or a laboratory! In the first instance the man is reprieved under the gallows because "proof" is forthcoming at the eleventh hour which invalidates the "proof" that sent him there. In the second, you add pink stuff to blue stuff in a test tube and it turns green. What have you "proved?" Nothing that some yellow stuff added will not "disprove." Shades of Puck, *"Lord, what fools these mortals be!"*

I was relieved to board the ferry and bid farewell to that clammy foggy isle, but just as I was on the point of departure, A.J. informed me abruptly, "I've met Richard." "Who? Richard III?" I queried. "Who? Where?" "I must not tell you," she replied. I was used to her erratic ways and cryptic comments, yet the statement puzzled me. I had been given to understand, in the course of the daily spirit communications while in Reading, that Richard had re-entered as the son of a housewife in Kettering (not surprising, so near Bosworth), and that he was a mere harmless student, trying to make restitution through impersonal service. This housewife had been *Eloyne,** then Cecily Neville, the *"Rose of Raby,"* Richard III's mother, then Queen Astrid of the Belgians, killed in a car crash in the earlier years of this century. It was not until 1994 that I became aware that two or more *thoughts* or *offshoots* from the oversoul can be incarnate at the same time.

An identical situation exists with the poet Shelley. I established, beyond cavil, in discussion with Paul Foot, that he is the latter's reincarnation; but a book recently published in America places him, most convincingly, in another environment. At first, when I read the book, and in view of A.J.'s statement, I was perplexed. No longer. An impetuous entity that died young could not hope to grasp everything within the framework of one brief lifetime, nor implement all the yearning aspirations. It must take two lifetimes, or more. Thus the semi-monad can, and sometimes does, throw in more than one "tea-bag" at the same time, just as it will sometimes introduce a further offshoot while its predecessor is still in physical form, as in the case of Clint Eastwood and Gary Cooper. I know too that it happened with my own father, in the person of the young lawyer in Arkansas who helped me with a court case against a fraudulent publisher, in answer to my father's sad frustration that he could not help me, when it was all he wanted to do in the world. Warner Taylor was so like Dad in every feature, it was positively uncanny. Spiritual comprehension is paid out, gradually, as and *when* the recipient is ready to grasp it. ◆

*See *Where Do We Go From Here?*

IX

Corruption in High Places

Reading was *quiet*. There was little opportunity for socialising. Most of my time was spent in astral communication, punctuated by nice swims in the Thames, and in writing the third volume of the trilogy called *Where Do We Go From Here?* whose predecessors were *True Tales of Reincarnation and Astral Rescue* and *More Astral Rescues.*

It was a different kind of communication from the startlingly objective clairvoyance I had had in my little flat in Brighton. It was not visual, but conveyed by a series of impressions and the written word in the vernacular or form of speech used by the communicants from whatever period they derived. I compiled files and dossiers for General Oglethorpe, Mary Fitton, Francis Bacon, Queen Elizabeth I and Charles I. These are preserved for Ian to use if he wants to. A double link was established between Henry II and Lord Dundee, "Fair Rosamund," * (Eleanor of Aquitaine) and the Marquis of Argyll, and on that account I had to make a special visit to Northumberland where two ladies were, astonishingly, receiving communications from Eleanor of Acquitaine at precisely the same time, almost identical in wording, which betokened a restlessness on the part of that strong character that brooked no inattention. They were Pat and Norah, and the latter had been one of my pupils in 1979, powerfully aware that in an earlier life she had been one of King John's soldiers posted on the city wall at Newcastle, huddled in sheepskins against the constant blizzard which filled the nooks and crannies of that grim wall with driven snow.

My friend Florence came once to Reading. She now lives in Chester, and I miss her considerably, a genial, fun-loving soul from the Brighton days, a

---

*See *Fragmented Incarnascopes*

friend of Ted and Richard too. She used to arrange lectures for me, and in 1992 invited me to give a lecture at the Chester Theosophical Lodge, and stay the night at her home. It was she who introduced me to Francis Carr, the Brighton writer and historian who was at the time, (about 1982), composing a biography of Mary Fitton. He eagerly petitioned me for information about the latter. Her ghost had been seen at Gawsworth Hall, her ancestral home near Macclesfield. At first I doubted my ability to obtain it; the period is not my specialty as the seventeenth century is, and I knew very little about Mary. To my amazement a passionate response was drawn forth, and she was in my auric-surround for several years. The passion of Francis in turn for Mary is not surprising, since he is the reincarnation of one Quentin Cézanne, a youthful lover of the handsome young woman. Records of the extensive communications are extant in the *Mary Fitton File*, and all I need to say is that if only Francis Carr had been able to open his mind to the esoteric, (he does in private, but will not admit it openly), he and I together could have produced a "best-seller," with my access to the hidden information and his scholarly research. But because he could not, and because the Curse of the O'Connors intervened again, the communicants withdrew, or were withdrawn by their respective guides, and the floodgates of that mysterious period were never opened as they could have been. There is a wealth of unrevealed knowledge "up there," which historians would give anything to possess. Francis, like so many not-very-brave people, wanted to pick my brains and purloin my knowledge without acknowledging it. His unpraiseworthy aim was to claim that he had made the discoveries and gained the knowledge by looking up documents and thereby obtained "proof" to satisfy a secular publisher. He wanted the resurrection without the crucifixion. I had had the crucifixion; I would not let him thus perjure his soul. He was, in lots of ways, too nice a man for that. He was good company; he had been an officer in the army. As mentioned, I like soldiers, and he was no exception; yet I withheld the treasure he so unethically craved.

There was an anagram, devised by Quentin Cézanne for Mary Fitton, which has never been deciphered, albeit scholars and historians have sat up late racking their brains in desperation for 400 years. I was given it straight from its source, and, in a sense, it belongs to Francis Carr, but he must earn it and not tell lies about it by saying, as he intended to do if I divulged it to him, that he, Francis Carr, had been the first and only one to "work it out." He would never work it out, and neither would anyone else, for that was not scheduled as the way of it. It was a gift from Spirit, with me as go-between. The exposition is in my file on Mary Fitton, but it seems the anagram will go with me to my grave. Such a pity! Such a **waste**! But people are so stupid, and often the clever ones are more stupid than the stupid ones. I am reminded in this context of a story I used to read to Meg about *Winnie the Pooh* by A.A. Milne. Pooh and Piglet were exchanging views on Rabbit . . .

"Rabbit's clever," said Pooh.
"Yes," said Piglet, "Rabbit's clever."
"And he has a brain."
"Yes," said Piglet, "Rabbit has a brain."

There was a long silence.

"I suppose," said Pooh, "that's why
He never understands anything."

I felt, and still feel, a sense of tragedy concerning my encounter with Francis Carr, but I am out of touch with him now. He will come to regret his paucity of spirit later on, as indeed will so many others. Better, notwithstanding, than jeopardising his soul and committing spiritual perjury. I truly wanted to hand over the anagram to him. It is of no use to me, and God knows I am no dog-in-the-manger. With that in view, I visited him in 1993, but the position had not changed one iota.

Nine years ago, we moved to Bristol. I missed the Thames, as I had missed the sea at Brighton, and even the cold sea in Northumberland. Here there is nowhere to swim. I hate closed-in swimming pools.

Weston-super-Mare is a wilderness of mud, and the tide goes out so far that you cannot even find the sea, still less enter it. Our River Avon is inaccessible and inhospitable. That is a great drawback. Otherwise, as cities go, it is preferable to Birmingham or Manchester or Liverpool. I couldn't live in any of those places, nor could I endure London now, though I once lived there. Ah well, one can't have everything. At least we have a mild climate and the Spring flowers are the earliest out.

We have exhaustively explored the West Country. One grows to like it; although I think County Sussex remains my favourite. One April, in 1991, I think, we spent a cold, wet, windy holiday in Dorset, renewing acquaintance with the Thomas Hardy country and Judge Jeffries* and the Romans; an evocative region. Glastonbury likewise came to mean a lot to me. I waged war there with the Church over Bligh Bond, and came up against extreme corruption in high places. (All this is described in the final chapter of *True Tales of Reincarnation and Astral Rescue*.)

*See *True Tales of Reincarnation and Astral Rescue*, Chapter II.

I had a nice friend in Glastonbury, Rose Dallaway. She had a little house in Benedict Street, beneath the Tor. I stayed there when I gave lectures in the town. She was a fine artist, very sensitive; too sensitive perhaps for this dimension. She died at Christmas in 1993 aged only fifty-three. She lives in my memory, and the long walks we had together in that atmospheric King Arthur land. She knew where the best blackberries were, and mushrooms as big as tea plates, and she showed me *Gog and Magog*, the two oldest oak trees in England. A thousand years have passed beneath their gnarled branches; what tales they could tell of England's history!

Rose was another graceful ship that passed in the night. She went out of my life as strangely as she came into it. Twelve years ago I gave my final television broadcast in Newcastle. She wrote me on the strength of it for an incarnascope. She waited five years before asking to discuss the results with me, stayed in contact seven years, then slipped away again. She always made her own dresses, so deft and creative she was. They were always pink, exactly like a rose. And her voice was soft and gentle to match.

I do not go to Glastonbury anymore. Last year, 1993, I sat on the Tor eating a sandwich, and for a moment loneliness engulfed me. It does not, usually, for I know how to shake it off, and I am in no way sorry for myself, no matter how hard the Curse of the O'Connors tries to make me. God knows, there are so many worse off, infinitely worse off; sometimes indeed I think it is almost everyone! Yet I could not dismiss the words of the poet Tennyson,

> *I have had playmates, I have had companions*
> *In my days of childhood, in my joyful schooldays.*
> *All, all are gone, the old familiar faces.*

and I went home, sensibly, I think, for the last time, because thus far I have not been moved to repeat the visit.

1990 was a significant year, embracing my final trip to America, and the karmic contact of my cousin Toby in the shape of Marc Lecordier,* the reunion with Mrs. Foster and Scout Hall in Yorkshire. Of late, the years have telescoped up, folding uneventfully one into the next, without meaning or stimulus. There is always work. All the while you traffic in problems, you can be sure of doing a roaring trade. I'm not sure that I want to. But even if you attempt to give it all up, people simply will not let you.

Beyond doubt, there is a "time" for everything. When I retrospect on the milestones of my life, I become aware that had they been differently spaced, I

*See *The Smiling Lady* File.

would not have bothered to do what I did. We do things when we are moved to do them, and that tallies precisely with the "time" when we are "meant" to do them. They had to be done, and our "mood" had to be just "right" to do them, for to leave them undone was simply not on the menu.

John Kempster, who helped me with *Operation Prince Charles,* was puzzled by this, and confided to me before he left for Japan, "I think everything I have done up to now has been a waste of time." "Not so!" I hastened to repudiate the suggestion. "All the time you want to do it, and consider that you should be doing it, it is not a waste of time. But if you go on doing it after you have reached the conclusion that it is a waste of time, then it *is* a waste of time." John saw the point at once, and took up residence in Japan in a happier frame of mind.

Thus it was with *Operation Prince Charles.* (It could justifiably have carried the subtitle, *Corruption in High Places.*) The incredible correspondence with Sir Laurence van der Post is faithfully preserved in the abovementioned file, and it would be painful as well as superfluous to resurrect it here. I did my best for Prince Charles; my motivation was wholly altruistic and in his interests. But such is the ignorance and blindness of the "Establishment" that it invariably impugns an unworthy motive, and his entourage did its utmost to prevent any vestige or fragment of the truth reaching him. God knows, he needs protection, not from me, but from those who seek to protect him.

Persons in high places go in constant fear of "social climbers," of those who hope to "get to know them." Again, God knows, in my case nothing could be further from the truth. I only wanted to help, to share. I would expect to get nothing out of it, only to put something into it; I never get anything out of anything. The loss is theirs, never mine. So all exerted their (very considerable) power to contrive that this unhappy scion of royalty who chances to be heir to the throne of Britain remained immune from any help that alone would be valid. All I can add to the van der Post file is that the task took me six years, from the moment in 1986 when I approached Barbara Cartland to solicit her cooperation, to the moment when I indited my terse paragraph to the prince himself, to convey his incarnascope to him, losing, in the process, two expensively produced copies of my book, *The British Monarchy and the Divine Right of Kings.* Can it be possible that Sir Laurence van der Post, reputable author and arm-in-arm friend of the Prince of Wales, could lie and cheat? *Yes.* In default of a satisfactory explanation of what actually took place, *it is.*

The Duke of Bedford adopted the same attitude at an earlier date. He was too lazy and indolent to bestir himself to assist his ancestor in distress, and too conceited to regard himself as responsible. Equally, the Marquis of Bath refused to allow the ghost at Longleat to be exorcised; he was too selfish to forfeit the ghost as an added tourist attraction.

And so on it goes.

111

In the arduous and thankless undertaking called *Operation Prince Charles*, I was grateful for the great help and support of John Kempster. He worked at the *Rowan Tree* bookshop in Bristol, and sold my books there. He proved a splendid artist and advertised my books and lectures about town. It was he who designed the cover of an edition of *British Monarchy and the Divine Right of Kings*. John was a professional book illustrator. He was sickened and disgusted by the theft of my two books by way of the secretarial judgements of Sir Laurence van der Post, and advocated litigation in court. But in view of the fact that van der Post was in "high places," I could not sue him, and in fact, was powerless to act at all. I simply had to accept the injustice and corruption of which I was the victim. It was a development of the Francis Carr theme, but on a larger scale, and more ruthless.

If you venture to state that people are unscrupulous predators, today's community eyes you askance, yet that is what they are, in more cases than is generally recognised.

Had it been today, *this* day, I would not lift a finger to help any of them. ◆

X

America: My New World

A Prophete is not withoute Honoure, excepte in his own Countreye

—Sir Thomas Mallory

It is necessary to go back to 1977, because for the next fourteen years, America was to be my second home. There's a saying, "Home is not where you live; it's where you're understood."

I was in fact suspended between two worlds, leading a double life; following the family 'round England like something tied on at the back of the caravan, and commuting twice a year, sometimes more frequently, to Arkansas, where, the minute I stepped off the plane, I was "home." It was quite extraordinary; all my friends there agreed that it was. Birtha Macon always wrote out a notice which she pinned on herself when coming to meet me at Tulsa Airport, "Welcome Home!" Karma of course had a great deal to do with it, marinating on that particular spot throughout the centuries, plus a natural affinity and mutual need, they for my knowledge, I for their love. So I am talking of two lives which ran concurrently.

To live with the people of another country is entirely different from staying in hotels, even if karma is not part of the agenda. There is no point of reference, and you get a wholly different picture. I am no tourist, and have not travelled extensively, or recently. I suppose that I travel in *time*, as opposed to space. But what I had to do in America was supremely important to me at the time. It began as a lecture tour, nothing more, and how that came about was by reason of the applicants' enthusiasm for incarnascopes, which, they averred, were invariably "right on the ball." I was racking my brains as to how to bring it about. They kept begging, "Come visit!" and I could not afford the fare. Then Uncle Jack died, and touchingly left me £1,000. Not much by today's standards perhaps, but it paid the fare, as I'm convinced he knew it would. Fate is strange,

113

sometimes inexorable, sometimes capriciously opportune. yet not strange at all really. I thanked him in spirit, and have communicated with him subsequently. (He is helping Eric, who was killed in the war, and is progressively ensconced in his individual reach of eternity.)

It certainly did not all end as a lecture tour. Once launched, I went back and forth again and again.

Sad that the *journey* is only exciting the first time. The novelty wears off. Flying over New York at night the lights looked like necklaces strung out in a jeweller's shop window. Even going through the Customs is amusing, where later it is irksome. Once they confiscated a slice of ham I had in a cellophane packet, teasing me that it would start a rabies epidemic; then there was the time when I took a little bunch of primroses, (my friends in Georgia had never seen any English primroses, and they don't grow anywhere else), and had to conceal it in my coat pocket lest they subjected it to forensic examination and insisted on its extradition; and once they asked if I carried any snails. "Snails?" I echoed, open-mouthed. "Where would they be? In my case?" "Oh," said the official, "someone brought a tank of snails last week."

But all that mattered, and all I could think of then, was the importance of spreading the message.

It no longer seems important; I am content to let people move at their own pace, and don't care whether they get the message or not. Neither is that callousness, but probably means that my karmic contacts have been dealt with, and none remain. The Theosophists had held up their hands in horror when I announced my intention of taking their message outside the rather cagey confines of their society, to take it on to the television, into schools and universities. "Don't do it!" they had vehemently adjured me, "They'll crucify you!"

They did, of course, but a crucifixion entails a resurrection, and although I was very vulnerable to start with, and truly was hurt by their antagonistic shafts, I was resilient and developed an armour-plated exterior. Concerning America, they were less worried. Yes, was their verdict, I could do it. The Americans would welcome it.

They did.

The initial trip might have been construed into an ill omen, but Fate turned it to good account. Ian was always so helpful and conscientious about escorting me to the airport. I don't know what I should have done without him. On this occasion there was a strike at Gatwick, a *serious* one, and all the 'planes were delayed. I had to wait six hours. I had a dreadful headache, and felt sick with anxiety. There was a lot hanging to it. I was going to meet a total stranger at Tulsa, right down in the heart of Oklahoma; I had arranged to carry one of my books for identification. She would think I wasn't coming, and would go away. I would be stranded, unable either to go back or forward. My mind began to boggle.

Ian could only come as far as the gate. After that I was on my own. The flight was ready at last, but it reached New York at one o'clock in the morning instead of the scheduled early evening. The season was Autumn, cold and dark, and foggy, and I have never felt so alone in my life. Somehow I had to get to La Guardia Airport, all across the vast city. It is much further than the distance between Gatwick and Heathrow. I was in a state of panic. The forecourt was deserted. No one helped. The officials at the airport were singularly disinterested. It was too late for a taxi, and I doubt if I could have afforded one anyway, all that way. I would miss the 'plane to Tulsa. Nancy, who was only a name to me, was to recognise me by the prominent position of *Call Joshua*. Suppose she just went home again? A hundred-mile drive! Whatever should I do? Thus my distraught mind tormented me, and the headache dealt me hammer blows from stress and strain. Physical fatigue, hunger and lack of sleep conspired to complete the picture of dejection I presented, standing forlornly at the deserted 'bus-stop with my cases and baggage all around, given up to despair.

Then one of those things happened that only happens once in a lifetime. They say that for a Sagittarian it can happen *twice* (shades of Arnold Blood); a figure emerged from the enveloping fog. It was a workman returning from a nightshift. He came up to me. . . "What's the matter with you?" he questioned without preamble. I confided my predicament. By way of response he put his fingers in his mouth and emitted a shrill whistle. As if he had rubbed Aladdin's Lamp, two more shadowy forms materialised. They were a Negro and his wife.

Beyond credulity it transpired that the man knew Brighton, while the woman, a member of the Samaritans, had visited Guildford, another of my youthful hunting grounds. I had to pinch myself to ascertain that I was not dreaming. They led me to their vehicle, they took me all the way to La Guardia, they bought me a cup of coffee and a "hotdog" (I think it was, but I was so grateful that a cold cat would have been just as welcome), and soothed my fraught nerves. "Just you relax, honey," crooned the woman, turning round from her seat in the front, Just you relax. You're going to good people, who are going to look after you!'

Oh, how prophetic those words proved to be! From that moment on, I met nothing but warmth and kindness such as I have never known since early childhood, and the words of Joan at Portsmouth came back to me: "You'll find more love and care in America than you've had all your life in England."

It was, indeed, like a dream. I caught the 'plane to Tulsa. Nancy had waited. She came straight up to me, brushed *Call Joshua* aside, and bending her taller form, hugged me in a close sisterly embrace. "I didn't need the book," she declared, in her Arkansasian voice with its unique drawl, "I'd have known you anyway!" She half-carried me to her car, and it was Nancy who, on a subsequent visit, when I had been shaken and battered for days and nights on a dreadful "Greyhound" bus (never do it, reader. If you cannot afford the 'plane fare, crawl on hands and knees, rather), waited hours and hours and met me at midnight in a God-forsaken haunt called Joplin, Missouri, and I literally fell off the 'bus into her comforting arms.

Nancy had failings. Many disparaged her. She embezzled the funds at Tyson's vast factory in "Chicken-Town" where she worked, to the tune of thousands of dollars. But she was kind to me, and I remain true to the old adage, *"Speak as you find."* Now she is dead. She gave me some happy times, and wrote in a book about the Buffalo River Country which was a present to me from all her family, "Remember us always." And I do. There is a long karmic story there, but it does not belong to this book, since I suppose, for me, she was only another ship that passed in a rather sad night. Her son David and his.wife Melissa were burnt to death in their home in 1992.

I was so tired that I fell asleep in the middle of a conversation. "Gee!" exclaimed Nancy, "I sure can't wait till you wake up outa that jetlag, and tell me the rest!" "The rest" meant *everything* . They were so alive, so alert, so keen and enthusiastic, such a contrast to my reserved and often dull countrymen; it's the sunshine no doubt! and of course they're descended from a race of pioneers, and like adventure, whether spiritual or physical. They are a breath of fresh air.

The second time, it was a Freddie Laker flight. He came on board, beaming comprehensively, to talk to his passengers. He distributed first-time largesse in the shape of little travelling cases as mementoes. He stopped in front of me and asked what I thought of Laker flights, and I said they were great. "You look great!" he said spontaneously, and he really meant it. I felt great. It is so long that I felt like that, it is difficult to believe that anyone said it.

He was indeed a ship (or rather an aeroplane) which passed very briefly in the night; but I've never forgotten him, and wonder what became of him. . .

My statement that I was leading a double life is not strictly accurate, because the American involvement is again subdivided. I was in Florida, in Georgia, in Arkansas, with excursions into adjacent states as well. Thus actually it was a *triple* life. It cannot be kept separate, because friends became interlinked; I seem to have been a specie of omsbudsman (omsbudswoman), and there was an ongoing interchange.

The continent is so vast that each state is a different nation, the language being the same, with amusing and delightful variations. Florida is vulgar and unsympathetic, a tourist centre; Georgia respectable, conventional, neatly laid out, reminiscent of its founder General Oglethorpe, its residents more sophisticated. Arkansas is rougher, the denizens näive, unspoilt, simpler, *nice*, I thought.

Bill Clinton has a bit of what I'm at pains to explain, with his babyface, soft voice, innocent expression and schoolboy haircut. He should not, of course, be the President of the United States; Hillary should. (But he's a poppet nevertheless.)

I could have lived there. With their lovely warmth and spontaneity they asked me to. They truly and sincerely meant it. It was simply another of those forks in the road that are our common experience, speculating in vain as to what might or might not have happened had we chosen the "other one." All we can cater for is what did happen. And what did happen was that they cordially pressed me to stay and make Arkansas my home, and that I bowed to the inevitable and knew that my karma lay in England. It isn't that I was not tempted. Birtha said, "This is your home. Everything is yours. Your room is always there."Susie, Birtha's daughter, said, "You can have my room forever; I will sleep on the couch forever. I don't mind. We love you." Americans do say that. In England we are more familiar with "How do you do?", and "yours sincerely." I performed healing for Susie, who although only twenty-one, suffered pain as the result of a diabetic condition. "I wish Mollie were here," she confided to her mother when I had returned to England between visits, "She wouldn't let me hurt like this."

As for the "holidays," the American Thanksgiving is worse than Christmas, if that were possible. They take the day off work, stay indoors and remorselessly eat.

Susie and her friends escorted me to a crowded house where the table had all it could do to maintain its upright stance by reason of its immense burden of indigestible comestibles. They are so hospitable that for one calamitous moment I was in terror lest Susie, who is big and strong, was going to hold me down while her friends stuffed buns and chicken legs down my throat.

I resisted that cordial gesture of a home in America.

Life would have been greatly more lively and stimulating had I taken it to my heart in 1977 as it came from theirs. I should have been able to bask in their lovely sunshine and the warmth of their affection, as opposed to the blighting east wind of my family and the British climate.

But I came back, and have no regrets about it, even though it has entailed a dull and often sad and painful programme.

There was, among other karmic commitments, Ian's little cat *Puss* whom I looked after until her death. I loved her so much. I had had her before, in mediaeval times, when as the ill-fated Marjorie Wollaston, I had adopted, (or perhaps more accurately *stolen* her) for company. Then, she had been jet black, a veritable witches' cat; this time she was fluffy white with little brown ears and tail. She had been involved in a long, drawn-out karmic situation with *Pinero Rothenbarel,* now Chris Miller, one which led to the execution of Marjorie

Wollaston and partially accounts for my sojourn with the family today. She was mine from every angle. I miss her terribly. She did not have a happy life; they shut her in the kitchen and did not understand her. Ian rescued her from her semi-wild habitat at the airport where he worked, when he himself was lonely in his flat in Bristol and was glad of her company. But when Ian's wife Marion came on the scene, *Puss* was ostracised. Marion does not like animals.

Ian until recently has not exhibited strength of character or purpose, albeit both are now noticeably developing. He did not then possess the capacity to make a stand, and poor little *Puss* , (that was her only name, though I often called her *Whitepuss*) , got caught in the crossfire.

Similarly with the Cosmic Law. Although Ian has been unresponsive, and has emulated Mavis and Chris in a timidly sedulous way, pretending to repudiate everything I say, and "siding with" Mavis and Chris in their cynicism and stupidity, deep down he knows perfectly well that what I say is the truth: the Eternal Verities and the ageless wisdom. Thus all I can do is patiently, laboriously and painstakingly let fall the odd remark from time to time, knowing that these must take root. But the insults and indifference strike deep. I know what they stem from, and so try not to be hurt too much. As far as strangers and the public at lectures are concerned, one can effectively grow an armour plate.With "family," the growing thereof takes longer, but it can be done, and I am pretty sure now that I have finally done it. In any event, I never allowed the pain to show when the shafts were directed against me at the *personal* level; but that, of course may be attributable to Sagittarian pride.

This may be a bewildering chapter altogether, because in it I appear to be in several places at once, dodging from Arkansas to Florida and back, and thence to Georgia, all interspersed with returns to England. It was impossible to part with America, because not only did I meet up with a whole crop of karma, but I formed such lasting and stable relationships that going back again and again was a foregone conclusion.

America is a notable venue for the implementation of karma, by entities from all periods. All my life I have been "led" for better or worse, to the people I have been destined to be involved with, and it was while staying on "the farm" in Oklahoma that I received the request for an incarnascope which led me to Florida.

Meanwhile, my "billet" at the farm in Oklahoma was supplied by the good offices of Dr. Arias, Imogene's friend. At first, they had accommodated me in an "apartment" in Fayetteville. That was before they knew me, and thought of me as simply an itinerant lecturer. But soon they transferred me to their homes, and one of these was that of Lee and Maria Ferguson who ran the farm near the Red Indian township of Tahlequah.

One of my happiest memories was of swimming in the creek not far from their house. I had been lecturing in the University at Tahlequah, and the following day doing card-readings for the students. The queues for card-readings were endless, I couldn't do it now, and by the end of the day I was totally exhausted, albeit I had recouped the fare to England, all in one day! I went to have a bath, and they pounded on the door, proclaiming,"There's a line for readings." "I'm in the bath," I told them. "Never mind; put a towel 'round you and come and do readings."That was how it was; everyone so light-hearted and gloriously inconsequential. Imagine my joy at escaping to the farm and the heavenly cool water of the creek. It was like heaven, that refreshing pellucid water with the white pebbles beneath and the green trees above and glimpses of the day-blue sky moving towards the pink of the sunset.An experience never to be forgotten, like so many in that wonderful continent.

There were many swims after that. Maria was very kind. The sun was very hot. I was so happy. They took me to *Tsa-la-Ghi,* the authentic Red Indian village, where there were Indians with raven-black hair down to their ankles, and buffaloes, fortunately in enclosures. I just happened to remark, "they look pretty mean," and one, who must have overheard, charged at the fence, straight at me, till the edifice shook. Maria and Lee tried to commemorate my advent; they asked me to plant three melon seeds whose product was to bear my name. A drought desiccated the ground and they did not show their noses.

Maria and Lee later named a cow after me, the daughter of *Ladybird.* She grew up to hate the sight of me, and lost no opportunity to get at me, even going so far as to wait at the bottom of the steps. And let no one tell me that cattle cannot dodge 'round trees, because they can and this one did.

I'm not particularly dog-orientated, but there was a dear dog whom I named *Shadow,* partly because he latched on to me like a shadow, and partly because he was grey like a shadow, a collie. All Maria's dogs had been rescued from the shores of the creek, or the highway, where cruel owners left them to be killed by wolves or by speeding cars. She had five. Of these, three were wantonly shot by a man living nearby. (Any irresponsible individual, even youths, can carry a gun in America.) One of them was my *Shadow.* I'm glad I was not there at the time, as I would have desired to inflict Grievous Bodily Harm on the perpetrator. *Shadow* had been my dog, and had accompanied me wherever I went, over the fields into the woods, teaching me how to avoid rattlesnakes.

The Fergusons kept pigs too, nice sunburnt pigs, with little golden hairs all over them, not like our pallid pink muddy ones. I learned a great deal about pigs while I was there. They are far more intelligent than we give them credit for. One day Lee confided to me, "I don't allow my pigs to behave badly."

"Oh, come on!" I teased him. "How can you stop them? You must be joking."
"Oh no," he assured me. "If I see them pushing and getting each other's food, I clout them." And they were the most orderly well-behaved pigs I have ever met

Tahlequah is the perquisite of the Cherokee, their one-time "reservation." One day, while I was engaged in reading cards after a lecture at the University, a student came rather apprehensively to announce that the Chief of the Cherokee wished to see me. "What for?" I queried. "Oh, just to look at you. They're all Indians here except for the University, and they haven't seen many English people."

The resplendent individual stood in the doorway, surveying me in silence. He obviously did not approve of what he saw. "Can I help you?" I enquired, somewhat superfluously. "I'm sure you don't want a card-reading." He continued to scrutinise me with contempt. "Huh! I can look in the stream and tell you your life-story!" "I know you can," I hastened to concur. "That's why I didn't think you wanted a card-reading.".

I thought for a moment that he was about to spit on the floor. Instead he turned on his heel with a further grunt, and left as abruptly as he had come.

The American Indians *do* harbour resentment. It was the same with the Seminoles in Florida, who manifested a parallel animosity. One has to concede that really they can't be blamed for that, but it was no excuse for their Chief Joe Dan Osceola to "borrow" my manuscript of *Manifest Destiny* and fail to return it. Doubtless he utilised the material for his own ends.

Anyway, I researched and wrote the esoteric story of the Red Indians while in Arkansas, and *Manifest Destiny* is still in print. The next summer, I alternated between the Fergusons' farm and Birtha Macon's home at Springdale and Imogene's home likewise, of whom more anon.

A request arrived by post at the farm from West Palm Beach, Florida, for an incarnascope. I duly completed it and in dispatching it, casually enquired if the correspondents knew of any groups or organisations which might be interested in a series of lectures, and if by chance they could recommend a guest house or individual who would consider a paying guest, and not to bother to reply if they didn't. But they knew all of it, and pressed me to stay with them. They turned out to be Deignan and Penelope, who were to play a major part in the ensuing phase of the story; Deignan was a friend of Leila, with whom I had stayed in Majorca. The karma with Deignan and Penelope was not so much of a personal kind, in that I could not trace connections at that level in former lives, but of an *evolutionary* nature, inextricably bound up with "the work." I stayed with them, not only on that occasion, but many times after that, even when they relocated to Georgia, as being a better proposition for employment; Penelope is a musician, Deignan an artist among other things. Like Iris Bryson-White Deignan enjoys the Multiplicity of Gifts. I'm not sure that she enjoys them, since some of them lead to her carrying the can for everybody. It does not always pay to be capable in a wide variety of fields. It is an exceptional combination of skills to be able to build a house, paint a picture, execute cartoons and write articles and lift weights. (Once I essayed to lift from the ground, with both hands, one of a pair of two formidable objects which Deignan was in the habit of raising above her head, one in each hand; it continued to repose there unmoved.) She is likewise versed in the art of self-defence Once, in Georgia, I nervously remonstrated about her leaving the doors open; they were not even equipped with a lock, and I was to be alone in the house all night. "I take my chances." she explained, whereupon I expostulated, "Yes, but your chances and mine are two different things!" (Charles I said something like that.) But in promoting books, and "The Work," we take our chances together.

The lectures in America were now on a much wider scale. In Tahlequah I had lectured to six thousand students. In Florida the girls organised lectures at the university at Boca Raton, and convened halls and venues where the lectures were advertised in neon lights on the highway and drew audiences from near and far. The results were sometimes explosive. People of all types and nationalities attended, and I was called "England's Mollie Moncrieff." It was strange, but electrifying, and wonderfully gratifying and stimulating. They packed the hall, stood in the doorways and all up the stairs, and it was necessary to speak through a microphone. I gave a number of television broadcasts, thereby incurring the wrath of Churchgoers and the Bible Belt and raising a storm. It was very exhilarating, though I would not find it exhilarating now. But most Americans are liberal, open-minded and eager, not dull and apathetic as they so often are in England. Deignan, albeit of Lemurian extraction, plus being an Aquarian Cat-year subject, wary and poised for flight, is paradoxically a fighter, believing in "direct action." Today she applies it to the rescue of animals, then she inaugurated an "Anti-Church" campaign. It was harder to prevail then. It grows easier now; there are more anti-Church campaigners as the century draws to its close.

Penelope and Deignan were wonderful. They drove me everywhere; they carried my books to sell at meetings; they acted as chairmen; they discreetly kept curious callers at bay; they cooked dinners for me; they showed me the countryside. I loved them. We formed a happy threesome, based on Shakespeare's immortals, Oberon, Titania and Puck. We fitted the parts uncannily well. Deignan at that time could have been the Principal Boy in pantomime. Penelope, with her long blond hair and not pretty but engaging countenance was to the manner born Titania, and I could only be Puck because I could make Oberon laugh. On one hilarious occasion years later, the two of them came to meet me at Hartsfield Airport in Atlanta fully clad in the raiments of these characters, to the astonishment of waiting passengers.

Deignan came from Massachusetts, giving as her reason for being in Florida that she had endured years of intense cold, and craved the sunshine.

121

Penelope, who at twenty-two had never seen any snow, encountered it for the first time in Arkansas. She stemmed from an old well-to-do Florida family, which had kept slaves. She showed me an eighteenth century account-book which set out details of the calico clothing and the medicaments purchased for the black slaves. The servants the family employ today are descendants of these one-time slaves.

An incredible circumstance linked me with Penelope. As children, Kath and I were frequently at Sir Philip Sidney's home, *Penshurst Place* in Kent. On the wall there hung a portrait which fascinated me—that of Lady Barbara Gamage. What *seemed* a lifetime later, thousands of miles away, I came into contact with Penelope, the descendant of that lady! There is no such thing as a coincidence. It *is*, once again, the Law of Synchronicity at work. It is a really ancient family, that of Gamage, dating back to 800 A.D. when an incident is recorded of a woman buried alive for poisoning her husband. A blessing that the custom has been discarded! Penelope's father is, or was then, (he has subsequently died), a circuit judge; a trifle incongruous, in that she is, or was, quite frequently involved in minor skirmishes with the police, who admittedly are ultra-officious in Florida and Georgia.

There were other friends. Mary Fleming was wonderfully helpful too. She drove us all the way to Arkansas, lots of times, crossing the mighty Mississippi whose ducks are as big as swans, among other fascinating scenes. She was a business girl. She could persuade anyone that in purchasing a hacksaw they were securing a privilege on a par with the acquisition of the Crown Jewels. She accommodated us in the "motels" which feature of those interminable roads unfolding before the motorist like a ribbon whose spool is inexhaustible.

Once Deignan had planned to take me to see Matt Dillon's town at Tombstone, with its Gary Cooper saloon half-doors and cowboy appurtenances, but we ran into an ice storm which daunted even Deignan; it was a most alarming experience; and we had to abandon the attempt and go straight to Arkansas via Little Rock. And once, returning to Florida from Arkansas, I swam in the Swanee River. Very few English people have done that I think. Actually, it is "Suwanie." The caress of that uniquely soft warm water was out of this world, and the manatees, (poor affectionate, innocent creatures often injured by reckless speedboats), came up to us and swam alongside. We did not have to be wary of these as we did of the far less approachable alligators in Florida.

On the subject of alligators . . . some contretemps arose in Florida over the Red Indians' "sport" of alligator wrestling. The Seminole Indians, as indicated, did not like us at all, and I can't say I liked them very much either. Their "sport" was sickening, just as inhumane as our fox-hunting and badger-baiting, and I published an article in the *Palm Beach Post* protesting against it which aroused the ire of the Seminole tribe.

The *Post* published at least one other piece of mine. I had written a

122

letter about my adventures while walking along the causeways connecting West Palm Beach with Palm Beach. Besides innocently collecting a variety of sports balls, (mostly golf), I had inadvertantly collected the interest of the local police. These zealous men pulled over their cars and questioned me about my "home address" and "point of origin," repeatedly. Within the "mobile society" of America, Florida distinguishes itself as a State running on petrol. It seemed that *walking*, especially so near the protected quarters of posh Palm Beach, is construed as "criminally suspect." However modest and direct my need for exercise may have been, my motives remained bewildering to the local authorities.

My letter to the *Post* was entitled, *"Trouble in Paradise."* The now deceased, but still famous Lewis Grizzard took up the challenge of my words and built a "column" around the general idea, printing my entire story within his print space.

Apart from verbal battles, we had heavenly times in Florida, when I was not doing readings, incarnascopes or preparing lectures; when Penelope was not rehearsing or performing; when Deignan was not slaving at awful commercial art and articles to earn a few bucks. We raced along the silver beaches among the sandpipers eternally grubbing for worms in the tideline, plunging into the turquoise sea and the beautiful tepid lakes and the pure cold creeks.

Penelope took me to her family's home in Sanford, Florida, near Orlando and drove me, Airies-style, anywhere I wished to go. I even "filled-in" part of her performance duties one night on the Dixie Highway, at a "nightclub." It was New Year's eve, and I sang Scottish songs, including a crowd-quieting rendition of *Auld Lang Syne.*

I was in Florida during both winters and summers and gained a taste of the true seasons. In between, we visited Alabama and at midnight gambolled in the fields of corn in the capacities of Oberon, Puck and Titania, and I laughed like a schoolgirl. There was something about the place!

And once, Deignan drove me half across America, or so it seemed, to track down a fraudulent publisher, over whom there was subsequently a court case conducted by Dad's successor, Warner Taylor. The solicitors and District Attorney had been endeavoring to run this elusive character to earth for an indefinite time, but as so often happens, it took a female actually to succeed. Deignan found him at last in his hideout in the wilds of the Ozarks. The tiny area was called Omaha.

It was all such fun! Certainly things can happen in America that would be unthinkable in England.

Digging up bones, for instance . . .It is difficult to see the reason for such macabre exercises being woven into the tapestry of one's life, as they certainly do not seem to lead anywhere. But we were informed in Boca Raton,

123

Florida, of the existence of an historic graveyard, and whether it was my idea or Deignan's I have not the remotest recollection; all I remember is that it all had to do with a report from Deignan's landlady's boyfriend, a construction-site supervisor. He had been concerned that the bones he and his crew had uncovered were being left unconsidered by his company's management and by the Indians' representatives. No one had proposed doing anything.

I next recall Deignan in a trench, frenetically wielding a spade, burrowing and excavating and tossing up to me standing at the brink, showers of bones. Authorities in such matters judged them to have been two thousand years old, Red Indians, then, obviously. As it turned out, the construction supervisor *was one of those Indians*, which may have explained his reluctance to simply plow the bones under the foundations of just another office building or "condo."

I carried home a little bag of bones. Miraculously, the Customs overlooked them, or I would have been in the Nick as a body snatcher, and the bones in hydrochloric acid to yield up their identity.

The only sequel that might or might not carry esoteric significance was the total and totally unexplained disappearance of the bones in question. One by one, over a period of "time," they vanished from the face of the earth. I am normally quite methodical about keeping things and knowing where they are. I thought I knew where these were, and had preserved one in particular to send to Deignan as a keepsake. But behold, when I went to get it, there was no sign of it, or any of its companions. This is Gospel truth as I stand here. So either the Red Indians called them back, as Custer's horse came back for his soul,[*] or else it was the Curse of the O'Connors enjoining me not to mess about with other people's bones. "There are more things in heaven and earth, Horatio . . ."

So I revelled in the glorious Florida sunshine. And even in the sudden torrential afternoon rains from which Deignan would drive out and rescue me.

Lots of karmic contacts were renewed. There was Richard Barnes, who lived at Boynton Beach, who in 500 A.D. had been the Roman soldier guarding a threshold, and observing the poor fourteen-year-old starveling that was me, in the forest near Camelot, and registered the unfulfilled wish that he could provide me with a square meal. He did, lots of them, in the sumptuous restaurants of Palm Beach County. His one heartfelt longing was to possess a twig of the Glastonbury Thorn. I procured one for him, the next time I was in Glastonbury. Ian helped, when the vigilant keeper's back was turned. I sent it to Richard, and he has reverently framed it, with my signature beneath it, and vows that now he can die happy. He is probably the only American citizen who has a piece of the true Glaston Thorn. The Glastonbury story is all in *True Tales of Reincarnation and Astral Rescue.* ◆

*See *Manifest Destiny*.

XI

America: My Second Home

Long ago, in days gone by
I did something . . . Was it I?

Do not ask, I have forgot
Whether it was I or not.

One could go on forever talking about America. As a generality, they are smarter than we are. The only thing they cannot do better than we can is to make a cup of tea. That stems from the Boston Tea Party, when the ladies recorded a resolution to boycott everything British, be it clothing, or tea. The upshot was that they are better dressed than we are and have become addicted to coffee, of which they consume more than is good for them. I taught my friends in Arkansas to make a cup of tea, and they have been fanatically making tea ever since, but I could not cure Americans of their incurable habit of driving on the wrong side of the road. They lag behind a little likewise in kindness to animals. Not that we are the "nation of animal-lovers" we are cracked up to be, but collectively our efforts to aid animals are better coordinated. As an overall humanity, we have made a signal failure of our most vital mission, namely the cherishing and developing of the next kingdom, and no one, so far, takes a powerful initiative.

But Americans are wonderful; their energy and vitality are such as to invigorate the dullest Englishman, and when your 'plane lands at Gatwick the pall of England descends on your shoulders again with a physical impact, till you marvel where the life-force could have evaporated to in the space of ten hours.

The happiest days of my life have been associated with cold streams, (Kath and the Darenth), and the Americans have access to the loveliest places and the coolest streams and creeks. There was an ice-green creek that Imogene took me to in Arkansas, whose waters glided out from beneath a bluff, so cold, so pure and clean that you could drink the water as you swam. And parts of it were so shallow that we could walk upstream for miles, beneath the rich over-arching trees. And once Imogene took me to some caves beneath a similar bluff, but there the temperature was quite the reverse, really warm, and unvarying at all seasons. There were lakes there, between the stalagmites and stalactites, full of fish which were all white, colourless as ghosts, because they had never seen the sun.

Who was *Imogene?* A fellow-Sagittarian, she had crossed my path in 8,000 B.C. in *Moelanta,* which was later metamorphosed into Africa. In the male embodiment, she had been a farmer, doubtless plagued by the tiresome small girl I then was. In a sort of way she was protective towards me as well, and looked after me when I caught a virus on my final visit. She was always so obliging, so accomodating. She worked long hours at her responsible job at Tyson's factory in Arkansas, yet always found time to drive me miles and miles to swim in the lovely warm and beautiful Beaver Lake. We had an easy rapport, and talked animatedly and intimately all the way there and back.

Imogene had spent her whole life looking after other people, then all these invalids died and she was left alone. The "farmer" took over, and she emerged as a natural gardener, kept dogs, and preserved endless supplies of fruit. Her sister, Estalene, had likewise been in Moelanta, and was jealous and suspicious of me. These emotions, stemming from that far-off time and doubtless justified, were aggravated by the incidence of her being a "manic depressive" in the current life.

Estalene's spontaneous dislike of me indicated that she was working off karma. I must have given her cause for dislike, and in order to redress a grudge, an individual will assemble for that purpose the type of "personality" that will permit of their doing so. She was chronically sick while I was there, and shortly thereafter died.

With Imogene, it was as if we had merely taken up the threads where we had laid them down, and that is invariably the way a karmic relationship can be detected, no matter how long anterior. In exchange for her selfless indulgence of me, I was able to communicate to her the esoteric intelligence she had long been eager to gain. And that's how it was all the time in America, so satisfyingly mutual. We need not feel beholden, or indebted, it was entirely reciprocal. I have not known that comforting relaxed feeling in England. After a lecture, when Imogene would charmingly act as chairman, people would come up to the platform with warm expressions of appreciation. One exclaimed, "You're spell-binding when you talk! I could listen to you forever!" It made English apathy seem a very distant discouragement. But in Georgia it was noticeable that lectures were far less sought after. Each State is like a different country, Arkansas, Florida, Georgia, all so diverse.

But in Arkansas, there was *Birtha*. She was Sandys Butler's "Leonora." This is all set out in detail in the Sandys Butler File, and the story began three hundred years ago. I was made aware of Birtha's existence long before I met her. She opened her home to me, and proved to be a focal point of a whole chapter of karma, introducing me to numerous characters who are on the Sandys Butler wavelength.* Susie, Birtha's daughter, is not on that wavelength. Susie is a kind, good-hearted girl, strong-armed (she would meet me at the airport, lift in one hand a case that I could not get off the ground with two, and dump it in the van like a feather-pillow.) Her hobby was catching catfish in the White River. She rented a cabin beside the Beaver Lake and dove in wearing her t-shirt with "ALCATRAZ" written thereon, which dried in the sun. We were so joyous there. Nobody cared about anything.

In order to pay Birtha for my board and lodging and recoup the fare back to England, I would do readings in Birtha's sunlit garden, or in the kitchen which was used as a club, when all manner of interested spectators would congregate. Some were rough and noisy, and exuberant, but there was one I really liked: Milton Holliman. He was a handsome businessman from Fort Smith; he always made a point of coming to see me, and professed a keen interest in *The British Monarchy and the Divine Right of Kings.* So I gave him a copy and signed it, and after that was signing books all the evening. So there was another gratified American!

Dr. Arias was very clever and accomplished too. She taught at the University of Tahlequah and drove a hundred miles daily to do it. She was of the Arkansas coterie, and very kind to me, tireless in her welcome and provision of comfort and meals out. Her cleverness was academic, not the same as Deignan's which was of a more intuitive calibre, and Deignan herself a sort of "Capability Brown."

Birtha's eldest son Ronnie lived on a ranch in Wyoming, thirty-seven miles from anything, school, shops, neighbors; only rattlesnakes sat on the doorstep, sometimes eight feet long; they can grow to twelve feet, like alligators. I was spared the sight of one, though there were horrific stories circulating about them. Arkansas has three snakes of note, the rattlesnake, the cotton-mouth and the copper-head; and the barn-snake which is harmless to humans and keeps rodents down. But the family could get steak at no cost at all, as thick as a doorstep.

---

*On this wavelength are *Kathleen Lyne,* her sister *Gladys*, Birtha's son *Donald* and *Carolyn*, his girlfriend, who was Sandys cousin *Eileen* of Westerham in Kent (seventeenth century) *Faye*, the deceased wife of *Jim Bunnell. Kath* is reincarnated in Fayetteville as an art-teacher and her grand-daughter, *Kath* is with my first husband Harold Lisle, part of whose opposite polarity she is.

Fayetteville was civilised, and in my "apartment," (before these kindly generous people transferred me to their homes), I lived on ice-cream for several days, because everything in America is on such a large scale that small sizes are often unavailable. It put me off ice cream for a considerable time. Here too, the "Jesus Boys" introduced themselves. Waiting one day for a client for a reading, I was suddenly surrounded by three youths who asked, *"Ma'am*, where's the Post Office?" "Right over there," I answered. (All the men in Arkansas address you as "ma'am.") At first I thought they must be making fun of me, as they would be in England. But Birtha said "No," adding darkly "It's a mark of respect. And they'd better, too!" That's how it was. Far from meeting with rudeness still less violence in America, as I had been warned, I never met such polite people; there were no louts; the men open doors for you. And Nancy, on being told how uncouthly some men in England behave, working on buildings minus a shirt, radios blaring beside them, calling out derisive remarks to girls, exclaimed "Heavens! If they did that here they'd be run out of town." Of course, in New York or Chicago it may well be different.

But that's in the nature of a digression. I was talking about the "Jesus Boys." "Is it open?" they continued, meaning the Post Office. "I think so," I rejoined unsuspectingly. "Ah, but, ma'am, are *you* open?" they cried. "Open to Jesus?" "Crumbs," I thought, I'd heard of them; worse than Jehovah's Witnesses. I backed towards the door; they followed. "Come to Jesus, ma'am, come to Jesus! Jesus will save you, ma'am, Jesus will save you!" There was no escape-route. Hadn't Mick Jagger said something? They were about nineteen: surely they'd understand that language? I said, "Boy, I'm English! I don't save easy!" It worked; they got into their van and drove away. Still, at least they were polite; an improvement on the charmless louts let loose in England.

The creeks in Arkansas yield no alligators, and once with Imogene and a stalwart friend called *Pat*, our long trek through the water terminated in an impossibly steep hill to the latter's house. Americans all seem to be so strong, unless it is that I am so weak. (Cleopatra, flattered by sycophants who said, *"but then, your Majesty is so clever . . . "* shook her head. *"It isn't that I am so clever; it is that the others are so stupid."*) Anyway, laboriously climbing, clutching tree roots, I suddenly found myself lifted bodily by Pat, using only one arm—she was stout and powerfully built—flying through the air and being deposited at the summit without having exerted any further effort. An extraordinary experience, one of many.

Two men once accompanied me on an exhausting walk in tremendous heat all through the State Park and into the Ozark Mountains. Neither Birtha nor Imogene felt equal to it. On the way back, dehydrated and palpably flagging, I observed buzzards circling overhead. "Gosh!" I exclaimed, aghast, "are they. . . ?" "Oh yes," said one of my companions. "Just reconnoitring . . . just in case. . . " What a relief to get home!

128

Nancy died. Some had disparaged her; but if anyone did so in my hearing, I thought of that awful Greyhound 'bus, and that remote shanty town, Joplin, Missouri, in the midst of nowhere, and of Nancy waiting, loyal and considerate, to pluck me from that detestable vehicle with it murky vitreous windows like a London fog shutting out the sunshine. . .

That is the other theory I omitted to mention; the Americans are *not* better than we are at 'Bus Services! Nevertheless, whenever I travel on *British Rail*, I am appalled by the abysmally low standard of public behaviour. It seems there isn't *anyone* who can just find a seat, sit in it till they reach their destination, then get out. They've got to be up and down all the time, slopping about with cups of tea and coffee and upending tins of Coke with heads tilted back till they stumble against the rows of seats, going to the toilet, up and down the corridor, treading on people's toes, coughing, sniffing, yawning cavernously without putting a hand before their mouth, smoking, chewing gum, sucking peppermints, stuffing buns and sandwiches and chocolate and strewing the wrappers widespread, while their uncontrolled and uncontrollable offspring scream and climb and spreadeagle all over the upholstery. While on the stations every available seat is invariably occupied by *men*. An inspiring picture of Great Britain in 1994! All travellers returning from abroad comment on it; heroes and empire-builders turn in their graves as the strains of *Rule Brittania!* die away and Brittania sinks beneath the waves she once ruled.

Nancy had been compulsively dishonest. It's an illness, kleptomania. She even stole from her friends. Never from me. There must have been a curious karmic connection between herself and Don Tyson, who was well known to Birtha and her circle. Her assessment of her despoilment of the firm was, unrepentently, "It took a lot of fancy footwork to do that," as if it were some brilliant achievement. She was genuinely shocked and outraged when Don Tyson reluctantly prosecuted her, ("Fancy, Don doing a thing like that to me!") She was sent to prison at Pine Bluff, a circumstance which led to the most poignant of all my experiences in America.

I was asked to deliver a lecture at the Women's Prison deep down in the heart of Arkansas. (This delectable State is exactly the same size as England!) Imogene drove me there; she was Nancy's friend, and never lost affection for her. It was an incredibly hot day, only one of many in the part of that globe.

On arrival, after leagues of endlessly unfolding tree-lined forest roads, the officials submitted us to a rigorous search of our persons in order to locate treasonable matter. Having satisfied themselves that we carried no files, pinned a label on me to the effect that I was *Guest Speaker*. And for being that, they afterwards presented me with an honorary certificate of thanks and appreciation. But meantime they seemed bent on treating me as a potential criminal, for when I petitioned to be allowed to walk in the glorious sunshine while awaiting the lecture, numerous dragon-like blue-clad females cast disapproving glances at me before grudgingly unlocking those grim doors and letting me out for a strictly prescribed interlude under their suspicious scrutiny. When I signalled my readiness to come in, they re-opened the doors, which uncompromisingly clanged shut behind me, and I was not let out again. I duly gave the lecture on reincarnation, and never before or since have I been so bombarded by so many frenetic demands and questions. "Was it possible," one besought, "to commit a murder while possessed by a devil?" She was serving a life sentence for murdering her husband. In company with another woman, she had shot him as he left his van. Not dead, he contrived to crawl out of the vehicle, whereupon she shot him again, this time fatally. I said I thought it possible that an entity could step aside temporarily from its own ego, and permit an outside entity's influence. She seemed calmed. All of them thrust trinkets into my hand to be psychometrised. I was utterly drained, depleted and exhausted, so desperate, so urgent were their vibrations. By the end of the session, what with the heat, and the fraught tension of the atmosphere, I was leaning over the table incoherent and incapable of speaking another word. Imogene took me home. "Home" I have always felt the house in Springdale to be. But the sadness and desperation of those women followed me, and is with me, on and off, to this day, while that one woman's ravaged face will haunt me forever.

Doors keep closing now, as those prison-doors did then, but much more finally and even more grimly.

Birtha and Imogene took me to Fort Smith, to see Belle Starr's notorious *Pull-Up for Cowboys*, (who ironically had to undergo a bath before being admitted!), and Judge Parker's lock-up and gallows, where he would hang six men at a time. He was called "the Hanging Judge," rather on a par with our Judge Jefferies. In the nineteenth century little sentiment was extended to criminals, as opposed to the leniency, in England at all events, which exists today.

Thank you, Imogene, again and again from the other dimension, for all these services that live so vividly in my memory!

Back in Georgia, I wrote my short biography of General Oglethorpe and its companion booklet about John Wesley. The two figures had met, and did not "gel" at all. At the time I was visiting, Georgia was celebrating the 250th anniversary of its founder's landing, and the said founder's ghost was said to be haunting the city of Atlanta as well as St. Simon's Island, where Penelope took me on a beautiful summer day to research by subsequent volume, *Oglethorpe of Georgia.* *

As always, Deignan and Penelope were veritable Towers of Strength. A typewriter was provided, accomodation convened and tape recordings arranged. Michelle Martin managed to arrange a location for printing several volumes of my books, with the help of many of the abovementioned friends. It was a determined network. Penelope drove me tirelessly wherever it was necessary to go. I am eternally in their debt.

Then, once more, some of us linked up with the Arkansians, travelling by way of Memphis, Tennessee, where everyone is expected to worship at the shrine of *Elvis*, at "Graceland." Mary Fleming, Deignan and I could hardly resist the compelling pull towards the popular local attraction.

Once there, an ardent fan, standing nearby asked me, "Aren't you over-awed?" When I rather tactlessly replied "No," she looked again, a little more closely, and observed, "Oh, <u>English</u>!" which is always used to account for eccentricity.

Much the same was the considered opinion of the Family when my lack of appreciation was again apparent in having viewed, without enthusiasm, a movie premiere on my flight into Atlanta. It featured Clint Eastwood and Sylvester Stallone. I thought it was rubbish. My response to a concert by Ray Charles in the park of Stone Mountain, ** Georgia was the same. For their part, it was all "wasted on me."

Meanwhile, in Arkansas, we all fraternised at Springdale and swam together in the Beaver Lake. Birtha's house was great fun, (*Birtha's Motel*, as it

---

* Recently combined into one volume along with the biography of *Wesley.*
** Such a quaint idea, to carve those faces in the Stone Mountain, Georgia. We haven't got anything like that in England; Tony Blair and Mr. Major would be sort of funny. We would swim in the lake there. It was a lovely lake, excellent for swimming, but there was a notice to the effect that it was prohibited. Penelope would dive-in off the notice. We would take our swim in rotation. The patrolling police would go 'round the park in their vehicle, and when they were out of sight, one of us would swim; as soon as they hove into view once more, he or she would come out, wait until they resumed their circumnavigations, then another would swim. One officer commented dryly that our hair was wet. "oh, well," Penelope would airily explain, "it was raining earlier." She was always ready with an answer. Another time, caught for speeding, "Well, we're on our way to an important rehearsal, Oberon and Titania and Puck, you know; Puck's in the back, under all those blankets and stage-properties. You know how it is." "Oh, yes," replied the officer, "we know how it is! We'd better look at your license."

was named), in that people used it as a general rendezvous. She had an enormous television which was "on" from morning till night, and unemployed youngsters would frequent the house to use it as a free cinema, until at length Birtha, indulgent up to a point, would unequivocally chase them out.

Here too I laughed so much, as I did in Georgia with Deignan and Penelope and their "extended family." These young woman did not adhere to the conventional *family concept,* which after all is nothing more than a "karmic cluster," *not* welded together by ties of affection or like-mindedness, but by the tiresome artificial "relationship" upon which our societies are still unfortunately based, despite Steiner's observation that we should by now be outgrowing such legislation.

And so the dreamlike days passed. And passed away, for Imogene is dead, and we are all scattered and have taken our varying ways.

My final visit was to ensure that the protagonists in the Sandys Butler saga understood their place and part therein, and I am satisfied that they did, and that the more sophisticated Milton Holliman grasped the significance of his programme, where it may have presented a degree of perplexity earlier. I was transported to Georgia soon after, to see the house in the wilds that Deignan and Julie built. They have since named a road after me. For the first time in my life, I am vouchsafed encouragement and appreciation as opposed to the apathy, indifference, negation and denigration that is the lot of the pioneer, especially from his or her own "family." ◆

XII

Ian and Mavis

No one can write another person's biography with any degree of veracity or certainty. Famous people have their biographies written by successors, in that an aggregate of information has already been amassed from a variety of sources. Even so, it is only reported speech. Dr. Johnson said so many things that his biography largely consisted of quotations, such as *"A fishing-rod is a stick with a worm at one end and a fool at the other."* Apart from that, each man is an island, and only he or she can accurately express his or her sentiments, and sometimes he or she is unable adequately to do that.

Ian and Mavis must write their own biographies, if they want to. They might view them from totally different angles than mine. All I know about them is that they both carried a chip on their shoulder for an exaggeratedly long time.

Mavis was, (or thought she was), disappointed in me as a "person" or as a "parent," and that Ian, as a poor Piscean/Lemurian/Female Principle/Pig-Year this time 'round, can only emulate and despairingly cling to what is familiar and stronger than himself, and accordingly emulates Mavis and Chris, while his inner and deeper self knows full well that what I have to say is true.

Mavis has undergone an astounding "personality-change." Until she was fifteen, she understood me perfectly, and was in total rapport; to such an extent that I could project a *thought* without voicing it, and she would pick it up and answer it without a word being exchanged. Even in sleep she could do that, and was indeed used by the guides as a channel for Spirit.

Today, overwhelmed by *normality*, and contaminated by materialism and politics, associated with silly people and an uninitiated partner, she hates me (or thinks she does) and resentfully accuses me of failure as a mother. Since she was thirty-six at the time, when one cannot expect much of one's mother, (who might not even be there), she was not only conventional, but unrealistic.

It would seem that she has been harbouring bitterness, as only a Leo-subject can, because ten years ago I may have said something which gave her

133

credit for more development than she possessed. She did possess the development at fifteen. I was not to know that she was going to take a header back into materialism and the interpretation of all things at the "personal" level. It is not in my nature to upset anyone, and whatever comment it may have been, it was not at that level. As soon as I made the discovery, I fell silent, and have remained so ever since. Ten long years.

At first, she was associated with Ian Gates, and seemed likely to team up with him. That was not to be. She was karmically led to a portion of her opposite polarity, its female aspect in the shape of *Chris*, and they became partners and produced two children. Once under the influence of this immature but capable person, she adjusted as only a Leo-subject can, if it wants to, and convinced herself, as again only a Leo-subject can, that together they were always right about everything.

Chris in his early twenties was possessed of a certain elementary sense of humour, which was a saving grace. That evaporated, and he grew bumptious and assertive and was for several years a trouble-maker. He imbibed silly, Marxist ideas; and both of them based their friendships on politics. In so doing one cuts out many very nice people and restricts oneself to a narrow and sterile coterie.

The cardinal mistake that Mavis made was to confuse her "personal" attitude to me, with my *work*. This is fatal. She is by no means the first to do it, and alas, at our present stage of evolution, will not be the last. Like kicking the postman down the steps because he brings you a letter from the Income Tax Authority, or, as in mediaeval times, hanging the herald when he conveys an ultimatum from the enemy. It is only shallow, unimaginative people who do this, and if Mavis has chosen to ally herself with such, she must dree her own weird.

Between them, she and Chris and their "friends," ill-informed, uncouth, uncultivated, uncultured types, including Chris's parents, subjected me to unpardonable insults. His parents would not have cast the incredible aspersions they had the effrontery to do, upon my friends, had not Chris and Mavis opened the door to that kind of thing by discussing me with them and making derogatory references.

The insult to me, "personally," would not have mattered, hurtful though it may have been and certainly was. But an insult to God's truth, the Cosmic Law, the Eternal Verities, is a thing that, **BY** that Law, can never be redressed. At all events, *in that lifetime.*

"When the pupil is ready, the teacher is waiting." Yes. But I offered my services, in all innocence, *too soon!* I repeat, the teacher does not apply for the same job twice. If he gets a kick, and is rejected, as I was, he can never re-apply, and the pupils must gain the knowledge from another source.

The tragedy is that Mavis will have to wait a long time before she meets another source. It is she who will suffer. Everyone has to learn the truth sooner or later. Unfortunately, so many people in today's unawakened societies choose to make it *later*. Mavis, brought up by me, knows better, but chose to convince herself that she did not.

Chris would say to me in that odious, denigrating way that such spiritual invertebrates employ, "How do you know it's true?" No one but a cretin would ask such a question, since he would be the very type who would be incapable of understanding it if you explained. And who is going to stick their neck out to explain it, or anything, to such persons, in whom ignorance and insolence always go hand-in-hand? How would Chris have liked it if I had said, about the reams of inconsequential trivia he writes about social work, *"How do you know it's true?"* Yet they will do it to me, who has forgotten more than they can hope to learn in a month of Sundays! His brother-in-law was the same, sniggering behind hands, exchanging the "superior," "tolerant" glance over my head! Christ! What fools! No wonder Jesus wept!

Mavis "extenuated" their unforgivable insolent behaviour by informing me, "We don't *set-up* as teachers!" God help her! She need not! If she travels the world over, seeking enlightenment, she will *never*, in this life, meet anyone, anyone at all, who is a better "teacher" than I! Privileged by the authority of a powerful guide, I have studied the *process* all my life. I know the thing, in and out, from A to Z. The tragedy is hers.

Mine too. Because between them they drove me into permanent silence. For eight solid years I sat alone, night after night, often crying my eyes out, because systematically they have deprived me of the opportunity to repay to them any deficit in my role as parent, of which I am aware, and more than anything in the world I have longed to discharge that debt; even more so *to Ian*, who has suffered so much more.

My life's research and experience would have repaid it with compound interest; a legacy infinitely more desirable than a fine house to live in, a fleet of automobiles and a fortune in the bank.

It is too late now. One passes beyond tears, beyond anger or regret, beyond everything. The **Law** is inexorable. It enacts that we do not cast pearls before swine, and no exceptions are made for "relatives." Mavis and Chris did indeed trample them underfoot, Mavis perversely and with spite and cruelty: Chris with that widespread dumb, numbing ignorance and stupidity and preference for football matches and loud teen-aged music.

The emotional content has to go out of all things; otherwise they would be unbearable. As it was, the eight years were well-nigh intolerable, mercifully punctuated by my visits to America, where the loneliness was mitigated, and there were receptive people with their warm welcome.

Now it is all 'round me. But it belongs to a bygone era. I do not think about it any more, and when I do, can dispassionately affirm, like Rhett Butler,

"Frankly, my dear, I don't give a damn!"

Ian likewise for a while, with parallel obtuseness and tenacity, pretended to maintain a callous attitude to what is esoteric, proclaiming his preference for "leaving it alone." This was purely sedulous. I told him in no uncertain terms to apply himself to just that attitude, and retreated into silence equally with him.

A cold anger at last possessed me. No longer remorse, no longer self-reproach. No longer karma. They had gone too far, and reversed the karmic order. It has rebounded upon themselves. No one can go on forever. The responsibility is no longer mine, the ball is now fairly and squarely in their court, and they must seek elsewhere for their eventual enlightenment. But it will be eventual, for they do not mix in circles where wisdom and lore is available or comprehended.

Right at the end of their lives, long after I am "dead," Mavis may be sorry, Ian somewhat before that. I do not know. It may have to come out in some far distant wash. I have done all I can do. I have left Ian the Pearl beyond Price, the Crock of Gold at the End of the Rainbow, in a record of the Process, and of man's identity as an ensouling principle. If even then he still elects to pretend that he does not want it, I cannot help it. He was only emulating Mavis in trying to hurt me through my work. But I shall be well out of it. *God is not mocked*, and Ian is going to need that knowledge, if anyone is! Albeit I longed to help *him*, and he too, would not let me.

But the heartbreak is over. Admittedly my heart is sick and tired, and I long to quit this dimension which has become a prison, with its sterile outlook, its injustice, spiritual limitations and suffocating weight of insensate humanity. But that is no longer *because* of Ian and Mavis. The compulsion of karma is no longer there.

None of it is at the "personal" level. I feel no rancour towards Mavis and we are on perfectly amicable terms. It is just that we cannot talk to each other because we have nothing to talk about. They are a complete foursome without me, and I am gratified that they have done so well, for themselves and for Meg and Laurie. There is nothing they need from me, at that level. But at the monadic level, my guide calls Mavis and me *Balin and Balan*, the unfortunate brothers in the Arthurian Cycle. Balin killed Balan, not knowing that they were brothers.

Chris and Mavis do their best now, at the "personal" level. If I accompany them on a walk, they help me up the hills and over the styles. At home they fill the house with visitors, and I just keep out of the way. ◆

Dad
Ernest Kipling

Mollie Moncrieff

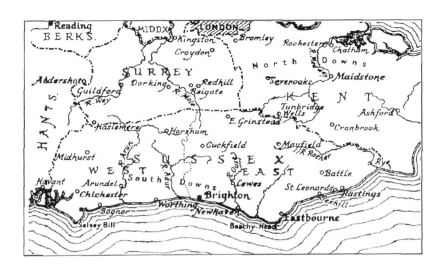

Auntie Madge's cottage at Ashurst (1995)

"The front room overlooked the road and had a little front garden into which the cows would sometimes stray and eat the flowers and churn up the sod. Nobody minded at all."

Kent Ditch

*"It marked the boundary between Kent and Sussex.
The gypsies were always stealing Uncle Bert's
chickens. Then they forded the stream, overnight,
into the adjacent county, where they could not be
prosecuted for misdemeanours perpetrated on Sussex
territory and vice versa."*

*oast
house*

*"Each season, the
hop-pickers came
down from London
. . . I was content
to watch, as the
curiously-smelling
plant was laid out
on racks, and that
unique Kentish
feature, the oast
house, came
into play."*

Sir Walter Scott's house at Abbotsford

"In Auntie Madge's bedroom hung a picture of Bonnie Prince
Charlie saying goodbye to Flora MacDonald. I used to sneak
in there breathlessly to gaze at it at every opportunity. . . .
Years later, I held in my hand a lock of Bonnie Prince Charlie's
hair. That would be impossible today; there are too many
people. But in those days things were more accessible and
humanity less prolific. It was . . . at Abbotsford. The curator,
noting my wistful expression, very kindly opened the glass
case and took it out for me. . . . It was a faded strand, that
might have belonged to anyone, it probably would not do
much for my disillusioned eye today, but then it did, and
it was with elation and reverence that I replaced it
in the case."

The Shambles of York

*"Who can pass judgement as to what
is 'better' or 'worse'? It was
much the same with the Shambles. . . .
I saw it, exactly as it was; as it
had been for centuries, just before
it was 'cleaned up.'"*

The Shambles of York

"Life has to go on. The new, the hygenic, secular and materialistic, is superimposed upon the old, the dirty, the mysterious and religious."

Shibden Valley

*"I knew my way over earthly territory which
in the current life I had never seen. . . .
I recognized all the seventeenth century
landmarks. I had covered that terrain
thoroughly in my life as Jennifer Butler. . . .
This beautiful area near Halifax . . . I called
'The Valley Time Forgot'. . . . All the farms
and cottages along its extensive length
are at least three hundred years old, and I
knew the names of all of them, and all
the landmarks, and no one told me."*

Scout Hall

"The dominating and most impressive feature
of Shibden Valley which my spirit urged
me to frequent, was Scout Hall, built
by one John Mitchell in 1680, and I
recognized it at once, and recalled John
Mitchell too, for as Jennifer Butler
I had seen him from a distance, when his
house was new, and the stone a creamy
colour instead of being smoke-grimed. . . .
It boasted 365 windows, one for each
day of the year."

24, Dyke Road, Brighton

"... another of Ted's rat-holes. ...
It had a chequered history.
... Drug-addicts, dogs, defaulters-
with-the-rent, and kindred weavers
of chicanery comprised his tenantry.
But I was from time to time among
them, and am grateful for the
asylum the strange house afforded me."

12, Old Steine, Brighton

*"There was . . . the phenomenon of
'deep breathing,' which can be most
disconcerting when one is alone with
it. I was, . . . it emanated from beneath
the buttress under the window where,
I understand, two women were killed
by the storm of 1848. . . . There was even
the ghost of a dog, 'Nelson.' Ordinary
dogs in fleshly form would not
enter the building."*

South Downs, Sussex

Bamborough Castle

*"Some say that Bamborough Castle was
Sir Lancelot's retreat, 'Joyous Garde.'
Others claim the distinction for Alnwick."*

Traquair House
*"The gates are locked because the laird in 1745,
heart-broken at the defeat of Bonnie Price Charlie
locked them and threw the key into the [River] Tweed,
declaring that they should not be opened again
until a Stewart held the throne of England."*

Penshurst
*"An incredible circumstance linked me with Penelope.
As children, Kath and I were frequently at Sir
Philip Sidney's home, Penshurst Place in Kent. On
the wall there hung a portrait which fascinated
me – that of Lady Barbara Gamage. What seemed a
lifetime later, thousands of miles away, I came into
contact with Penelope, the descendant of that lady!
There is no such thing as a coincidence."*

7, Trelawney Road, Bristol

*"I am glad of the proximity
of Ian. He . . . never fails
to 'phone or call when
the family goes away
and I am left alone in the
house . . . as it is unnerving
here at night."*

Road sign
Homer, Georgia, USA

"I was transported to Georgia
. . . to see the house in
the wilds that Deignan
and Julie built. They
have since named a road
after me."

Mollie Moncrieff Road

XIII

Ian

I suppose it was just my share of the Curse of the O'Connors.

Yes, Ian had a deprived childhood, going from pillar to post cheated of what he felt to be his birthright. That is undoubtedly true. Yet no one individual is ever " to blame" for everything. I was "to blame" for some of it, Robert Moncrieff for some of it, Lambodhar Zutshi for some of it. But the easiest, unthinking course is to appoint a scapegoat, and Ian saw fit to blame me for everything, in that I was *there*, the only one to whom he had access to apportion "blame."

Theoretically, as an adult with a quick, responsive and analytical mind, Ian can rationalise it. But where it's a question of *emotions*, even the cleverest of people remain like children, and never forget, never fully "get over it," and nurture a chip on their shoulder apparently indefinitely.

Where Ian has lacked wisdom, is in getting entrenched in bitterness for too long. It is wearing off now, but has damaged him, just as his dead-end job at Gatwick Airport damaged him. In middle life now, it is thankfully not too late for him to repair the damage. And already his life shows signs of becoming more structured.

I was, when Ian was young, passionately dedicated to the acquistion of the esoteric knowledge which I am now in a position to bequeath to him. Once you have *that*, you have everything. It is the only thing that can enable you to withstand the slings and arrows of outrageous fortune, and ride out the storm.

In this dedication to esoterics, I may have, or appeared to have, neglected the children. Not *neglect* in the recognised connotation. They were always fed and warm, and had a roof over their heads, and I was always *there*;

they were not latchkey teenagers. But possibly I was not sufficiently involved in their activities, and did not help them with their homework or solicit interviews with the headmaster. Perhaps I did not attach enough importance to formal education. I suppose I still don't. Most people would be more imaginative without it. And certainly in Ian's estimation I did not attach enough importance to money. There he had a point. I, having had money, did not value it, whereas he, poor little devil, hated poverty and had to endure it. Yes, he felt he had the right to be bitter. He could not, or course, in youth, assess the price he and all three of us would have had to pay by the sacrifice of our freedom had we remained where the money was. *But*, and here is the crunch; *if only he*, as an adult, could have appreciated the superlative, indeed *supernal* value of the *Pearl beyond Price,* he need never have dissipated so much time and energy in feeling bitter!

Others appreciated it. I have sheaves and cupboards full of letters from young people all over the world, thanking me, recognising the worth of what I taught them. Only from my own children, sneers, contempt, indifference. God help them—even ridicule!

Mea Culpa? Oh no! Not any more! Never again!

It is all so long ago.

Everything that was real, or had any meaning, seems so long ago now.

I think Ian is beginning to find himself. He may have lost his job, but it was a job well-lost, and now at least he can look round and think about things, and sleep at night, whereas had he gone on using himself up in that dead-end capacity, he would have had no chance to develop, and would have been prematurely aged and destroyed.

Certain Laws operate in the universe. There is the Law of Synchronicity and the Law of Distribution. We all, at varying stages of our lives, possess some things and lack other things. What Ian did not have in childhood, at the material level, he can obtain now. Ice creams, and things he likes to eat, holidays abroad, a better home and a car. Assuredly, things are not the same out-of-season, and he never outgrew his sad denial of the pleasures of childhood. But the Laws work in spite of that. I, on the other hand, knew plenitude in childhood and lost it later.

If Ian goes about it in the right way, he will be able to make an income out of my work after I am dead. That, however, is a secondary consideration; he has the legacy of more knowledge than most people can hope to come by in many lifetimes.

138

Years into the future, when Meg and Laurie are grown up, he may well prove to be a tower of strength to them, and convey to them the help that I would gladly have given, had not Mavis and Chris deliberately precluded it, not only depriving me of the opportunity to pay a karmic debt, thereby incurring adverse karma for themselves, but equally denying Meg and Laurie an invaluable asset.

If Meg and Laurie show no interest, that is a different matter. It will mean that they are not ready for it, and I have no responsibility for them, only a residual quota for Ian, no more for Mavis. I have bestowed upon Ian all I have in exoneration, if only he has the sense to value it.

Then too, if Meg and Laurie express a need for it, he can compensate them for the wanton stupidity of their parents.

The foregoing paragraphs were written in the early part of the year. July 1994 finds them superseded by hopeful signs from Ian. Almost, one might imagine, as if he had undergone some sort of psychic experience . . . one of these *"Road to Damascus"* affairs. I don't know. But he evinced interest in the tape recordings! It is hard for me to believe, after such protracted repudiation. Sometimes I still cannot grasp the fact that it has actually happened. While he, quite probably, does not, outwardly and in the daytime, realise that anything world-shattering *has* happened! He is not spontaneous, enthusiastic or responsive. But then, he is a water-sign, and the rest of the family is not. But he is kind and good in his own way, and tries to help, and does things for me, and takes me out, none of which he is obliged to do, and I am grateful, and more than satisfied, as I do not expect anything of him. It is not his place to look after me; nor Mavis's, and I could not bear that they should be thus burdened. If only I can feel assured that my legacy, (under-estimated, belittled and denigrated as such treasures are in this dimension) will stand him in good stead in the time to come, I shall be content.

In the sleep-state, of course, he realises fully now, everything that has happened! And what kind of comfort or security his day-time self-deceptions or pretences afford him, is for him to discover.

The foregoing comments may seem to belie my earlier statement that my *Memoirs* cannot be committed to paper until all emotion has been drained out of them; for glancing back at it, I observe that it held some vehemence. But that was born of pain, now assuaged, in that Ian and Mavis were the central tragedy to my life.

Not now, but possibly until recently. Now, even my sadness has been consigned to limbo and handed over to Providence. After all, everything comes right in the end; all is under control, and there is plenty of "time." We have all the *time* in Eternity to work out our evolution and fulfill our destiny, and perhaps I was unduly impatient, anxious or eager.

I have learnt, again recently, to be none of these. There may still be a sadness, or heaviness, but that is because daily living is bereft of interest, and we seem to have to wait so long even for the smallest development. Then a sort of despair can set in, and we grow depressed, forgetting the longer term emergence, overlooking the wider canvas. Of course I know that there's a "time" for everything, and that each individual entity is allocated its own ration of "time." It was just that I was so desperately disappointed that Mavis and Ian were so *slow*, so ready to subscribe to the stultifying stupidity of today's spiritual climate. They knew better, of course, and therein lies the tragedy, but because the wisdom came from me, and their aim was to flout me at the personal level, they saw fit to try to be clever and flout the Divine Wisdom too.

Mavis and Chris have done well, in the worldly sense, overcoming disadvantages, and I wish for them the very best of everything, which they deserve at that level; and for Meg and Laurie too. None of my regrets or sentiments are personal, and if for the present they do not wish to transcend that level, I must accept it, and bear with the restricted communication it necessitates. Mavis and Chris work together admirably; they work hard, and co-operate on all points. They are perfectly integrated within today's society, and foster *normality* in Meg and Laurie, and this may well be for the best, since they too have to integrate likewise with today's world. Far be it from me to impose upon that any breath of something different.

Now I shall put this part of the script away, and think no more about it. There is a sort of peace which comes with acceptance. I do not use the word "serenity," for that betokens happiness, and I do not lay claims to that. But neither am I unhappy, and am aware of feeling a comfortable, detached goodwill to all men. ◆

XIV

The Last Tea-Bag

Crabbèd age and youth cannot live together.
Youth is as the Spring, age like winter weather.
Youth is full of joy, age is full of sorrow.
Age is yesterday, youth is all tomorrow.

—Shakespeare

Trust The Bard to have an apposite quotation to fit every human situation.

Any reader who has borne with the book so far, may have formed the impression that my life has been a wonderful adventure-packed exciting saga, full of fascinating contacts, ripe with experience.

So it has, I suppose, compared with many. I know it's the final entry, and that is always the most difficult and complex. But much, almost I think *most* of it has been spent *"wandering lonely as a cloud,"* some of which times were happy, probably the best, in their own way. Because when one is young, one is not living entirely in the present, but in the future, and when the present is pleasing, and the surroundings beautiful, the mystery of the future is pleasant too, not a programme to be dreaded, but anticipated as a joyous challenge.

Whereas when one is old, one has only the past to draw upon, and the unpleasantness of the present detracts even from that. It was Colonel Stewart who said to me, more than twenty-five years ago, *"most people die of boredom."* I did not fully fathom, then, the measure of the remark, and thought it rather a sweeping statement. But I certainly do, now, when the days just seem to fold uneventfully one into another.

I am reminded now, of a communicant who addressed me "out of the blue" in the Autumn of 1995.

"I was waiting for you to tell me that!"

"What? I questioned, startled, "Who?"

"Don't you remember *Wilhelmina Stirling?*"

My thoughts went racing back, over more than thirty years, when a famous authoress had written to me in connection with a series of articles I had published in *The Daily Sketch.* She was, she told me at that time, the oldest living writer, aged ninety-eight. We corresponded, though we never met. She wanted to hear of my psychic experiences. Her many fine books are filled with queries, but no conclusions. I kept her letters but have no copies of my own. Indeed, during those years I confess with shame that I was rushing about like a maniac. People do, until they learn more sense.

Ian and Mavis were young, I was pressed for money and trying to fit in twenty-five different commitments at once—a common enough story. I did not attach enough importance to the request; I do not think I even bothered to read the book she sent me, one of her last, *A Scrapheap of Memories.* Now I've routed it out from a forgotten shelf. It is a brilliant book, but as intimated, lacked the *answer* she sought. In extreme old age and illness, she was appealing to me to supply it, through our correspondence. Doubtless, I must have written to her about reincarnation.

The letters dwindled then came to a stop. Clearly, she had died.

My recollection of Mrs. Stirling made me realise how much we miss by our endless rushing about—how many important matters and people we neglect and overlook in the course of it.

I think it was not altogether a good day for mankind when he discovered the principle of Internal Combustion; it enables him to transport his physical form (with its accompanying *"personality equipment"*) from place to place at a speed wholly incommensurate with his pitiful quota of wisdom.

Speaking of travel, and formidable journeys, my "Extended Family" in Georgia urges me to move there, join their animal-care organisation, *Argus,* and help animals, among friends. Much as I'd wish to, I dare not dig up my roots, such as they are. How nice it would be if their abode were here, in Devon, or Dorset, or Sussex, or, as Coleridge lamented,

> *If I had but two little wings*
> *And were a little feathery bird,*
> *To you I'd fly, my dear,*
> *But thoughts like these are idle things,*
> *And I stay here.*

What a horrid century this has been for the world. Little wonder Noel Coward wrote his song *Twentieth Century Blues*. Its very first year opened with a war in China, followed five years later by a "natural" disaster in San Francisco. The *Titanic* was surely, on a lesser scale, the most poignant episode of our time! Not on a par with the sheer calculated evil of Hitler's machinations, but confronting individuals with the most agonising impossible choice that could ever be made. Then the First World War with its ineffable carnage, (they were still talking about that while I was growing up), then, the respite of the thirties, although one heard that there were *strikes*, but not the truculent selfish and greedy affairs that they are now, and Hitler building up to the Second World War that some of us can remember, though there is scarcely anyone left now who could remember the First. And after that, constant sporadic wars in other parts of the world, and Hiroshima, and an upsurge of crime and lawlessness unprecedented since the press gangs jettisoned all such instigators into the Navy and obviated the necessity for house-holders fearing for their property and women and children for their lives.

God knows what is amiss with today's people! It is true that the mission of our fifth root race* was to develop the intellect, and this we have done, to the detriment of all else. Thus it is their alarmingly *literal* outlook which makes people so difficult to help. They need the help as never before, and are continually soliciting it, but as soon as it is offered, they discredit it, and clamour for "proof". There is **NO** "proof", of the kind they mean, the kind you get in a Court of Law or in a Laboratory. The proof is within yourself, in fact it *is* yourself. Plato exhorted his contemporaries, "MAN KNOW THYSELF!" and added for good measure, *"The Proper Study of Mankind is Man."* Yet they will study anything and everything except that! Our planet abounds in clever fools and educated idiots. Jesus further reminded them, *"There shall be **NO SIGN** given to this generation. It is a generation of vipers."* By "generation," he meant, not 33 years, but an Evolutionary Cycle, and was referring to the Age of Pisces, which has been engulfed in the Kali Yuga.**

A further unfortunate factor which militates against today's people taking control of their own lives and deaths is the inability of our fifth root race to die when it has discharged its quota of karma for the existing entry, or implemented its commitment. The end of one's work should synchronise with the end of one's "life," that is, the physical shell and its accompanying "personality-surround" wherein that portion of the soul's work was accomplished. In default of that, ignorance or non-recognition of one's scheduled work must be the cause, or else one has some residual karma to work out,

---

* See *Prisoners of Time*.
**The "Black Age," from 100 A.D. to 1899.

143

something yet to infiltrate or impart, or a bit of both. But it is much tidier and more economical when the two can synchronise, besides the inestimable benefit of reducing the population and making room for another entity which has no option but to enter.

Thus people are not able to get out before they get old, and a contributory cause of this is our loss or forfeiture of the faculty of dematerialising the physical form. Jesus, who was the last Avatar, knew how to do this. In all his so-called "miracles," he was only applying faculties it is our human birthright to possess, which were possessed by the races of antiquity. And this of course explains his disappearance from the tomb. There is no such thing as a "miracle;" nothing can transcend the laws of nature. It is simply that by the time Jesus appeared on earth, humanity had dipped down to such a low ebb of awareness that anything they could not understand—which was almost everything—would be classed as a "miracle."

I have just, (in October 1994), witnessed a television broadcast of Doris Stokes. What a medium, at the *Spiritualist* level! and what supreme courage! It makes one feel humble and ashamed of one's grousing. I know that if I were as ill as she was, I would be making my own life a misery and everyone else's as well. It would seem that certain very special souls are sent in, or choose to come in, at specified junctures, to demonstrate selfless service and sacrifice in the face of what we lesser mortals would call impossible odds.

New friends have come into my life at this mature stage when I feel I have very little left to offer. *Mary,* who is well-dressed and charming, Aquarius, spiritually inclined but too busy and burdened with responsibilities to indulge in such a luxury. She was I believe sent into my orbit to drive me to Colyton to free my mother Queenie from an astral fixation in the one-time farmhouse at *Bonehayne.* Stranger things have been known to happen. But Mary has proved more persistent; I do not yet quite know why: unless it be that her equally persistent associates, (termed loosely "boyfriends" by today's loosely orientated society), need something that *I* , in some obscure way, can still supply.

At all events she has been a friend for more than eight years without drifting away as people do if there is no karmic tie. She attracts numerous admirers, as is to be expected, and of these, two recur in my life to the extent that I feel there must be some reason for it. *Michael,* who is the husband of Annie, the television-presenter who took her own life in 1990 by way of an overdose of a drug, and *John,* who is rich, money-wise, lost his wife, and is lonely. I have yet to discover the reason for these being in my path. John and

144

Mary are kindness itself, hospitable and ever-ready to help.

On an October day in 1994, the last link with Uxbridge was severed. Kath Berryman died in the Hillingdon Hospital. She had been in failing health for a long time, but even while she was ill, she continued to make her little home a notable "power-point" and focus for Spirit. Not consciously. Oh, no, Kath never did anything self-consciously. She was so innocent, simple and modest that she did not even know she was a *medium*. At last, she did, but it would never have occurred to her to tell anyone about it, still less exploit or advertise or commercialise the faculty. She was an outstanding transfiguration medium, on a passive wavelength, whose task was to aid discarnate entities rather than incarnate ones.

Kath had a long and lonely life. But again, she did not complain of loneliness; nor would she have consciously described herself as lonely; the house was always full of spirit-contacts. She never complained of anything, but would make matter-of-fact statements concerning situations that would have driven anyone else mad, including myself. She was never sorry for herself either, but was always neatly dressed and composed.

At one time, over a period of years, I worked with her, exorcising the visitants who used her as a channel. I would communicate with them, and arrive at the nature of their needs, after which there was no difficulty in setting them free. It was in fact a ghost which led me to Kath in the first instance, (it so often is!) And on these occasions I used to travel up from Brighton, stay with Iris at Iver Heath, then with Auntie Gay and Uncle Jack at Gerrards Cross, walk miles and miles to Uxbridge to stay the night with Kath, then take the coach back to Crawley and so to Brighton. The region of Uxbridge is very old, very historic. Apart from the martyrs who were burnt at the stake there during the Marian Persecutions, the zone, being flat, was used in the seventeenth century for military manoeuvres. I was "called in" by Barbara and Lionel Futers of Woodingdean, who were indirect connections of Kath, to exorcise a young soldier who had died on the site of Kath's house, thought his discharge-papers were hidden there, and was in a "state," haunting the premises and creating a disturbance. That episode, in 1960, sparked off a chain of similar hauntings, and Kath's work began.

Prior to that, she had led a simple life, assisting her parents in their modest "General Store" at Cowley. That is what her family had done for centuries. Her direct ancestor was not called "Berryman" as Kath's parents were, and the manner of that alteration was divulged to me by Kath's guide. It is an unusual name, which I have not encountered since. Until mediaeval time, people did not have surnames, but were identified by their trade or vocation, as "Smith," "Baker," "Fisher," "Shepherd," "Farmer." It would be about the year 1520 when young John *Sturgis* set out from Middlesex to seek employment. He found it at last, on Henry VIII's estate at *Nonesuch*. And there, man and boy, he worked all his life. A capable gardener, he soon gravitated to the responsible post of steward. The other servants did not call him "Sturgis," but *Berryman*. He was the King's berryman, in charge of the bushels of strawberries, raspberries, blackberries, cranberries, elderberries, red and black currents, gooseberries and cherries that went to the distilling of wines, jams and preserves for the royal ménage. He likewise superintended the orchards, fishponds and the weedless, velvety lawns, remnants of which can still be discerned, though the palace itself has vanished. Kath showed me a ring which she had in her possession, given to John Berryman by Henry VIII. It would not have been presented directly by the king, who in any case would have died by the end of the latter's term of service, but it seems to have been the quaint custom to bestow upon a long-serving retainer some item or token from the royal household as a keepsake, where today there would be a gold watch or a pension. The ring was not pretentious, nor jewelled, but mounted with a heraldic design, of a griffin or allegorical beast, in greyish metal, of exquisite workmanship. And thus the family inherited its surname *Berryman*, and rendered sterling service to England to this day, as yeomen, shopkeepers, solid London folk, never dwelling anywhere else, unquestioning, unanalytical, expecting nothing other than that, nor recognition or reward for their unremitting toil.

Kath too, expected nothing. And in this dimension, that would appear to be precisely what she got. She never to my knowledge had a "holiday," which most of us regard as our due from time to time. And yet the saying is that *"he who is not content with little, will be little better with more."* She did not marry. There was someone she might have married who I believe was killed in the Second World War; but she seldom spoke about that. The one love of her life was her father, with whom clearly she had a marked karmic affinity, to the extent of possibly having been his opposite polarity. * Kath was always talking about him, and his picture hung in the bedroom where I used to sleep when I stayed there. A gentle face, the female principle to her male one. She was so much aware of his presence that when she was admitted to the hospital under the care of her next door neighbor, very confused and having lost track of days of the week, she could only reiterate "October 27th." That was the anniversary of his death, and the day of her own.

Kath must have comforted hundreds of discarnate entities in her little anonymous centre in its secluded flower-filled garden. Henry VIII, as might be anticipated, was a frequent despairing applicant for the assailment thus far systematically denied him. His misdeeds haunt him, and he cries out about a rain of blood which he cannot stem. That of Sir Thomas More and Katherine Howard, and outstandingly Anne Boleyn. *"The Trumpets sound on the Other Side,"* and if ever those words applied to any person, they did to Kath. But the

* Similarly, Charles I and his daughter, Elizabeth.

146

irony is, she would not have wanted them to! Left to her own devices, there is nothing she would like better, at first, at any rate (and I am prepared to hazard an "educated guess" that that is exactly what she *is* doing) than to be back in the "General Store" at Cowley, helping her Dad to weigh out a pound of sultanas, or dispensing peppermint humbugs to the local juveniles; then, at the end of the day, putting everything away, so tidily (for Kath was born under the Sign of Virgo), knowing meticulously where to put her finger on it the next day, turning the simple key in a door innocent of bolt or burglar alarm, confident that all would be well and safe in the morning; walking home in the dusk to the little house and the uneventful evening, at peace with a world of whose ways she mercifully knew so very little. And of such is the Kingdom of Heaven.

Now my "life," (if one can call it that), pursues the even tenour of its way. It holds neither hope nor stimulus, and anticipates only termination. I am glad of the proximity of Ian. He has overcome his antipathy, and his emulation of Mavis to the extent of being *kind*. He never fails to 'phone or call when the family goes away and I am left alone in the house. He does not have to, nor do I expect it. Yet I am glad of the attention, as it is unnerving here at night, the house having a very accessible ground-floor. We have had three burglaries, and the front door kicked down and smashed in with the unprecedented savagery and venom that only today's unbridled thugs and louts seem capable of.

God knows what is the matter with them, or whence they derive. Karma and the violent swing of the pendulum plays a part, but in their abysmal ignorance of all spiritual laws, they are only succeeding in manufacturing more adverse karma which must rebound upon themselves, and thus it takes many lifetimes for the balance to come to rest. In addition, there is a major influx of Luciferic offshoots now into the physical dimension, just as there were in the third epoch of Atlantis.* These are given over to evil *per se,* and their advent is disquieting; children killing other children, criminals whose equipment is deficient in the attributes which militate against the enactment of evil. Then there is no deterrent, either from within or without. At one time, the incidence of "religion" posed a warning. A lingering superstition precluded vandals for instance damaging or stealing from the church. The old Parish churches were open day and night. Today doors are locked. Contemporary vandals do not fear for their immortal *souls* in that they are unaware that they possess such an appendage. This foregone awareness, combined with an uncompromising legal system, once furnished a cogent deterrent. All that has gone, and Mob Rule is the order of the day, here in Britain.

* See *Prisoners of Time.*

Ian's knee is a source of concern. It has never been perfect since the Marines' doctors bungled the operation, and he may need further surgery. I distrust surgery, and always recommend those who come to me for advice, to steer clear of it if at all possible. As for today's policy of prolonging "life" (as currently accepted); it seems utterly senseless. No one is the same once a portion of the anatomy has been removed; while "transplants" represent a futile concept. Each individual has its equipment and its appointed lifespan, and another's equipment, *still less* that of *animals,* is not valid. At best, an agonising two or three years can ensue, and to what possible purpose? If it were *youth* that were prolonged, it might be different. But it is *age* that is prolonged, and people are living to horrendous ages. Heavens, in this country a person can subsist on a pension for forty years!

Ian is only forty-seven, and I hope and pray that he may be able to retain some measure of "normality" (whatever that may signify in this world) and not be held back by any physical disadvantage.

Of the numbers whose existences are prolonged beyond the allotted span, many are not aware that their life's work is completed, or even that they had any specific mission in life. The ones who do, notably actors and actresses who have experienced fame and success, will simply fade out, to wit Bette Davis, who subsisted on orange juice and chocolate and then died. Others commit suicide. Yet others, exhibiting courage or foolhardiness, stage a "comeback" rather than peter-out into obscurity. Growing old gracefully* does not emerge as a universal achievement. Had they lived in very early antiquity, they would have been able to quit the physical vehicle before any such desperate recources commended themselves.

Ethel Mannin observed, *"you spend all your life trying to get somewhere, and then, when you get there, where are you?"* Another cited the definition of a celebrity as *"one who works hard to get known, and then wears dark glasses to avoid being recognised;"* while another affirmed that *"it is better to travel hopefully than to arrive."*

The last assertion certainly rings a bell. I made that discovery. After all the adulation in America, and the fuss that was made of me in many quarters; there is nothing at the end of the road, as far as this dimension is concerned, and as Napoleon declared, *"nothing counts except what you leave behind, your own imprint upon history."* That is wholly true. As an entity, you are of no account, and are soon forgotten, and may well have to come in again, more than once, to learn another trade. Most "great" people, that is, authentic geniuses, have been notoriously bad citizens, merely imperfect channels for divine inspiration. Even Jesus Christ admitted, *"of myself I am nothing."*

---

* See *Prisoners of Time.*

Psychic "gifts," if you wish to call them such, come and go, or are conferred and withdrawn as we need to exercise them or cease to require them, or change course and adopt a diverse approach to the same goal, perhaps via the intellect in writing or lecturing, whatever is most useful to the human race and whatever we accomplish to best advantage.

Now, I am simply an observer, not a participant. Auntie Florrie used to deplore, with a sad shake of the head, "it isn't our world any more!" Of course it isn't. One can't expect it to be. Change is an indispensable part of the package deal. It would not be possible for things to stay the same. I don't feel sad about it, except for the fate of the planet. I have my memories, and they are on record for anyone who wants to share them, and for those whose paths intersect them. Boredom and fed-up-ness, inevitably, there is. There's nothing to look forward to, except more of the same—serving as a catalyst, until one freaks out altogether, then sits down and waits to die, or possibly, like Queen Elizabeth I, refuses to sit down, ejects doctors with contumely, and dies upright, in a chair. It really doesn't make much difference in the final analysis.

I suppose it is part of the proverbial "lesson" to experience each phase of life in practice. I recall Ted Smith's observation when we sat together over our hand-gathered wood fire in the weavers' cottage in Yorkshire. I commented jokingly that we looked like Darby and Joan. "One day we'll be old," he replied, "might as well start thinking about it." And I had protested in alarm, "Oh, gosh! I'd prefer not to think about it!"

As for death, it is not the thing itself one dreads, but the path that leads up to it. Because we do *not* in fact experience death in this dimension at all. It is simply a transfer from one state of being to another, although at first in many cases there will seem to be little difference between the two states.

We can, if we want to, experience "death" *consciously*, in the alternative dimension, and that deliberate undertaking is termed the "second death" we read about in orthodox scriptures.

As far as "I" am concerned, it will be a relief from boredom to be in the alternative dimension. I am only "cliff-hanging" for Ian; otherwise I would whole-heartedly "ask" to be there. But I can't leave with a free mind until I am assured that he is "all right," that is, not in point of "jobs" and money—that will take care of itself, but in respect of the possession of awareness of his origins, his purpose and his goal. I don't feel inclined to write, and feel written out. I don't feel disposed to paint in water-colours anymore. I go for walks, but not to Glastonbury; it isn't the same without Rose. In Autumn I pick blackberries and make lots of jam, which I give away. In Spring I gather primroses and take them to people who can't get out much. I give the odd lecture; I attend the Theosophical Society; heaven knows why, the standard has fallen so low. Years ago, they didn't have such pretentious premises, but they had knowledge; now they have forfeited the knowledge in favour of "better" surroundings; and this commercialised element has crept into everything, both here and in America, even Findhorn. Such a pity, such a retrograde step. I look at the television. I used to ration this stringently, to interludes when I could not do anything else. These interludes grow more frequent, and thus I see, vicariously, rather more of the world than when I participated. Needless to say, I don't like what I see. Much of it is rubbish, and I don't look at that. Sometimes there is something really brilliant; there are wonderful wildlife features. It is a repetitious phenomenon that humanity always leaves everything too late for redress. He decimates his environment beyond redemption, by sheer weight of his overwhelming numbers, plus ignorance as to how to treat his planet, then wakes up with a bump to the devastating fact that half of it has disappeared, and the urgency of trying to do something about it. Thus, mounting extinctions in the wild.

Then there is the "News." This reads like a horror movie, but anyone with aspirations towards being a good citizen, is aware of some commitment to keep abreast of it. Here again, goodness knows why! It is beyond measure depressing. We're unconscionably sick of the Middle East and wish it were off the map. Then AIDS, and Cancer, and the bizarre experimentations to prolong "life" that are constantly mooted because mankind has sacrificed all cognizance of the alternative dimension.

We are expected to feel sorry for the Third World—people staring with blank eyes into space, waiting for us to supply them with sustenance. Yet they have the energy to produce children. No power on earth will stop them, or anyone else, from doing that! And its cessation is the **ONLY** thing that can solve the problem of our lunatic asylum. Animals, when conditions become adverse, cease to breed, and die out. That is because animals have the advantage of the group-soul instinct. Their thinking is done for them at the higher level, and very wise thinking it is too. But man has perversely denied that inestimable privilege. He is *an individual,* and is supposed to think for himself. The trouble is he doesn't, and in fact does not think at all. He simply reproduces, until he brings into being the situation deplored by Thomas Hardy, of the smothering preponderance of *"Shapes, like ourselves, hideously multiplied."*

Today, there is no excuse for it. Earlier generations had no escape routes. All generations within the Kali Yuga had no recollection of that spiritual rapport which precluded surplus population. Each generation has its peculiar problem. The 1939 generation had the Second World War, the one before that the First World War to contend with. The current generation has, fairly and squarely on its shoulders the issue of over-population. It is not facing up to that responsibility, and all the while it fails to do so, the planet will suffer, to the very point of extinction. If people, whether of the Third or Western world, simply will not attempt to find out what they are, *an ensouling principle;* and will not apply the one valid remedy for all our problems, *drastic universal reduction in our numbers;* then suffering will continue to form an integral part of their lives. The two things are inseparable, and at this stage of evolution it is still only by suffering that we learn, egregiously slowly at that!

What else does the "telly" tell us? A few years ago it was Lebanon and Beirut and the Gulf. It's always been Northern Ireland. Now it's Bosnia, *ad nauseam,* till one feels inclined to exclaim like George V,* "Bugger Bosnia!" How would such sentiments be interpreted? As sheer callousness, no doubt, lack of sympathy, even "racism," or the crotchety cantankerous outpourings of "crabbèd age." I don't know, and I have to confess I no longer care. Such unworthy thoughts! Of course it isn't that one wishes anyone ill. One could equally readily swing to the other extreme and assert that *"any man's death diminishes me, because I am involved in mankind."* Needless to say, I am sorry for the victims of Bosnia, and for the Third World, and for Prince Charles and Princess Diana, and for homeless beggars, but I confess that I am greatly more diminished by the death or suffering of <u>an animal,</u> since human beings at least are equipped with reasoning power and the capacity for perceiving what is happening, plus the ability to shift for themselves, and the majority of them are so selfish that they do, exclusively; while the others who can't or don't want to utilise these advantages, sit and wait helplessly for someone else to shift for them.

Whereas <u>animals</u>, poor wretches, are wholly defenceless and at the mercy of our stupid and unimaginative humanity. Nor do they have many champions to come to their aid, while the horrid, charmless and out-of-hand progeny of the proletariat, in Western Society, at all events, is accorded illogical and arbitrary priority. Accordingly I work for animals, writing letters of protest to Governments and European M.P.'s about atrocities and criminal negligence and kindred thankless undertakings. Similarly I am diminished by man's multiple depredations and his stamping out of wildflowers and creatures, and sometimes even by the futile if well-intentioned efforts of *Greenpeace* and *Friends of the Earth,* whose members often have three or more children, thereby cancelling out their own otherwise praiseworthy endeavours, and I think of Wordsworth, who said, *"to me the meanest flower that grows can give thoughts that do often lie too deep for tears."*

* It *was* George V, wasn't it? I'm, sure George VI would never have said "Bugger Bognor!" unless he were undergoing an unwonted lapse from grace. The Queen Mother would know, of course, but I haven't been in touch with her lately.

151

I verily believe that the Curse of the O'Connors is thinning out now; its one-time virulence no longer makes itself apparent in the thinning ranks of the family. When I go to London, which is seldom, because the place is a nightmare, and no longer human, I am brought into touch with one of its minor and most amusing ramifications in the house at Putney where Margot lives in solitary state.

Margot, if any reader remembers, came to England from Germany many years ago to seek work and probably, as is the normal procedure, someone to marry. She found both, work in my husband's household at Brighton, and marriage in the shape of Val, Lambodhar Zutshi's man-of-all-work. Now Lambodhar Zutshi, who was rich, did not like Margot. Not for herself, for she is quite nice, but out of resentment in that she took some of Val's attention and undermined his very considerable usefulness. This jealousy smouldered for an appreciable time, and he at length conceived the idea of issuing a specie of ultimatum to the couple that unless they left Brighton and came to live nearer London so that Val would be on hand and accordingly on call, he would not exactly disinherit them, but pay them noticeably less. The upshot naturally was that they came to London, and my husband's reward, or bribe, according to where one may be standing, took the form of a very large house in an affluent area of Putney, wherein they were installed in 1959. They had two sons. To cut a long story short, Val died prematurely. Lambodhar had left him a lot of money. It went to Margot, along with the house. It was the last thing Lambodhar would have wanted! But Fate moves in mysterious ways its wonders to perform! So the little German girl who came to work as a maid, now resides in a mansion. But Margot, who is practical, capable, placid and very literal, enjoys her fortune, and knows nothing of Fate or the Curse of the O'Connors, and has never intimated by one word or suggestion, that she is aware that anything out-of-the-ordinary has transpired! But she is happy and content, and it is refreshing to find anyone who is, when so many are not, in London or anywhere.

Travel, not only to London but anywhere on *British Rail* these days is an ordeal. It is partly because there has been such a pronounced decline in manners or even basic decency in the standard of public behaviour. Whenever I have occasion so to travel, I am repelled by the unedifying spectacle of every available seat being hogged by *men*. *Young* men; the older generation was taught not to . . . while elderly or infirm people stand. Many of the men have their feet sprawled out before them and their baggage sprawled too, on the adjoining seat, so that no one else can use it. Doubtless their glib reasoning would be "it's to do with Women's Lib."

Rubbish! A woman of eighty leaning on a stick has nothing whatever to do with any "Movement" which is referred to as "feminist." The idea has never touched her; it means nothing to her. It is simply that they are uncouth selfish louts who should have their backsides kicked. But they in turn have never been taught anything. Their parents were out to work all the time, endlessly grubbing for money. They learnt nothing at school; there are too many of them, there isn't *time*, and the teachers probably don't know anything either, so it's another dead-end.

At my last encounter with *British Rail* (there was a strike for two months, so encounters were brief), Brighton Station was packed. I have never seen so many young people congregated. Students of all nationalities, male and female, cramming the seats, jamming the doors, clambering and sitting all over each other, shouting, jostling, pushing, hilarious, unthinking, uncaring, unaware of the existence of anyone except themselves.

All this has arisen and escalated during the last quarter-century. I've always noticed it, but never until now actually been its victim. Because I've enjoyed reasonably good health, and it didn't greatly matter to me whether I sat down or not. Now it does. The weather was hot, and I have a "condition" known as "Hyperglycaemia," which renders one liable to grow weakened at untoward junctures, and precludes one's presence on an airplane. That is why I gave up going to America in 1990, a veritable bereavement. Therein lies the difference: theoretical or abstract impersonal disapproval as opposed to practical involvement. I longed for one of the seats to be vacated, so that I could stave off the horrid panicky sensation engendered by the "condition." So now I began to see why old people are reputed to become crotchety and cantankerous, and resentful of youth, and why younger people avoid them. It is all too easy to become depressing and a hostage to aches and pains. hence the gulf that exists between the generations. Older people see the world as a cruel, unkind place which has no regard for their infirmities; younger ones as a stamping-ground wherein to try out their skills and exploit their potential.

At the "personal" level, the gap is unbridgeable. At the spiritual level it is less noticeable. It has always been my experience in associating with the young, that "the work" has the effect of ironing out discrepancies, and I am their companion. Whereas with my own family, which has repudiated the knowledge and will not acknowledge the monadic level, I keep to myself, and there is no point of reference, and no communication. Indeed in the house where I now live, which is perennially full of people as gregarious as my daughter and son-in-law, I feel for the Ancient Mariner who complained (with apologies) of *"People, people everywhere, nor any word to speak."*

Notwithstanding, there are lots of very nice young people about. It is just that they don't make headlines, while the obnoxious fraternity does.

153

Life is a lonely journey.

Each man is an island.

You don't really know anyone.

All these are clichés, and no one disputes their veracity. Theoretically, that is. But it may well be that the number of us who actually experience that veracity is comparatively few.

Because people delude themselves. It is only "natural," or "human nature," to hang on to someone or something that is familiar, to which they can relate, to which they feel they can claim to "belong." it is a fundamental need to _belong_; to *something*, a "family," a club, a political party, a religious sect. It takes more courage than most of us possess to acknowledge the fact that we are starkly alone.

Those who have lost everyone who "belonged" to them by the time they are thirty-five or thereabouts will have a more realistic grasp of this truth than those who still have parents or brothers and sisters or husbands living when they themselves have reached a mature stage. It means that not all their ships have quite passed in the night, but are still cruising in neighboring waters, creating the semblance of company, tossing a comforting red herring into the breakers that harass their bows. And inevitably these will view life in a somewhat less harsh perspective.

But if we analyse our position, isolation is what it amounts to. Our "belonging" is artificial. It is the product of expediency, of our man-made institutions. The "family" trap is a salient instance of it. "Families" are merely *karmic clusters*, thrown together as the outcome of past indiscreet or mistaken involvements, and the mandatory necessity for their disentanglement. Rudolf Steiner stated that we should by now have outgrown the concept, but are at least half a century behind schedule, and still, in the types of societies we have built up, the kingpost, albeit crumbling, is still the structure of "family." "Relatives" are the only resource to which we dare to appeal to bury us when we die, to "look after" us if we become ill, or infirm or deficient in funds. Our "friends" can in no wise foot that bill, nor should we expect them to.

But these distasteful compulsions are not valid, nor have they any spiritual content. Nothing is of any worth at all unless it be freely given, and these "obligations" seldom are. And why should they be? The reluctant family is only implementing an onerous duty which by a contemporary man-made law has devolved upon it. They don't really know *you*, and don't want to. The only one who has known you all your life is yourself.

Thus, according to the phase of your life at which people meet you, they form their impression of you. Everyone beholds you in a wholly varying light, often to an almost ludicrous extent. Your parents see you as a baby, a small child in need of "looking after;" your brother as a charmless teenager who loses no opportunity of being nasty to him; your husband, (or husbands) as a

154

lively pretty young person who they thought would be nice to marry, (until they discovered their mistake); your children as a back-number and failure whom they have no intention of emulating; your best friend as a congenial companion and confidante, sharing activities and enthusiasms, exchanging goodwill and mutual promotion during the years in which your paths happen to intersect; your worst enemy as a pain in the neck. For your grandchildren, you don't exist at all, except possibly as a negligible source of revenue at birthday and Christmas. But then, as the scriptures remind us, *"No man is your friend, no man is your enemy; all are alike your teachers."*

And thus you don one mask after another, and you project whatever image may seem expedient or advantageous at the time. If people meet you when you are young, that is how they will think of you, and if they are likewise young, they will include you in their interests and pastimes. If you are old when they are introduced to you, they will envision you as a sympathetic experienced listener to whom they can pour out their emotional problems and derive benefit from your wise counsel. And if you are old and they are younger, and you have nothing to offer, either of counsel or substance, they will studiously avoid you. And why shouldn't they? Our society is essentially a selfish one, because its need is great. There are so many more "out there" in need of help than there are those prepared or able to give it, and thus it follows that our society is not a philanthropic organisation—that is not overlooking the praiseworthy and notable exceptions who strive to carry out altruistic work in the shape of what is fashionably dubbed "community service."

And if you take into account all the previous lives you have had, and the entities and characters with whom you were then associated, you realise what a minuscule portion of your monadic being is dropped down each time (like a *tea-bag);* you grow aware that at the monadic level each little lifetime is insignificant except for the quintessence that is distilled from it.

But lonely it most certainly is, especially if you happen to be one whose contacts have all died at early stages, leaving you with no continuity in your life at all, and not one single individual who has watched you grow up, or grown up concurrently, or remembers anyone or anything that you can remember, or to whom anything that you remember means anything at all.

However, another cliché is *"Not a Sparrow falls . . ."* And that would be contradictory indeed, or just blasphemous rubbish, if applied in the context of this dimension. For millions of sparrows, and not only sparrows either, and "your Heavenly Father," (whoever he may be when he's at home), does not stir a finger to rescue them. So it obviously applies to the wider canvas, and then, of course, it *is* the case, in that "your heavenly father" signifies the *Universal Wisdom,* and the sparrow renders up its tiny quota of experience into that, where it is absorbed and reserved for the sparrow in its next emergence. And while on the topic of sparrows, it is now given out by certain schools of thought, notably

155

the Arcane School, that since the meridian of global clearance and denudation has been attained to and passed, namely *now*, at this specific point in serial "time," animals and birds will become respectively human and devic in the impending Jupiterian Cycle, without having recourse to intermediate animal and airborne forms as hitherto. An onerous responsibility for the leaders of this ensuing humanity, to educate and develop so many elementary entrants. But at least they will not have to contend with the horrible ramifications of the Luciferic intervention which have dogged the steps of this humanity and continues to do so, seemingly beyond all possibility of redemption.

Maugre the foregoing, there has been much in a lifetime to appreciate and be thankful for. There are the dear and delightful *sounds* which evoke the richest associations. The cuckoo's magic call in the Spring when one was among the primroses, the clamour of "the blackbird and thrush, all the birds of the bush," the purr of a contented cat, the purl of a stream, the murmur of rivers and calm sunlit seas, the turquoise waves on Miami Beach, Scottish bagpipes, and the songs one sung in one's youth. All fade, but are recorded elsewhere.

Then too, there are the fine actors and actresses who have given so much first-class entertainment, if one is of the generation that admires pure theatre. Gregory Peck, Robert Mitchum, Kirk Douglas, Stewart Granger, Charlton Heston, Barbara Stanwyck, Deborah Kerr, Margaret Lockwood, Phyllis Neilson Terry, Gielgud, Olivier . . . even Boris Karloff and Basil Rathbone! The television is an asset, when one is too tired to do anything else, but a mixed asset when it comes to crime and violence. There is the marvellous grace and poetry-in-motion of Torvil and Dean, of the little youthful earnest Lemurians in the Olympic Games, who demonstrate before a breathless audience how the physical form, subservient to the spirit, can perform miracles. And long ago, the air astir in the cosy chicken-huts, with the chorus of Uncle Bert's baby chicks and their soft, happy cheeping. Or just *silence*, now at such a colossal premium!

Regarding the "New Age," there was, twenty or thirty years ago, inordinate enthusiasm anent the fabled "Age of Aquarius." This, in the light or perhaps rather, *darkness* of events, has somewhat abated, much as the post-war fever abated when gradually it was borne in upon us that the rather sententious and nauseating predictions of Vera Lynn were not to be implemented.

Five years brings us to the twenty-first century, thirty years to Aquarius. After that, it will take five hundred years for the new cycle to become fully entrenched and established. It may be that during that inevitably confused and probably turbulent span, the present Armageddon situation will subside in some degree as freedom of thought and action renders fighting superfluous. It is even possible that something will be done about overpopulation, (and God help the planet if it isn't!), as we move towards our next hermaphrodite cycle.

The current crazed obsession with sex will diminish. it is always darkest just before the dawn, and people, subconsciously *sensing*, without being conversant with the mechanics of it, that something is on its way out, will desperately strive to hang on to it, since it is all they have known, and they are fearful of change. The mob rule that now bids fair to prevail, may well worsen, and the emphasis will be on the group, not on the individual.

Ouspensky's observation that *evolution is not necessarily improvement, but only change,* will be highlighted while the cycle is in process of steadying down into its evolutionary pattern. While, like Auntie Madge, *I am very glad I won't be here to see it,* I can point to some of the changes to which those who are here will have to adjust.

There will be more vegetarians. Homosexuals and Lesbians will increase in number. These are much truer to the emergent prototype than are their heterosexual counterparts. Very few "divorces" take place among homosexual partners, who "get on" together far better than so-called "married couples." That is because they are usually opposite polarities or off-shoots from the same monadic oversoul, and thus experience no difficulty in staying harmoniously together.

The next physical prototype is neither male nor female but a blend of both. Ideally combining the best qualities of each. The Age of Aquarius prepares for its advent, though it will probably not be perfected until the sixth root race is established.* Aquarius will notice that boys are getting like girls and vice versa. Already the metamorphosis grows apparent, and the term "unisex" crops up with increasing frequency.

New Age denizens will see a gradual re-introduction of some of the arts and sciences of the fourth race; the science of sonics, of levitation, of trapped solar rays, even, in some cases, of the faculty of dematerialisation.

The symbol of Aquarius is the Man with the Pitcher of Water, which Jesus mentioned at the Last Supper. The pitcher contains, not $H2O$, but the *Pranic Essence* or *Water of Life*, to be poured out to wash away the ills of Pisces. These ills, tyranny, oppression, class distinction and racism, will cease to apply as the cycle unfolds.

* See *Prisoners of Time.*

The targets for Aquarius are:

1. The End of War;
2. The End of Marriage and the War between the Sexes;
3. The End of Organised "Religion;"
4. The Attainment of Universal Brotherhood.

There is no guarantee that these targets will be reached. They are not, always, and then a legacy is handed down to the ensuing cycle for redress. Assuredly the myriads of souls currently pouring in, will have to take their chances! And whether their chances will be "better" or "worse" than those of their predecessors, or whether they will be equipped to expedite them successfully, who is to hazard a guess?

1995 has dawned, bleak and grey.

They are talking about getting rid of the Monarchy, at least the "Republican" element is. Silly monkeys. As if they could wipe out thousands of years of history by their shallow, wishful thinking. Already, we have mob rule, mediocrity extolled, criminality condoned. What more do they want?

At the same time, the current manifestation of the Monarchy deserves to be got rid of. It has wholly lost sight of the Object of the Exercise, just as the people of England have. It wants it both ways; it claims the "perks" without honouring the obligations. It is no longer conversant with the origin and meaning of the Monarchy.* The Queen and Prince Philip have done the job to the best of their abilities and limitations, as a pair of fossils sunk in tradition without knowing the significance of the tradition; but the recently imported material has reduced the concept of kingship to the lowest common denominator. The Duchess of York is a glorified prostitute, the Princess of Wales an insipid suburban housewife, ever bemoaning the absence of "love" from the opulent package deal. "Love" has never formed an ingredient of the royal wedding cake recipe. While the Prince of Wales, who could have been so different, is a damn fool. And there we have it, in a nutshell.

Why should we pay for them, and their too-numerous offspring, to indulge in skiing holidays at Klosters? Why indeed? "Royal" progeny is no less charmless and prolific than that of the ubiquitous proletariat; their achievements are equally insignificant.

Let them go, by all means. And let England, like the Gaderene Swine,

*See *The British Monarchy and the Divine Right of Kings.*

pursue her headlong career to the cliff's edge, her more sensitive units to drown in despair, the cocksure "republican" types to swim ashore and be cheerfully swallowed up by Europe, if that is what they (think they) want.

Who cares? It won't make any difference to the ancient prophecy that eventually into this House of David will incarnate that evolved soul who, in company with a parallel soul from America, will be instrumental in leading the world back to some sort of cognizance of sanity.* That, by the look of things, will be by no means yet! But why chop down a tree because some of its leaves are attacked by blight?

Once, I loved my country, passionately, patriotically, and with deep joy, for its green-ness, its unique serenity, its insularity. Now, I would not willingly contribute two pence towards its upkeep. Once, they would say, *"The Englishman's home is his castle," "The Englishman's word is his bond,"* and lots of other complimentary things. If you went abroad, they would not even bother to look at your passport, but would smile, *"English?* That's all right." Now, looking askance, they mutter, *"English?* Football hooligans! We don't want *them!* "* All within the span of half a century!

I am not alone in my thoughts. I am not unlike an ancient Roman despairing amid the ruins of his crumbling empire; or a Greek, fleeing from the incursions of barbarians; or an Egyptian, witnessing the demise of his culture. The sense bears expression. All great civilisations go the same way. And I guarantee that today, more than one Englishman, treading his litter-strewn pavements, breathing fumes instead of air, contemplating the unending vista of bricks and mortar his environment has become, and recalling the England he knew, will be echoing them.

We must not mind, at the "personal" level. We can no longer afford to function at that level, since, as Christopher Fry observes, *"affairs are now **soul**-size."*

And, at the monadic level, we do not mind, because we know that it is all part of evolution, and is inevitable; and as Ouspensky points out, evolution is not necessarily improvement, but only *change.*

And change is an indispensable part of the process. All is illusion, and this dimension is simply a school. Once we have assimilated what the school has to teach us, we need not come back. And assuredly the conditions prevailing on the planet, (not in England alone), scarcely conduce to tempt the ex-student to return for a further dose.

As far as I am concerned, the "republicans" can go to Hell along with the dregs of the Monarchy. They are a bunch of whining malcontents, spinelessly blaming the "Government" for everything, because they lack the guts to make any effort themselves, still less reduce their obscene numbers and solve

*See *The British Monarchy and the Divine Right of Kings*

the one, solitary, besetting problem! What in the name of Heaven do they expect the Government to do? "Create" jobs for them when there are no jobs and too many applicants for the jobs there are? build houses for them to live in, bestow handouts upon them to live *on,* deface still more countryside to contain them, wipe out more wild flowers where they trample, so that they can continue to multiply unchecked? Developing such a programme to its logical conclusion, they are confident that if the scientists work hard enough, they will open up other planets, so that when they have crowded themselves off this one, and submerged the last grass blade in concrete, the "Government" will find them a nice Council-house on Jupiter where they can reproduce themselves ad nauseum.

Alas for these dreams! There is no room for us on other planets and never will be. Transportations to other planets are collective and divided by aeons of "time." The planet <u>Earth</u> is our arena, and whether we like it or not, we are forced in the end to work out our karma in Piccadilly Circus.

These optimistic prophets have so much to learn, such a long way to go! They will require so many lifetimes to reach any conclusions at all, that they will destroy the plant before they reach them.

In any case, the "Republic" will not happen. It is not in accordance with the aforementioned prophecy, which cannot be gainsaid.

What, then, can we envisage? Queen Camilla? Perhaps a mature, sensible woman might help Charles to stop the rot? Or, then again, perhaps not!

If they make William king prematurely, the old warning would apply: *"Woe to the land whose king is a child."* * If they make him king at all, the reversion to the Angevin name will militate against the spirituality that Charles, had he not gone off-course, could have supplied.

Thus, whatever emerges from the prevalent chaos, it is bound to take a long, long time before England recovers from the silliest, most trivial and ignorant mood she has ever been in, and before *she*, no longer "England" as we have understood the term, (but a karmic cluster of selected souls assembled on these islands, in the far distant future), again takes the lead.

I can't do much for England. All I want now is a bit of peace. Thank God one can at least retain a sense of humour!

Two things recently made me laugh. One, that Mavis and Ian have "taken up" Buddhism! God knows, I could have told them all they needed to know! Once you have the truth, you need no more "ists" or isms." I recall in the autumn of 1993, Mavis's strident accusation, as she thrust her face, distorted with hate, close to mine, "You and your 'theories' about Reincarnation!" Now I observe her perusing the *Tibetan Book of the Dead!* Supreme irony! Or, as Lady Thatcher remarked, upon being betrayed by her own party, "It's a funny old world!"

*See *The British Monarchy and the Divine Right of Kings*

The second was the spontaneous return of Howard, who died unexpectedly in May 1995. He was Chris's brother-in-law, who likewise had subscribed to the snigger-behind-the-hand brigade. His death was sudden, his return equally sudden. I meant nothing to him, but he had nowhere else to go. This kind of thing has happened so often.

"I didn't intend any insult," he volunteered. (They grow more perceptive quite quickly in the other dimension, before they embark upon their new and more real experience.)

"Oh, that's quite all right," I said. "What are you going to do now?"

"Nothing for ambition. Travel again I suppose. I see now why you ostracised yourself from the family. You were an unknown quantity at the time. You're not now."

"Well, that's something!" I replied. "And I see why you were taken out at the age of fifty-two. You weren't getting anywhere. Like my brother years ago. He realised it afterwards. He was only forty-nine. Nice scenery," I added. "All these spikey cactuses, and strange animals and birds. Lovely blue river, and the trees absolutely beautiful . . . so green . . . "

"Yes. Australia."

"Still moving on, then?" I said.

"So far. More or less. I always was at a loose end."

"There's plenty of time," I pointed out. "No hurry. If you want anything else, come back, won't you?"

"Will do," he promised, and headed for the comfortable "hotel" the guides had conjured into being for him. Doubtless when he encounters the next hang-up, he will approach me again for one of those short, disjointed interviews that help novices on their way.

I have in the course of the book touched many times upon the karma engendered between parents and children. This, like all karmas, works itself out at widely diversified speeds, some fairly quickly, others as a far longer-term proposition. Doubtless the Curse of the O'Connors had some bearing upon ours. I was persecuted at school by reason of my mother's Socialist leanings. I did not have time to tax her with the damage done to me. Queenie left the scene before I could formulate the customary judgmental and one-sided broadside of condemnation, which was just as well, since I have completely outlived the desire to do so. Mavis and Ian exacted full retribution for any shortcomings I may have had as parent, to the extent of taking the skin off my back by issuing unremitting innuendos at all opportunities. The do not do it now, and doubtless had I had a partner, or "husband," as the saying is, (not that I have minded being without such an appendage), they would not have done it at all. But surely it has exhausted the karma at last; only what an *age* it has seemed!

To satisfy the karma between Mavis and Chris and Meg and Laurie will take infinitely longer, for the process of *denouement* has not yet even commenced! It may well claim more than one lifetime, in that ostensibly there is none. They have at the material level bestowed upon them the best possible equipment and start in life. Yet their karmic burden for depriving them of the vital knowledge their maligned grandmother could have given them will be very grave.

The saying, *"the Sins of the Fathers shall be visited upon the Children"* would make perfect sense were it not for mankind's persistent misuse of the words.

"Sin" simply means ignorance. It derives from a Greek term used in archery, which means to miss the target, not to know. Parents at varying stages of evolution do not possess the wisdom and knowledge requisite to understand the needs of their children, and consequently do harm. Or, as Philip Larkin expresses it,

> *They mess you up, your Mum and Dad.*
> *They may not mean to, but they do.*
> *They pass on all the faults they had,*
> *And add a few more, just for you.*
>
> *But they were messed up in their turn*
> *By fools in old-style hats and coats,*
> *Who half the time were soppy-stern,*
> *And half were at each others' throats.*
>
> *Man hands on misery to man.*
> *It deepens like a coastal shelf.*
> *Get out as quickly as you can,*
> *And don't have any kids yourself.*

One can only legislate for oneself, and for myself, I hope there will not be much more to record. I suppose it is the approved thing to conclude on an appreciative note, positive as opposed to negative, proton and neutron or something akin.

So, before I close, I have taken the precaution of detaching from my bed-post my first two slogans: Montrose's brave one of my youth, about being prepared to win or lose it all, and the cautious counselling of middle age, about not putting one's trust in princes, etc., and substituting for them the sagacious dictum of Abraham Lincoln,

"THE BEST THING ABOUT THE FUTURE IS THAT IT ONLY COMES ONE DAY AT A TIME."

THE END

Appendix A

The Sandys Butler Story

Recounted in Arkansas, 1990, on my final visit there, the month being September.

I have to go back more than 25 years, to a time when I was very clairvoyant, and would always see in the mirror a face other than my own.

The face I saw repeatedly and outstandingly was that of **Sandys Butler**, whom I, (then *Jennifer Whittaker*) married in the seventeenth century.

I had already been apprised in detail of all my past incarnations.

The appearance was of a man in his thirties with fair hair, brown eyes, and the wide-brimmed hat and orange scarf of James II's army.*

In 1688 Sandys and Jennifer were married at the Cornhill in London, but Jennifer, who was looking for something else, did not stay with him. Instead she removed to Yorkshire, where she lived out a long and rather pointless life with the Whittaker relatives in a farmhouse at Luddendenfoot (which is still standing.)

Sandys was lost and unhappy, and could not understand why this had happened, until recently, when enlightenment supervened.

Sandys was born in Gloucester in 1661, and was employed firstly at *Petersfield* in Hants, as a steward of an estate—secretary, accountant, jobs of that nature, until eventually, as a Roman Catholic and competent executive, he secured a post as secretary to one of James II's entourage. Thus in 1690 he was involved in the Battle of the Boyne. This meant exile, and on James' defeat, he fled to Rome, as being the only safe refuge for Jacobites.

Albeit terribly lonely, he was able comfortably to maintain himself for five or six years, having excellent credentials and references. But towards the end

---

*Reference Tipperary, 1970's, when the very clairvoyant villagers described exactly what I had seen in the mirror: *"A Jacobite gentleman, a Roman Catholic, who was so glad that I had agreed to attend 6 o'clock Mass."* I had done this, quite reluctantly, to please Mrs. Guiry, with whom I was staying in Carrick-on-Suir.

of the decade, matters took an adverse turn for the Jacobites, whose credit and finances were diminishing. Sandys could not afford to live for long on his resources, and found that he could no longer count on work in Italy.

Airing the matter with acquaintances in Rome, he was recommended by them to try his luck in the *New World*. People were very persuasive, "talking without their book", as people so often do, averring with confidence that he would be sure to find work there.

Sandys was a Gemini subject. He often acted upon impulse. He believed them, and fell into the trap of expected good luck.

Not that he had much alternative. It was too early to return to England, as measures against the Jacobites were still in force.

Using the last, or nearly the last of his resources, he braved the hazardous voyage across the Atlantic, which took several months, sailed up the Arkansas River, and purchasing a horse, and travelled overland in search of employment.

His hopes were wholly dashed. There was no work at all, of the kind for which he had been trained. He had chosen the wrong place.

Arkansas offered nothing but vast tracts of empty land, a few poor farms, and Red Indians. These were not yet hostile to the few English and European settlers who passed that way, and helped where they could.

Sandys was in desperation. He had worked a little on the land, for a pittance; but the farmers could not continue to pay wages. He had no money left to buy food; he and his horse were exhausted. It is doubtful whether he would have lived, had not an elderly widow, occupying a poverty-stricken cabin in a small remote settlement called *Shiloh* (now Springdale!) taken him in, engaged him to help with the garden, the meagre harvest, the animals and vegetables, and shared her life with him for the space of nearly two years.

He was killed by snake-bite at the age of thirty-seven in the late Summer of 1698.

My first intimation of any of this was some 25 years ago, when during one of many communications with Sandys Butler and his guide, he suddenly remarked, "LEONORA LOOKED AFTER ME."

He meant that the elderly widow, Leonora, who was skilled in medicine, herbal remedies, and knew what to do for snake-bites, looked after him, as best she could, but was unable to save his life.

I knew nothing of Leonora, and did not know where Arkansas was.

But I recalled that at the very beginning of my adult life, before anything happened to me at all, I had consulted a medium, one *Alice Rixon*, in London, who told me, among other things, "You will go to America."

I did not believe her. I had no money, and in those days no one went to America, except a few businessmen and commercial travellers. My father used to go. He went twenty-two times in all, on the Cunard Line, the *Mauretania*, *Aquitania*, *Berengaria*, etc. Now that I live in Bristol, I sometimes go to the restaurant whose walls are decorated with the very timbers and dining hall of the *Mauretania*, and it gives me a strange feeling to be looking at the self-same surroundings in which my father crossed the ocean so many times.

"Oh yes," the medium insisted. "You will go to America. And you will go to the West of America where the cowboys used to be."

It was not until a lifetime later that her prophecy was borne out.

In 1977 I went to Arkansas to give lectures. That was all. I did not expect to stay, or to return again and again. As it transpired, I stayed with Birtha Macon and her family at Springdale. I knew all these people; I returned again and again. it simply worked out that way.

Birtha is *Leonora*. Sandys is *Donald*, her younger son.

Naturally, Sandys had wondered about Leonora, and naturally would want to get a step nearer, to find out more about her.

On seeing Donald, I might have been looking at Sandys, exactly as I had seen him in the mirror. Donald's wife Carolyn was Sandys' cousin *Eileen* and again the resemblance was astounding. In the seventeenth century she lived at Westerham in Kent. Sandys could have married, but she was too strong a character for him, and he preferred Jennifer (me), to his cost.

During his lonely exile in Rome, Sandys temporarily teamed up with an Italian singer in a tavern, called *Rosa*. They had a son called *Arnold*. Sandys knew nothing of the existence of the boy, until a few years ago when astrally in my presence they were brought together.

Arnold, naturally eager to know more about his father's sufferings and wanderings and the woman who gave him shelter, accordingly incarnated seven years ago as Birtha's granddaughter, *Jamie Dawn*.

Birtha is bringing this girl up,* in lieu of the parent, *Susie*, Birtha's daughter, who did not feel equal to the responsibility and did not wish to marry Jamie's father.

On this my recent visit in 1990, I restored Sandys to his (karmic) family, so that he can watch over Arnold (Jamie!), and make up for his' unawareness of the latter's existence, *and* help and influence Birtha in return for her help to him 300 years before. And, incidentally, to help *Eileen* , who, as

---

*When a grandparent brings up a child, it indicates a very special kind of karma. The only way Arnold could gain access to Birtha at closer quarters was to be brought up by her under the same roof.

Carolyn, spontaneously understood exactly what I meant when I rendered the explanation.

Birtha would naturally be anxious to ascertain what manner of woman it could be who could leave so nice a man as Sandys, and had been perplexed. That is why I was sent to Springdale, so that she could get a closer look at me.

I did not know until 1993 that Birtha's friend *Jim Bunnell* * who lives at Gentry, was part of the Sandys Butler network. I only met him once, at Faye's farm at Gentry, and he was always in the background.

In 1698, he was the humble curator of the little burial ground at Westville, when Birtha (Leonora) took Sandys there for burial. It was in that capacity that he met Birtha. It was called *St. Joseph's,* and the present burial ground, where Jim's uncle was a preacher, is on the site of it.

Jim and Birtha met again, circa 1849, when both were laying railroads or *plank roads*, and building log cabins. Both were male on this occasion. Hence their karmic bond today.

In 1995, another entity joined the network.

I had returned to Arkansas year after year for fourteen years. there were many children who used to come to Birtha's house. Each time I returned, they were a little older. Among them was *Tammy*, the daughter of Carolyn (*Eileen*). The last time I saw her, in 1990, she was fifteen. Now, at twenty, she has emancipated herself from parental influence, and requests to know where she fits into the Sandys Butler network.

Not directly involved, but coming in as a second generation, as this time, she was Eileen's daughter at Westerham, after Sandys left for Rome and Jennifer for Yorkshire. She would only hear about all that later. Her mother Eileen, having married someone else, probably Tammy's father, (now *Mr. Carnes,*) was skilled with the spinet and virginalls, and taught her daughter to play what is now the piano. The girl became quite proficient in music, married and went to live in London.

*Jim Bunnell's wife *Faye*, who died some years ago, had a granddaughter who was the reincarnation of my childhood friend Kathleen, who took her own life at an early age. I recognised the paintings. This girl became an art teacher in Fayetteville, and is part of the opposite polarity of my first husband Harold, a painter and an A.R.A. At the time I saw the pictures on the wall at the farm at Gentry, the granddaughter would have been about sixteen. Now she would be nearer thirty.

Appendix B

Incarnascope of Mollie Moncrieff

Principle: *Female* (the monadic core)

Ray: *Twelve.* Teach the King: Guide, Advise, Influence

Doorkeeper: *No longer required.*

Early Origins: *Adamic*

It is seldom a viable proposition for purposes of a brief outline, to trace pre-human entries. Such entries follow a distinct and logical sequence however, so that the forms prepared for each entrant follow consistent patterns. Each form is designed to support the strength or weakness of the entrant.

Throughout these manifestations, the group over-soul retains control of the monads. Once the stage of man is reached, the monad breaks away from the group altogether, and thereafter is recognised as a self-responsible unit.

Early Form: *Cat*

First (human and traceable) incarnations: *Atlantis.*
       Drowned at age three, in the first cataclysm.

Second: *Moelanta*, (now Africa).
       An immediate post-Atlantean life.
       Duration: 18 years.

Third: *Egypt*
       Duration: 17 years.

Fourth: *Hungary*
As a barbarian.
Duration: 14 years.

Fifth: *Britain*
Camelot region. 500 A.D. Name: *Kirolie.*
Duration: 14 years.

Sixth: *Ditchling, Co. Sussex, England.*
As *Margorie Wollaston.*
1501-1518

Seventh: *London and Yorkshire.*
As *Jennifer Butler.*
Late seventeenth century.

Eighth: *England.* The current life.

Index

169

Buddhism, 160
Bulls, 28, 48, 96
Bunnel, Jim, 127n, 166
"Bunny" (cousin), 9
Bunratty Castle, 94
Burns, Robert, 32
Bus services, 116, 129
Bute, Isle of, 105
Butler, Jennifer, 8, 51, 53, 104, 163-66
Butler, Rhett, 135
Butler, Sandys (*see* Sandys Butler)
Butterflies, 13, 27
Buxton, 54
Byron, Lord, 29, 45, 86

C

Call Joshua, 91, 94, 115-16
Campbell, Archibald, 80
Carlisle, 102
Carnes, Mr., 166
Carolyn *(Eileen),* 127n, 165-6
Carr, Francis, 79, 108-9
Carrick, 94, 163
Cartland, Barbara, 84, 111
Caterham, 19
Cats, 72, 75-6, 100, 117-18
Channing-Pierce, Dr., 12, 54, 58
Charles I, 15, 82, 85, 103, 107, 121, 146
Charles II, 74, 85
Charles, Prince, 73, 89, 111, 151, 158
Charles, Ray, 131
Chatsworth Road, Brighton, 44
Chatterton, Jasmine, 68
Cheltenham, Ladies' College at, 25
Chester, Wales, 95, 107
China, 143
Chodewise, Colonel, 79
Chris Miller, 87n, 98-100, 103, 117-18, 134-40, 153, 161

Church, The, 40-1, 68, 71, 89-90, 109
Churchill, Winston, Intro., 48-9, 52
Chiddingstone, 30
Chipstead, 19
Cinema, 20
Cirencester, 96
Clandon, 9
Clarke, Mr. and Mrs., 17-18, 30-1, 73-5
Claverhouse, John of ("Bonnie Dundee"), 53, 79-80, 83
Cleopatra, 128
Clinton, Hillary, 117
Clinton, President Bill, 117
Cliteroe, Margaret, 31
Cochrane, Jean, 53
Coleridge, Samuel, 100, 142
Colonel Stewart, 67, 81, 102, 105-6
Colyford, 27
Colyton, 27, 144
Communications (with discarnates), 19, 53, 57, 66, 68-71, 80-5, 105-8, 145, 160
Compton Marldon, 27
Cooper, Gary, 106, 122
Corelli, Marie, 9
Cornhill, 163
Cornwall, 26
Cousins:
  Deidre, 8
  Denys, 9
  Eric, 47, 114
  Ernest, 8
  Joan, 8
  Joyce (Joy), 9-10, 26, 40
  Phil, 8, 9
  Toby, 14, 22-3, 28, 47
  Viola ("Bunny"), 9
Coventry, 54
Coward, Noel, 143
Cowley, 145, 147
Cows, 16-17, 119
Craster, 101
Crawley, 145
Creel, Paul, 29

171

M

P

Paignton, 27
Paisley, 53
Palm Beach, Florida, 123-4
Pandit, Mrs., 60
Pankhurst, Emmeline, 40
Parker, Judge Roy, 130
Parsons, Nicholas, 84
Past lives, Intro., 8, 22, 25, 29-30, 40, 48, 51-4, 71, 75-6, 84-5, 99, 102, 105, 117-18, 122, 124, 126, 155
Pat (and Norah), 107
Pat (Arkansas), 128
Patchin, Robert, 43
Patons and Baldwins, 56
Patriarchy, 10
Paul Foot, 106
Pavilion, The Royal, 82
Peak District, 12
Peck, Gregory, 156
Peet, John, 144
Penelope Williams, 120, 131, 131n, 132
Pennines, 102
Penshurst, 122, *photo*
Perivale, 61
Perthshire, 11n
Petersfield, 163
Peters, Mary, 102
Pethick-Lawrences, 40
Pevensey Beach, 30
Phil (cousin), 8-9
Philippa, 83
Piccadilly, 160
Pickles, Joyce, 50
Pigs, 119-20
Pine Bluff, Arkansas, 129
Pisa, 100
Pisces, the Age of, 92, 143, 157
Pitlochry, 53
Plague, the Great (of London), 25

Plato, 91, 143
Poets:
    Browning, 51
    Burns, 32
    Byron, 29, 45, 86
    Coleridge, 100, 142, 153
    Graves, 105
    Keats, 13n, 29, 46
    Kipling, 11, 52
    Masefield, 22
    Noyes, 29, 72, 88
    Shakespeare, 141
    Shelley, 29, 86, 106
    Tennyson, 79, 110
    Wordsworth, 29, 100, 151
Poland, 104
Police, American, 122-3, 131
Polio, 9, 12-13, 18, 43
Politics, 12-13, 38, 40, 100, 134
Ponds, 17, 23
Portsmouth, Joan of, 85, 115
Post, The Palm Beach, 122-3
Poynings, 44
Predictions:
    Auntie Florrie's, 16
    Joan of Portsmouth's, 115
    London medium's, 88, 165
    Winnie's, 94-5
Princes:
    Edward VIII, 39
    Charles, 73, 81, 89, 151, 158, 160
    Philip, 158
    William, 160
Princesses:
    Anne, 81
    Diana, 151, 158
Prisoners of Time, 30, 58, 143, 147-8, 157
Purley, 12, 17, 19-21, 27-8, 30, 44, 65, 72
Puss the cat, 117-18
Putney, 152

Toby, 14, 22-3, 28, 47, 110
Tonbridge, 30
Torvil and Dean, 156
Trafalgar, Battle of, 33
Traquair, Locked Gates of, 104, *photo*
Trees:
    Gog and Magog, 110
    Queenie's, 40
Trevor, 60, 63, 67
True Tales of Reincarnation and Astral Rescue, 25, 82, 85, 92, 107, 109, 112
Tsa-la-Ghi, 119
Tulsa, Oklahoma, 113-15
Tunbridge Wells, 17, 22, 30
Tweed Country, 80
Tweed-dale, Marquis of, 80
Tynemouth, 101
Tyne River, 101
Tyson, Mr. Don, 129
Tyson's Farms, 116, 126

U

"Uncle" Bert (*see* Bert, Uncle)
Uncles:
    Ernie, 7, 47
    Herbert, 38
    Jack, 37, 80, 88, 113, 145
    John, 39
Upper Warlingham, 22, 24
Uxbridge, 80, 145

V

Val, (*see* Balbadhar), 60, 152
van der Post, Sir Lawrence, 111-12
Varndean, 72, 74, 88
Vegetarians, 157
Victory (ship), 54, 69

Viola (cousin), 9

W

Wales, 95
Walking, 12, 27, 44, 48, 51
Ward, Leila, 120
Warr, Earl de la, 13
Washington, George, 11
Waterford, 94
Waterloo, Battle of, 33
Webb, Beatrice and Sydney, 40
Wellington, 50
Wellington, Duke of, 33
Wesley, John, 14, 130
Westerham, 127n, 165
West Palm Beach, 120, 123
West Pier (at Brighton), 84
West Riding, 51
Westville, 166
Weston-super-mare, 109
Westville, 166
Where Do We Go From Here?, 80, 106-7
Whitby, 51
White River, 127
Whitley Bay, 100-1
Whittaker, Johnstone, 97, 104
Whyteleafe, 19
Wight, Isle of, 26
Wilberforce, Wilbur, 41
Wildflowers, 15, 23, 88, 109, 151
Wilkinson, Ellen, 13
William, Prince, 160
Wimbleton, 49
Win (and Barry), 83
Winds, 40
Wingfield Manor, 61
Winnie the Pooh, 104, 108
Withyam, 13, 30
Woe Water, 25
Woking, 93

X

Y

Z